Using
Excel & Access®
FOR ACCOUNTING
2007

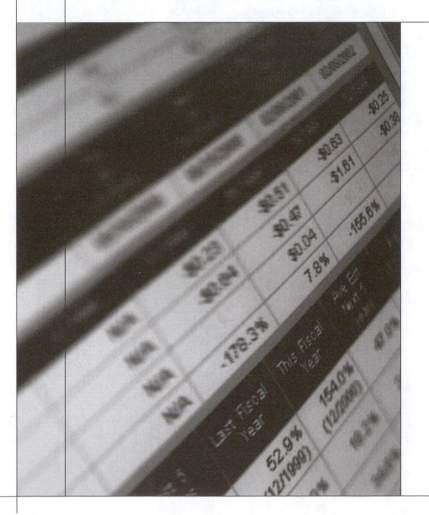

Glenn Owen

Allan Hancock College

*University of California
at Santa Barbara*

SOUTH-WESTERN
CENGAGE Learning™

Australia · Brazil · Canada · Mexico · Singapore · Spain · United Kingdom · United States

Using Excel® & Access® 2007 for Accounting, 2nd edition
Glenn Owen

VP/Editorial Director: Jack W. Calhoun

Publisher: Rob Dewey

Acquisitions Editor: Sharon Oblinger

Marketing Manager: Steve Joos

Content Project Manager: Jana Lewis

Manager, Editorial Media: John Barans

Technology Project Editor: Robin Browning

Manufacturing Coordinator: Doug Wilke

Production Service: Newgen

Art Director: Stacy Shirley

Cover and Internal Designer: C. Miller Design

Cover Image: © Getty Images

Printer: Globus Printing

For product information and technology assistance, contact us at
Cengage Learning Academic Resource Center, 1-800-423-0563

For permission to use material from this text or product,
submit all requests online at **www.cengage.com/permissions**
Further permissions questions can be emailed to
permissionrequest@cengage.com

Library of Congress Control Number: 2008930101

Student Edition ISBN 13: 978-0-324-78440-4

Student Edition ISBN 10: 0-324-78440-6

Student Edition with CD ISBN 13: 978-0-324-59439-3

Student Edition with CD ISBN 10: 0-324-59439-9

South-Western Cengage Learning
5191 Natorp Boulevard
Mason, OH 45040
USA

Cengage Learning products are represented in Canada by Nelson Education, Ltd.

For your course and learning solutions, visit **academic.cengage.com**
Purchase any of our products at your local college store or at our preferred online store **www.ichapters.com**

Printed in the United States of America
1 2 3 4 5 6 7 11 10 09 08

Brief Contents

Contents

Preface

What if you could integrate two critical business software programs into your accounting classroom without using confusing and complicated manuals? What if your students could use these programs to reinforce basic accounting concepts in an interactive case setting? What if you could do both without spending a fortune and a vast amount of time preparing examples, cases, and illustrations? *Excel and Access for Accounting* by Glenn Owen is a textbook that fulfills and expands upon all three of these "what ifs."

Why Is This Textbook Needed?

Many accounting educators are looking for ways to incorporate more business software into their accounting curriculum without displacing basic accounting instruction. They have tried to accomplish this by creating a stand-alone computer-based course, a lab component course, or by adding business computer software to their regular accounting curriculum. Current texts in this field are very generic in nature, spending little if any time on accounting-specific issues. Those that do address accounting issues address only worksheet or database issues but not both. Some texts that have a worksheet focus deliver a wide array of financial and managerial topics but lack a natural case flow. Some with a database focus emphasize the creation of accounting systems but do not address how databases are used to support the accounting function.

Moreover, employers expect today's college student to be computer literate in commercial accounting, worksheet, and database software. The demand for this type of training is growing daily as more and more businesses employ business software to solve real-world problems.

Instructors often want to incorporate business software into the first course but are reluctant to invest the time and effort necessary to accomplish this goal. Existing materials are often "preparer" driven in that they focus on the creation of worksheets and databases without addressing the effective use of these tools. Students are often discouraged in their use of computers because of the complicated and confusing manuals that concentrate on using the software without any business or accounting context.

This text responds to all of those needs. It provides a self-paced, step-by-step environment in which the students use a worksheet (Excel®) and a database (Access®) to solve real accounting and business problems. The text is designed to reinforce the concepts students learn in their first accounting courses and to show how worksheets and databases can help users make better and more informed business decisions.

What Are the Goals of This Textbook?

This textbook takes a user perspective by illustrating how worksheets and databases are used and created. Both Excel and Access are user friendly, with extensive help features and helpful toolbars to aid in accessing commonly used functions. The textbook uses a proven and successful pedagogy to demonstrate the features of both software programs and to elicit student interaction.

The textbook's first goal is to help students apply the accounting concepts they've learned to real-world problems, aided by the use of a worksheet and/or database. The content complements the first course in accounting and therefore should be used either as a supplement to that course or as the primary textbook in a stand-alone course that follows the first course in accounting. Some instructors have found this textbook and the *QuickBooks for Accounting* textbook or the *Peachtree for Accounting* textbook ideal matches for a stand-alone "Computers in Accounting" course.

The second goal is motivate students to become more familiar with and more at ease using a worksheet and/or database to solve accounting and business problems. Using this software application in an accounting context maintains student interest and provides additional incentive for pursuing an accounting degree or emphasis.

The third goal of this text is to reduce the administrative burdens of accounting faculty by providing a self-paced environment for their students to learn how important software applications are used in business. Accounting faculty must manage different learning styles of students as well as teach accounting concepts and practice techniques. The additional task of integrating computer applications into the classroom will be made simpler by using this text.

What Are the Key Features of This Textbook?

- The chapters incorporate a continuing, interesting, realistic case—Coast Jewelers, Inc.—that helps students apply Excel and Access features.

- A tested, proven, step-by-step methodology keeps students on track. Students enter data, analyze information, and make decisions all within the context of the case. The text constantly guides students, letting them know where they are in the course of completing their accounting tasks.

- Numerous screenshots include callouts that direct students' attention to where they should look on the screen. On almost every page in the book, you will find examples of how steps, screenshots, and callouts work together.

- *Trouble?* paragraphs anticipate the mistakes that students are likely to make (or problems they are likely to encounter) and help them recover and continue with the chapter. This feature facilitates independent learning and frees the instructor to focus on accounting concepts rather than on computer skills.

- The end-of-chapter material begins with questions intended to test students' recall of what they learned in the chapter.

- Chapter Assignments follow the Questions and provide students additional hands-on practice with Excel and Access skills.

- Two continuing Case Problems—Kelly's Boutique (a retail store) and Wine Depot (a wine distributor)—conclude each chapter. These cases have approximately the same scope as the Coast Jewelers chapter case.

- The Instructor's Package contains an Instructor's Manual that includes solutions to end-of-chapter materials, a test bank, and a CD with student files and completed assignment files.

Using This Text Effectively

Before you begin, note that this textbook assumes you are familiar with the basics of Windows XP or Vista: how to control windows, how to choose menu commands, how to complete dialog boxes, and how to select directories, drives, and files. If you do not understand these concepts, please consult your instructor.

The best way to work through this textbook is to read the text carefully and complete the numbered steps, which appear on a shaded background, as you work at your computer. Read each step carefully and completely before you try it.

As you work, compare your screen with the figures in the chapter to verify your results. You can use Excel 2007 and Access 2007 with either Windows XP or Vista. The screen shots you see in this book were captured in a Windows XP environment. If you are using Windows Vista, you might see some minor differences between your screen and the screens in this book. Any significant differences that result from using the different operating systems with Excel or Access will be explained.

Don't worry about making mistakes—that is part of the learning process. The *Trouble?* paragraphs identify common problems and explain how to correct them or get back on track. Follow the suggestions given *only* if you are having the specific problem described.

After you complete a chapter, you can answer the Questions, Assignments, and Case Problems found at the end of each chapter. They are carefully structured so that you will review what you have learned and then apply your knowledge to new situations. Feel free to page back through the text to clarify how each task should be accomplished.

Your Student CD

To complete the chapter and exercises in this book, you must have a Student CD. The Student CD contains some practice files you need for the chapters, the Assignments, and the Case Problems. Your instructor or lab manager may provide you with a Student CD, your instructor may require you to make your own Student CD, or you may be asked to use the disk that accompanies this text. See your instructor for specific details. In any case, this text will assume you have a Student CD that contains the aforementioned practice files.

Excel and Access Versions

The text and related data files created for this text were constructed using Excel 2007 (12.0.6024.5000) and Access 2007 (12.0.4518.1014) Series Release 1. To check your version and release number Click the Microsoft Office Button and then click Access Options or Excel Options. Click Resources, and then click the About button. All references to Excel and Access throughout the rest of this textbook are to Excel 2007 or Access 2007.

Excel and Access Options

Excel and Access have many options that can be altered by the user. In a lab environment, or in an environment where different people use the same computer, these options may have been altered from the default settings set when the software was first installed.

About the Author

Glenn Owen is a tenured faculty member of Allan Hancock College's Accounting and Business Department, where he lectures on accounting and information systems. In addition, he is a lecturer at the University of California at Santa Barbara, where he has been teaching accounting and information systems courses since 1980. His professional experience includes five years at Deloitte & Touche and seven years as vice-president of finance positions at Westpac Resources, Inc., and ExperTelligence, Inc. He has authored many Internet-related books and accounting course supplements. He is the author of the popular *QuickBooks for Accounting* and *Peachtree for Accounting* texts and teaches both regular and Internet-based courses in financial and managerial accounting. His innovative teaching style emphasizes the decision maker's perspective and encourages students to think creatively. His graduate studies in educational psychology and 33 years of business experience combine to yield a balanced blend of theory and practice.

Dedication

I would like to thank my wife Kelly and my sons Nathan, Kyle, and Casey for their help in the development of this text—and, in particular, their support and understanding of my deadlines and late night case writing. You continue to be what life is all about.

Excel for Accounting

Excel Tour

In this chapter you will learn:

- Excel's capabilities and new features
- How to start, navigate, and work with Excel files
- How to use Excel help
- How Excel is used in accounting

Case: Coast Jewelers, Inc.

Nathan Peters and Meagan Lopez own Coast Jewelers, Inc., located in Santa Barbara, California. They've been in business for five years and have developed a number of repeat customers. As is typical in the beachside resort town, they also cater to the tourists who flock to the community each summer. They specialize in diamond jewelry manufacturing and sales, both retail and wholesale, and are eager to expand their customer base and their supplier pool. Their local C.P.A., Kyle Ski, has suggested hiring a local college student to help them computerize their operations. He suggests they use QuickBooks to keep their accounting records but also encourages them to use a worksheet software application to help them analyze their business situation and support their accounting operations. Nathan, excited to get started, places an ad in the local college paper.

As an accounting student at the local college, you've become fairly adept at using computers to complete homework assignments but you're eager to broaden your horizons. You'd like to combine your accounting and computer skills with some practical experience. Lucky for you, an ad in the college paper for part-time computer and accounting help falls on your desk one afternoon. After an intense interview and background check, you're hired!

Your initial meeting with Nathan, Meagan, and Kyle reveals some unfamiliarity with the software application Kyle has suggested you use. Kyle has agreed to coach you through the basic use of the worksheet program after Nathan and Meagan reluctantly agree to pay his fees. They're hoping, of course, that you can learn the worksheet application quickly and help them use it to further their business expansion.

First off, Kyle introduces you to Excel, a powerful worksheet application he has been using since the mid-eighties. Kyle explains that this most recent incarnation of Excel is far more than a simple calculation program.

Understanding Excel's Capabilities and New Features

You have often used paper worksheets in your accounting courses and ask Kyle if Excel is just an electronic version of that same worksheet. He explains that, in essence, you are correct. In your beginning accounting courses a worksheet might have been used to adjust a trial balance for accrual accounting and to create financial statements like the income statement, balance sheet, and statement of cash flows. You added columns of numbers, subtotaled them in places, drew lines, created titles, and so forth.

Excel is, however, much more than an expensive calculator or place to put information. Built-in functions can help an accountant create financial statements, pivot table reports, analyses, depreciation schedules, loan amortization schedules, cash flow budgets, cost-volume-profit analyses with charts, and more. But first, you need to become familiar with the multitude of Excel commands and procedures.

New features in the 2007 version of Excel include a completely redesigned user interface, conditional formatting, and a new file format.

The new results-oriented user interface makes it easy for you to work in Microsoft Office Excel. Commands and features that were often buried in complex menus and toolbars are now easier to find on task-oriented tabs that contain logical groups of commands and features. Many dialog boxes are replaced with drop-down lists that display the available options, and descriptive tooltips or sample previews are provided to help you choose the right option.

You can use conditional formatting to visually annotate your data for both analytical and presentation purposes. In order to find exceptions easily and to spot important trends in your data, you can implement and manage multiple conditional formatting rules that apply rich visual formatting in the form of gradient colors, data bars, and icon sets to data that meets those rules. Conditional formats are also easy to apply—in just a few clicks, you can see relationships in your data that can be used for purposes of analysis.

Excel now has expanded and easier-to-use charts and pivot tables, which make it an ideal and necessary part of an accountant's arsenal of analytic tools.

Starting, Navigating, and Working with Excel Files

To begin, Kyle asks you if you are familiar with starting programs in Windows XP. Since Nathan and Meagan admit to very little knowledge of computers, you offer to demonstrate. First you explain that some of the company's computers use the Windows Vista operating system but that the one you are most familiar with uses the Windows XP operating system. In either case, you explain that starting Excel is the same in either operating system. You then offer to demonstrate the process for starting Excel in Windows XP.

To start Excel:

1 Click the **Start** button.

2 Select Microsoft Office Excel 2007. Your window may look like Figure 1.1.

Figure 1.1

Starting Excel

3 Click **Microsoft Office Excel 2007** to start the application.

Trouble? Your start menu may be completely different from that shown in Figure 1.1. See your instructor or lab personnel for instructions on starting Excel.

Kyle explains that Excel always opens an empty workbook upon starting. In this case, a workbook is a set of three blank worksheets as shown in Figure 1.2. Each worksheet is a grid of rows and columns into which you enter information. You can add additional sheets to a workbook if necessary.

Nathan has been replicating Kyle's actions on his own laptop, which has Excel installed as well. He notes that his screen does not exactly match Kyle's, whose Quick Access toolbar and Ribbon seem different than Nathan's. Kyle explains that screen size can change the appearance of the Ribbon and that both the Ribbon and Quick Access toolbar can be customized.

To illustrate, Kyle has captured his Excel window in Figure 1.2 and provided callouts and an explanation of the Excel window characteristics.

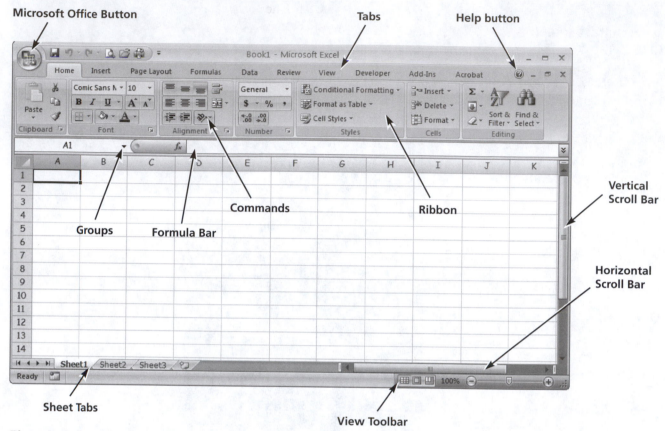

Figure 1.2

The Excel Window

Microsoft Office Button – This button, located in the upper left hand corner of the Excel window, is available in all the Office 2007 applications. The Microsoft Office Button replaces the File menu and is located in the upper-left corner of these Microsoft Office programs. When you click the Microsoft Office Button, you see the same basic commands available in earlier releases of Microsoft Office to open, save, and print your file.

Quick Access Toolbar – At the top of the Excel window is the Quick Access Toolbar, which is designed to give you an easy way to execute the commands used most often. The default setting in Excel provides access to the Save, Undo, and Redo commands. You'll note that in Figure 1.2 the Quick Access toolbar has been modified to include the Print Preview, Open, and Quick Print commands as well. This is accomplished by right-clicking the Quick Access Toolbar and selecting Customize Quick Access Toolbar (or by right-clicking any command on the Ribbon and selecting Add to Quick Access Toolbar). Don't adjust your Quick Access Toolbar yet; we'll get to that shortly.

Ribbon – There are three basic components of the Ribbon, as follows. *Tabs:* There are seven of them across the top. Each represents core tasks you do in Excel. *Groups:* Each tab has groups that show related items together. *Commands:* A command is a button, a box to enter information, or a menu. The principal commands in Excel are gathered on the first tab, the Home tab. The commands on this tab are those that Microsoft has identified as the most commonly used when people do basic tasks with worksheets. For example, the Paste, Cut, and Copy commands are arranged first on the Home tab, in the Clipboard group. Font formatting commands are next, in the Font group. Commands to center text or align text to the left or right are in the Alignment group, and commands to insert and delete cells, rows, columns, and worksheets are in the Cells group. Groups pull together all the commands you're likely to need for a particular type of task, and throughout the task they remain on display and readily available instead of being hidden within menus. These vital commands are visible above your work space.

The commands on the Ribbon are the ones you use the most. Instead of showing every command all the time, Excel 2007 shows some commands in response to an action you take. When you see an arrow (called the Dialog Box Launcher) in the lower right corner of a group, there are more options available for the group. Click the arrow, and you'll see a dialog box or a task pane.

Other Excel Window Items – As with all Windows screens, scroll bars control your view of the worksheet (horizontal and vertical). Formulas contained in each cell are displayed in the Formula Bar. The View Toolbar gives you quick access to viewing your worksheet in Normal layout (shown in Figure 1.2), Page layout (shown in Figure 1.5), or Page Break preview layout.

To demonstrate some of Excel'S features, Kyle suggests you follow along while he opens an Excel file:

1 Open Excel, if you closed it previously.

2 Click the **Microsoft Office** Button, and then right-click **Open.**

3 Click **Add to Quick Access Toolbar.** Note that your Quick Access Toolbar now shows a folder icon that will enable quicker opening of new files.

4 Click your newly created folder icon in the Quick Access Toolbar to open a new file. (*Note:* if you are using Excel in a computer lab environment, your changes to the Quick Access Toolbar may not reappear the next time you start Excel.)

5 Navigate the Open window to the location of this text's student files. (The location would be the CD provided with the text or from your computer lab's server.)

6 Double-click the file **ch1-01**, which should be located in a Ch 01 folder. The workbook shown in Figure 1.3 should appear.

7 Click the **Microsoft Office** Button again and then click **Save As.** (This is done to keep your original student file available in case you need it again and also to provide a unique name for your file.)

Figure 1.3

Sample Workbook

8   Add your name to the file name using the underscore key as shown in Figure 1.4. In this example the file will be saved as ch1-01_student_name (replace student_name with your name).

9   Click **Save.**

10   Click in cell **A1.** This is now the active cell.

11   Hold the Shift key down and then click in cell **F1.** This should then highlight cells A1:F1. Alternatively, you could click in cell A1 and, with the mouse button down, drag the cursor to cell F1.

12   In the Font group, click the **B** icon to make the text in those cells bold.

13   In the Alignment group, click the **center text** icon to center the text in those cells.

14   Click in cell **D2** and then with the mouse button down, drag the cursor to cell **D29.**

15   In the Number group, click the $ icon to format the text in those cells in currency format.

Figure 1.4

Saving a Worksheet

Bold button

Center button

SUM function
formula for cell D31

Click here to launch the
Numbers group dialog box

Borders
button

	A	B	C	D	E	F	G	H
10	50333	Kmart	9/9/2009	$ 71,433	A. Foreman	AZ		
11	50334	Target	9/10/2009	$ 54,275	S. Moore	WA		
12	50335	Costco	9/11/2009	$ 16,276	R. Clemens	OR		
13	50336	Kmart	9/14/2009	$ 21,028	A. Rod	TX		
14	50337	Kmart	9/15/2009	$ 32,809	A. Foreman	WA		
15	50338	Wal-Mart	9/16/2009	$ 22,663	R. Clemens	FL		
16	50339	Kmart	9/17/2009	$ 39,509	A. Rod	AZ		
17	50340	Target	9/18/2009	$ 26,616	S. Moore	WA		
18	50341	Costco	9/18/2009	$ 57,573	G. Sammy	OR		
19	50342	Sears	9/21/2009	$ 36,967	A. Rod	FL		
20	50343	Wal-Mart	9/21/2009	$ 35,274	R. Clemens	OR		
21	50344	Kmart	9/22/2009	$ 63,419	F. Lemming	CA		
22	50345	Target	9/23/2009	$ 23,817	S. Moore	AZ		
23	50346	Costco	9/24/2009	$ 39,705	G. Sammy	FL		
24	50347	Sears	9/25/2009	$ 70,546	A. Foreman	AZ		
25	50348	Wal-Mart	9/28/2009	$ 60,482	R. Clemens	WA		
26	50349	Kmart	9/28/2009	$ 47,847	A. Rod	OR		
27	50350	Target	9/28/2009	$ 57,965	R. Clemens	FL		
28	50351	Costco	9/29/2009	$ 16,441	A. Rod	OR		
29	50352	Sears	9/30/2009	$ 65,793	S. Moore	CA		
30								
31	Total			$ 1,194,672				

D31 f_x =SUM(D2:D29)

Sales Data | Sales by Salesperson | Sales by Customer | Sheet2 | S

Click here to view
SUM function in action

Figure 1.5

Ch1-01 Student File as Modified

16   In the Number group, click the arrow next to the Number group name to launch the Dialog Box Launcher.

17   Type **0** in the decimal places text box, and then click **OK.**

18   Use the vertical scroll bar to move down the worksheet until you can see row 31.

19   Click in cell **D31.** Note the formula =SUM(D2:D29) which appears on the formula bar.

20   In the Font group, click the **Borders** icon and then select the **Top and Double Bottom Border** icon. Depending on the size of your Excel window, your screen should look like Figure 1.5.

21   Keep this file open.

Kyle further discusses and then illustrates the changes in Excel's appearance when a different view is selected and when the screen resolution or size is changed.

Page Layout View – In Page Layout view there are page margins at the top, sides, and bottom of the worksheet as well as a bit of blue space between worksheets. Rulers at the top and side help you adjust margins. You can turn the rulers on and off as you need them (click Ruler in the Show/Hide group on the View tab). With this new view, you don't need Print Preview to make adjustments to your worksheet before you print. It's easy to add headers and footers in Page Layout view; when you type in the new header and footer area at the top or bottom of a page, the Design tab opens with all the commands you need to create them. You can see each sheet in a workbook in the view that works best for that sheet. Just select, for each worksheet, a view on the View toolbar or in the Workbook Views group on the View tab. Normal view and Page Break preview are both there.

Screen Resolution and Window Size – The figures displayed so far should match your version of Excel if your screen is set to high resolution and the Excel window is maximized. If not, things look different. If your screen is set to a low resolution —for example, to 800 by 600 pixels—then a few groups on the Ribbon will display the group name only, not the commands in the group. You will need to click the arrow on the group button to display the commands. The groups that display only the group name in a smaller resolution are those with less frequently used commands. At any resolution, if you make the Excel window smaller, there is a size at which some groups will display only the group names and so you will need to click the arrow on the group button to display the commands.

To examine the affects of page layout view and screen size:

1   Scroll to the top of the worksheet so that row A is visible in your ch1-01 file.

2 Click the **View** tab and then select **Page Layout** from the Workbook Views group. Alternatively, you could have selected the Page Layout icon from the View Toolbar. Your screen should look like Figure 1.6.

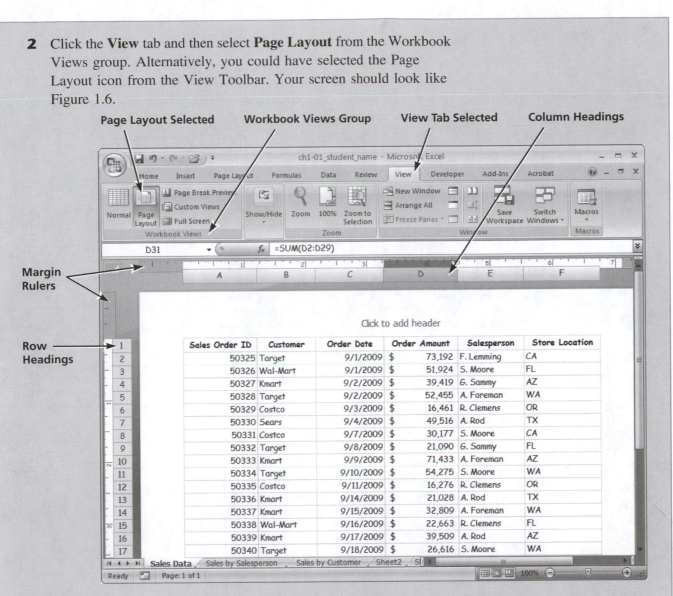

Figure 1.6
Page Layout View of the Excel Window

3 Click the **Show/Hide** group to see the expanded menu in Figure 1.7.

Figure 1.7

Show/Hide Group on the View Tab

4 Uncheck the Ruler, Formula Bar, Guidelines, and Headlines checkboxes to modify the look of the worksheet as seen in Figure 1.8.

5 Click the **Show/Hide** group and then check the Ruler, Formula Bar, Guidelines, and Headlines checkboxes.

6 Click in the text **Click to add header** and then click in the left header box.

Uncheck these boxes

Figure 1.8

Modified View of the Sales Data Worksheet

7 Type **September Sales** as the new header.

8 Select the **September Sales** text, click the **Home** tab, and click the **B** (Bold) button.

9 With the text still selected, select **12** in the font size text box.

10 Click **A** (to select column A) and then click the center text button in the Alignment group twice.

11 Click **F** (to select column F) and then click the center text button in the Alignment group twice. Your modified screen should look like Figure 1.9.

Figure 1.9

Modified September Sales Worksheet

12 Keep this file open.

"What are the tabs at the bottom of the worksheet?" Meagan asks.

"Those are different worksheets contained in our workbook" Kyle explains. "I create those using Excel's Pivot Table feature, which I'll explain later. For now I'll have you look at them to see what they tell us."

Kyle then explains that the Pivot Table feature in Excel allows you to view data in multiple ways. In the Sales by Salesperson worksheet, he organized the sales data (located on the sales data worksheet) by salesperson, providing a total of the month's sales by individual salesperson. In the Sales by Customer worksheet he reorganized the sales data by customer, providing a total of the month's sales by individual customer. In both cases Kyle has used Excel's new conditional formatting feature to reflect graphically the values for salespersons and customers relative to each other.

To view additional worksheets in a workbook:

1 Click the **Sales by Salesperson** tab to reveal the worksheet shown in Figure 1.10.

Figure 1.10

Sales by Salesperson Worksheet

Row Labels ▼	Sum of Order Amount
A. Foreman	$ 227,243.00
A. Rod	$ 211,308.00
F. Lemming	$ 136,611.00
G. Sammy	$ 157,787.00
R. Clemens	$ 209,121.00
S. Moore	$ 252,602.00
Grand Total	$ 1,194,672.00

2 Click in the down arrow next to the Row Labels text to view alternative ways of sorting or organizing this information.

3 Click the **Sales by Customer** tab to reveal the worksheet shown in Figure 1.11.

Figure 1.11

Sales by Customer Worksheet

Row Labels ▼	Sum of Order Amount
Costco	$ 176,633.00
Kmart	$ 315,464.00
Sears	$ 222,822.00
Target	$ 309,410.00
Wal-Mart	$ 170,343.00
Grand Total	$ 1,194,672.00

4 Again, click in the down arrow next to the Row Labels text to view alternative ways of sorting or organizing this information.

5 Click on the **Sales Data** tab to re-open the Sales Data worksheet.

6 Keep this file open.

Now that you've had a brief view of how to start, navigate, and work with Excel files, it's time to become familiar with Excel's help features.

Getting Excel Help

Excel's help features are quite extensive. Anytime you are working with Excel and are not certain how to accomplish a task—for example, format a cell, write a formula, or create a chart—then you should press the **[F1]** function key or click the blue and white question mark on the Tab bar. To illustrate, Kyle decides to show you Excel's help feature when trying to create a new chart.

To view Excel's help to create charts:

1 Press the [**F1**] function key or click the blue and white question mark to open Excel's help window as shown in Figure 1.12.

Figure 1.12

Excel's Help Window

> *Trouble?* You do not have to be connected to the Internet to get Excel help. However, the online help is much more extensive. This example assumes you are connected to the Internet. If you are not connected, click the text **Show me offline help from my computer** to view Excel help, keeping in mind that your window may not match the Figures shown in the text.

2 Click **Charts.**

3 Click **Creating Charts.**

4 Click **Create a Chart.**

5 Scroll down the window until the text **1. On the worksheet, arrange the data that you want to plot in a chart** is positioned at the top of the window as shown in Figure 1.13.

Figure 1.13

Excel Help for Creating
a Chart

6 Click the text **How to arrange data for specific chart types** to expand the help text.

7 Note that the text now displayed give you more details on how to arrange data for specific chart types. Close the Help window.

Now that you're familiar with Excel's help feature, Kyle thinks it is a good idea to explore how Excel is used in the accounting field.

Examples of How Excel Is Used in Accounting

There are an unlimited number of ways Excel can be used in accounting. This text will focus on building worksheets by using formulas, functions, and features available in Excel to create and analyze financial statements, calculate depreciation and create depreciation schedules, create loan and bond amortization schedules, and create cash flow budgets.

You may have previously learned how to create financial statements from a trial balance. For example, the trial balance in Figure 1.14 contains data that, through the use of cell references, formulas, and other Excel features, might be used to create the income statement shown in Figure 1.15. However, in most cases, accounting programs like QuickBooks and Peachtree are used to gather and

	A	B	C
1	Kelly's Boutique		
2	Trial Balance		
3	December 31, 2009		
4			
5	Account	Dr.	Cr.
6	Cash	$ 10,000.00	
7	Accounts receivable	15,000.00	
8	Inventory	50,000.00	
9	Prepaid expenses	1,500.00	
10	Supplies	400.00	
11	Land	30,000.00	
12	Building	100,000.00	
13	Accumulated depreciation: Building		$ 20,000.00
14	Equipment	15,000.00	
15	Accumulated depreciation: Equipment		9,000.00
16	Accounts payable		14,400.00
17	Income taxes payable		2,000.00
18	Notes payable		80,000.00
19	Payroll liabilities		2,000.00
20	Mortgage payable		70,000.00
21	Common stock		1,000.00
22	Retained earnings		1,600.00
23	Dividends	1,500.00	
24	Sales revenue		300,000.00
25	Cost of goods sold	150,000.00	
26	Advertising expense	6,000.00	
27	Depreciation expense	8,000.00	
28	Interest expense	7,000.00	
29	Income taxes	2,000.00	
30	Payroll expense	90,000.00	
31	Supplies expense	6,000.00	
32	Utilities	7,600.00	
33	Total	$ 500,000.00	$ 500,000.00
34			

Trial Balance / Income Statement

Figure 1.14

Trial Balance

	A	B	C	D
1	Kelly's Boutique			
2	Income Statement			
3	For the Year Ended December 31, 2009			
4				
5	Sales Revenue		$ 300,000.00	
6	Less: Cost of Goods Sold		150,000.00	
7	Gross Margin		150,000.00	
8	Expenses:			
9	Advertising	$ 6,000.00		
10	Depreciation	8,000.00		
11	Interest	7,000.00		
12	Payroll	90,000.00		
13	Supplies expense	6,000.00		
14	Utilities	7,600.00	124,600.00	
15	Net income before taxes		25,400.00	
16	Income taxes		2,000.00	
17	Net income		$ 23,400.00	
18				

Trial Balance / Income Statement / Statement of Retained E

Figure 1.15

Income Statement

summarize information to create financial statements. In this text we will focus on how to use Excel to support the creation and analysis of those statements.

In Chapter 3 you'll learn how to perform a financial statements analysis. For example, income statements between 2008 and 2009 are compared via a horizontal analysis in Figure 1.16, which includes a "percent of change" column. An analysis of expenses for a given year is depicted in the pie graph of Figure 1.17.

In Chapter 4 you'll learn how to perform depreciation calculations and create a depreciation schedule. For example, you'll use Excel's SLN (Straight-line

Figure 1.16

Horizontal Income
Statement

	A	B	C	D
1	Kelly's Boutique			
2	Income Statement			
3	For the Year Ended			
4				
5		12/31/2008	12/31/2009	%
6	Sales Revenue	$ 290,000.00	$ 300,000.00	3%
7	Less: Cost of Goods Sold	140,000.00	150,000.00	7%
8	Gross Margin	150,000.00	150,000.00	0%
9	Expenses:			
10	Advertising	$ 7,000.00	6,000.00	-14%
11	Depreciation	7,500.00	8,000.00	7%
12	Interest	6,000.00	7,000.00	17%
13	Payroll	92,000.00	90,000.00	-2%
14	Supplies expense	5,000.00	6,000.00	20%
15	Utilities	6,500.00	7,600.00	17%
16	Net income before taxes	26,000.00	25,400.00	-2%
17	Income taxes	1,500.00	2,000.00	33%
18	Net income	$ 24,500.00	$ 23,400.00	-4%
19				

Income Statement Horizontal / Expense Chart / Expense Comparison

Figure 1.17

Expense Chart

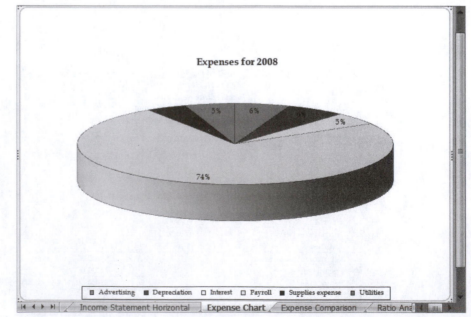

Expenses for 2008

74%   5%   6%   5%

Advertising   Depreciation   Interest   Payroll   Supplies expense   Utilities

Income Statement Horizontal   Expense Chart   Expense Comparison   Ratio Ana depreciation function) to calculate the depreciation expense for each year and related accumulated depreciation, as shown in Figure 1.18. You'll also use Excel's DDB (Declining balance depreciation function) to calculate depreciation expense for each year, as shown in Figure 1.19.

In Chapter 5 you'll learn how to perform loan amortization schedules and calculate loan payments given an interest rate, term, and loan amount. For example, you'll use Excel's PMT (Payment function) and formulas to produce the loan amortization schedule shown in Figure 1.20.

Finally, in Chapter 6 you will learn how to prepare cash receipts budgets based on a pattern of expected cash collections; see Figure 1.21 for an example.

	A	B	C
1	Kelly's Boutique Depreciation Schedule		
2			
3	Asset #	101	
4	Asset	Shelving	
5	Date acquired	1/1/2007	
6	Cost	$ 4,000.00	
7	Depreciation method	S/L	
8	Salvage value	$ 100.00	
9	Estimated useful life	3	
10			
11	Year	Depreciation Expense	Accumulated Depreciation
12	2007	$1,300.00	$1,300.00
13	2008	$1,300.00	$2,600.00
14	2009	$1,300.00	$3,900.00
15			

H ◀ ▶ H **Asset 101** / Asset 102 / Asset 103 / Asset 102

Figure 1.18

Straight-line Depreciation

	A	B	C
1	Kelly's Boutique Depreciation Schedule		
2			
3	Asset #	102	
4	Asset	Computer	
5	Date acquired	1/1/2007	
6	Cost	$ 15,000.00	
7	Depreciation method	DDB	
8	Salvage value	$ 1,000.00	
9	Estimated useful life	5	
10			
11	Year	Depreciation Expense	Accumulated Depreciation
12	2007	$6,000.00	$6,000.00
13	2008	$3,600.00	$9,600.00
14	2009	$2,160.00	$11,760.00
15	2010	$1,296.00	$13,056.00
16	2011	$777.60	$13,833.60
17			

H ◀ ▶ H / Asset 103 / **Asset 102 DDB** / Asset 102 SYD

Figure 1.19

Double Declining Balance Depreciation

Figure 1.20

Loan Amortization
Schedule

	A	B	C	D	E
1	Coast Jewelers, Inc.				
2	Loan Amortization Schedule				
3					
4	Amount	$ 325,000.00			
5	Rate	8%			
6	Term	10			
7	Payment	$48,434.58			
8					
9					
10	Payment #	Payment	Interest	Principal	Balance
11					$325,000.00
12	1	$48,434.58	$26,000.00	$22,434.58	$302,565.42
13	2	$48,434.58	$24,205.23	$24,229.35	$278,336.07
14	3	$48,434.58	$22,266.89	$26,167.70	$252,168.37
15	4	$48,434.58	$20,173.47	$28,261.11	$223,907.25
16	5	$48,434.58	$17,912.58	$30,522.00	$193,385.25
17	6	$48,434.58	$15,470.82	$32,963.76	$160,421.49
18	7	$48,434.58	$12,833.72	$35,600.87	$124,820.62
19	8	$48,434.58	$ 9,985.65	$38,448.93	$ 86,371.69
20	9	$48,434.58	$ 6,909.73	$41,524.85	$ 44,846.84
21	10	$48,434.58	$ 3,587.75	$44,846.84	$ 0.00
22					

Sheet1 / Sheet2 / Sheet3

Figure 1.21

Cash Receipts Budget

	A	B	C	D	E
1	Kelly's Boutique				
2	Cash Receipts Budget				
3					
4					
5			Jan	Feb	Mar
6	Total revenue		$50,000.00	$55,000.00	$60,500.00
7	Collections in month of sale	40%	20,000.00	22,000.00	24,200.00
8	Collections in 1st month following sale	50%	8,000.00	25,000.00	27,500.00
9	Collections in 2nd month following sale	10%	2,000.00	2,000.00	5,000.00
10	Total cash receipts		$30,000.00	$49,000.00	$56,700.00
11					

Sales / Purchases / Selling and Administrative Exp / Cash Receipts / Cash Disbur

End Note

The three of you are somewhat overwhelmed by your first exposure to Excel but are pleased with what you've accomplished. You've learned some of Excel's capabilities and new features; how to start, navigate, and work with Excel files; how to use Excel help; and how Excel is used in accounting.

In the next chapter you will learn how to enter information, create formulas, use functions, and print in Excel.

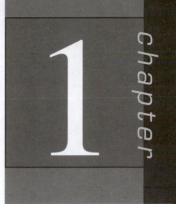

Chapter 1 Questions

1 Identify some new features in the 2007 version of Excel.

2 Why would you use conditional formatting?

3 Explain the difference between a worksheet and a workbook.

4 What and where is the Microsoft Office button?

5 What and where is the Quick Access Toolbar?

6 Describe the Ribbon.

7 How do you modify the Quick Access Toolbar to add the Open command?

8 What is the Page Layout view?

9 What is the quickest way to get help while in Excel?

10 What are the key accounting topics addressed in this text that relate to your learning Excel?

Excel Basics

In this chapter you will learn:

- How to enter information into a worksheet
- How to use formulas more extensively
- How to manipulate data and structure worksheets
- How to print a worksheet

Case: Coast Jewelers, Inc.

After providing you a tour of Excel, Kyle suggests you all practice entering information into Excel using some formulas, functions, and features that are common to almost all accounting applications. He has created a preliminary trial balance for you to work on.

Entering Information

To complete the trial balance it will be necessary to enter additional text and numbers. The basic data entry container for Excel is a cell. Each cell has an address determined by its location on the worksheet grid. The column number and row number determine the address.

Entering Data

Kyle explains that, before putting data into a cell, you must first select the cell by clicking on it. As you type, the data is also automatically entered into the formula bar. Text entries into cells are often referred to as *labels*, whereas numbers or formula entries are referred to as *values*.

To open the trial balance file and enter data into the worksheet:

1 Click the **Microsoft Office** button and then click **Open.**

2 Navigate the Open window to the location of this text's student files. (The location would be the CD provided with the text or from your computer lab's server.)

3 Double-click the file **ch2-01**, which should be located in a Ch 02 folder. The workbook shown in Figure 2.1 should appear.

Figure 2.1

Partially Completed Trial Balance

4 Click cell **B7**, type **84245.25**, then press the [**Enter**] key. Note how the number is automatically formatted for you (more on this later). Note also that the active cell is now one row lower, at cell B8.

5 Type **125351.45** in cell B8, and then press the [**Enter**] key.

6 Click cell **C20**, type **1527515.65**, then press the [**Enter**] key. Note that the cell value may show several # signs. If this happens, you will need to resize the column width (more about this later).

7 Click cell **A26**, type the label Total, then press the [**Enter**] key. We'll format this cell later.

8 Continue to fill in the remaining empty cells so that your worksheet looks like that shown in Figure 2.2.

9 Click the **Microsoft Office** button again and then click **Save As.** (This is done to keep your original student file available in case you need it again and also to provide a unique name for your file.)

10 Add your name to the file name using the underscore key as you have done previously. In this example the file will be saved as ch2-01_student_name (again, replace student_name with your name). Be sure to save your file to a location (e.g., a USB drive) from which you can later retrieve it.

Figure 2.2

Almost Completed Trial Balance

	A	B	C	D
1	*Coast Jewelers, Inc.*			
2	*Trial Balance*			
3	*December 31, 2009*			
4				
5	Account	Dr.	Cr.	
6	Cash	25,412.35		
7	Accounts receivable	84,245.25		
8	Inventory	125,351.45		
9	Prepaid expenses	15,625.26		
10	Supplies	10,245.15		
11	Land	120,000.00		
12	Building	300,000.00		
13	Accumulated depreciation: Building		60,000.00	
14	Equipment	65,000.00		
15	Accumulated depreciation: Equipment		8,000.00	
16	Accounts payable		75,182.10	
17	Long-term debt		400,000.00	
18	Common stock		10,000.00	
19	Retained earnings		15,000.00	
20	Sales revenue		######	
21	Cost of goods sold	993,900.30		
22	Advertising expense	54,215.45		
23	Depreciation expense	16,000.00		
24	Payroll expense	240,451.45		
25	Utilities	45,251.09		
26	Total			

Sheet1 / Sheet2 / Sheet3

You have thus entered both values and labels into your worksheet. Now you can make changes to the data already entered.

Changing Column Width and Row Height

Perhaps now is a good time to fix that sales number on the trial balance as Kyle suggests. The problem occurred when a number entered in cell C20 was wider than the column permitted. The result was a cell filled with # signs. To fix it, Kyle explains, all you have to do is resize column C. However, for uniformity, you should not only column C but also column B.

To change the column width and row height of a worksheet:

1 Place the mouse pointer between column C and column D at the top of the columns so that the mouse pointer cursor changes into a line with two arrows pointing left and right.

2 Click and hold the mouse button down to reveal the column width as being Width: 10.88 (92 pixels).

3 While still holding the mouse button down drag the column width to the right until the width is 13.00 (109 pixels).

4 To resize both column B and C point the mouse pointer to the B of column B and click once. (This selects the entire column B.)

5 Now click and drag from the B of column B to the C of column C. (This selects both columns B and C.)

6 With both columns selected, place the mouse pointer between column B and column C at the top of the columns so that the mouse pointer cursor changes into a line with two arrows pointing left and right.

7 Click and drag the column width to the right until the width is 13.00 (109 pixels). Both columns should now be the same width 13.00 (109 pixels).

8 To resize the height of row 4, click between rows 4 and 5 at the far left of the worksheet until the mouse pointer cursor changes into a line with two arrows pointing up and down.

9 While still holding the mouse button down drag the row height down until the height is 21.00 (28 pixels).

"If you are like me," Kyle admits, "you will find yourself making a few mistakes along the way."

Editing Data

Nathan agrees and wants to know about correcting errors. He claims he's not very good at typing and has made some mistakes when entering previous information. Kyle explains that you can always edit the information entered into a worksheet regardless of whether you've already pressed the Enter key or not.

Excel gives you two ways to edit data. You can either edit the formula bar or edit data directly in the cell. For instance, let's assume the utilities expense number you entered in cell B25 was 45251.09 when it should have been 45251.90. Also assume that the prepaid expenses entered in cell B9 was 15624.26 when it should have been 15625.45.

To edit data in the worksheet:

1 Click once in cell **B25**.

2 Double-click the value you entered into the cell. Note that this opens up the cell for editing.

3 Double-click the value again and the entire value is selected.

4 Type **45251.90** and the press the [**Enter**] key.

5 Click once in cell **B9**.

6 Double-click the value you entered into the cell. Note that this opens up the cell for editing.

7 Double-click the value again and the entire value is selected.

8 Type **15625.45** and the press the [**Enter**] key.

9 Since you actually did enter in the correct values you should undo your changes. Click the **Undo** button from the Quick Access Toolbar two times.

Meagan says she will probably have to use this procedure often because her keyboarding skills are rather weak. Fortunately, it is easy to use this process for correcting errors and making changes to a worksheet.

Controlling the Appearance of Data

You ask Kyle why the numbers on the trial balance are formatted with commas, since you didn't type commas when you entered the values. He explains that initially he formatted both columns B and C to be in the "comma" format. Formatting does not change the text or numbers in the cell itself; rather, it changes the way the text or numbers appear in the worksheet. To experiment, he suggests you modify the format of cells B6, C13, B26, and C26 to a "currency" format, since the top and bottom of a column of accounting numbers are usually formatted with the $. He further suggests that you replace the format with a "comma and cents" format using the format painter.

To apply the currency format to specific cells:

1 Click cell **B6**, then click the **Accounting Number Format** tool (it looks like a $) on the Number group in the Ribbon. Note how the number still has the comma and cents formatting from before but now contains the $.

2 With cell B6 still selected, click the **Format Painter** tool (it looks like a paintbrush) on the Clipboard group. Note that cell B6 now has ants dancing around the border of the cell and that the mouse pointer has an added paintbrush.

3 Click cell **C13.** You have now painted the Accounting Number Format to that cell.

4 Click cell **C13** and then click the **Format Painter** tool again.

5 Click in cell **B26** and, with the mouse button still down, drag it to the right to include cell C26; then release the mouse button. You have now painted the Accounting Number Format to cells B26 and C26, which will soon contain the total of each column.

Kyle also explains that it is common practice to total the debit and credit columns of a trial balance and include a double underline under such totals. Because you are in the midst of formatting cells, he suggests you format the two "total" cells before you create a formula adding a column of cells.

To format the "total" cells with a double underline:

1 Click and highlight cells **B26** and **C26** by clicking first in B26 and then dragging the mouse to C26 while holding down the mouse button.

2 Place the mouse pointer over the Borders tool located on the Font group—specifically, over the small arrow located on the right of the Borders tool. Click the arrow to reveal several border options.

3 Click the **Top and Double Bottom Border** tool to format the cells.

To finish the trial balance, all you need now is a total for each column.

Entering Formulas and Using Functions

Formulas in Excel always begin with an equal sign (=). These formulas can use numbers; math symbols to add, subtract, multiply, or divide (+, −, *, /); cell references; and/or functions. Nathan asks if Excel has a calculator built in so one could add the column and then put the result in the total cell. Kyle explains that the disadvantage of such an approach is that, if your numbers later change, then you'd have to re-add the column. Meagan asks if the best way to add a column of numbers is therefore to add each *cell*. Kyle explains you could certainly do that by typing a formula like this: =B6+B7+B8 et cetera.

However, Kyle explains that Excel includes some functions that accomplish this task in a more efficient manner. The SUM function, for instance, will sum up specified series of cells.

"Hold on," you say. "Functions sound like programming and I'm just an accounting student who has no desire to learn computer programming."

"Don't panic!" Kyle advises. "Excel's functions are fairly simple. Each function reacts to certain arguments you provide. For instance, the SUM function is written as follows: =SUM(argument). The argument is a series of cell references you want summed. Let me show you how to add the sum function to your trial balance to add up the debit and credit columns."

To use the SUM function to add a column of numbers:

1 Click cell **B26.**

2 Type **=SUM(B6:B25)**, then press **[Enter].** The result of that function should be the amount $2,095,697.75.

3 Click cell **C26.**

4 Alternatively, you can enter the argument by clicking and dragging the mouse pointer over the cells to be added. Click the **AutoSum** button in the Editing group of the Home tab.

5 Dancing ants should now be marching around the cells C15 to C25, as shown in Figure 2.3.

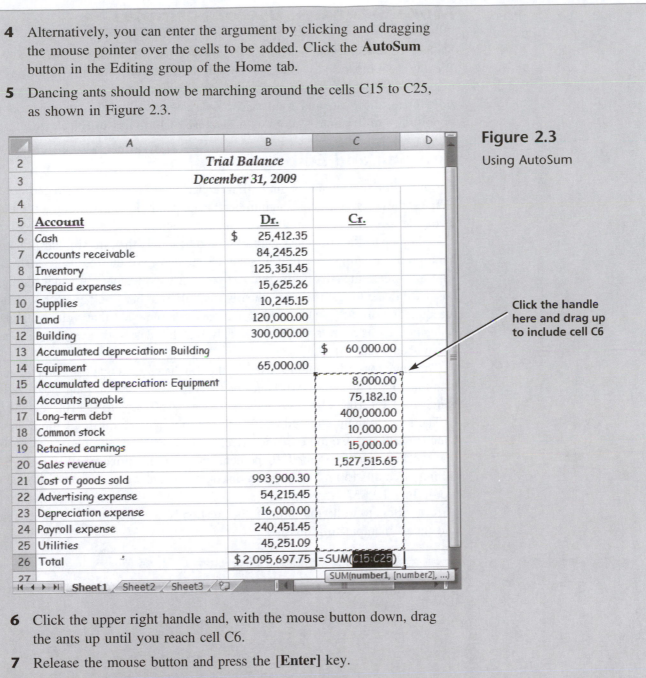

Figure 2.3

Using AutoSum

Click the handle here and drag up to include cell C6

6 Click the upper right handle and, with the mouse button down, drag the ants up until you reach cell C6.

7 Release the mouse button and press the [**Enter**] key.

8 Click the **Microsoft Office** button and then click **Save** to save your file. (Alternatively, you can click the **Save** button on the Quick Access Toolbar or press [**Ctrl**] [**S**].

Kyle explains that now you've used two different methods of entering a sum function to add up both the debit and credit columns. In both cases the resulting formula is the same; you've simply used different methods to achieve the same goal. Moreover, if you enter different data in the cells B6 to B25 or C6 to C25, the SUM function will automatically add them up.

More Extensive Use of Formulas

Nathan comments that he envisions another use of this worksheet software. Weekly he prepares, by hand, a "watch sales" worksheet that identifies how many Citizen watches have been sold each week as well as their cost, markup, sales price, discount, and total sales. Kyle suggests that this might be a good opportunity to illustrate a more extensive use of formulas in Excel.

Entering and Editing Formulas

Formulas in Excel always begin with an equal sign (=). As explained earlier in this chapter, these formulas can use numbers; math symbols to add, subtract, multiply, or divide (+, −, *, /); cell references; and/or functions.

Kyle prepares a worksheet with titles and headings that are similar to Nathan's hand-prepared worksheet. In it he includes the names of the four types of watches sold that week, the cost or price Coast paid for each watch, the usual markup on cost used to determine the price, the discount offered that week on each watch, and the quantity of each watch sold. Kyle then recommends that you, Nathan, and Meagan use this form to prepare a weekly Watch Sales worksheet for the week of November 6, 2009.

The price for each watch is based on the watch cost and markup percentage. For example, if a watch costs $100 and the markup is 50 percent, then Coast sells the watch for $150 (the $100 cost plus a markup of 50 percent × $100, or $50).

The total column is the product of the price less discount times the number of watches sold. For example, if the price (as previously determined) was $150 but that week it was discounted 10 percent, then the net price would be $135 (the selling price of $150 minus the $15 discount). If five watches were sold, the total would then be $675 (5 × $135).

Kyle offers to walk you through the creation of formulas, the use of references, and (later) manipulating the data.

To enter and edit formulas for the Weekly Watch Sales worksheet:

1 Open **ch2-02.xls** to reveal a file that should look like Figure 2.4.

Figure 2.4

Watch Sales

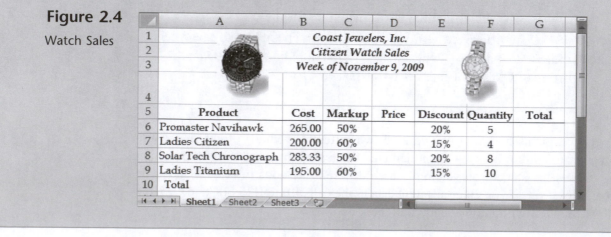

	A	B	C	D	E	F	G
1			*Coast Jewelers, Inc.*				
2			*Citizen Watch Sales*				
3			*Week of November 9, 2009*				
4							
5	**Product**	**Cost**	**Markup**	**Price**	**Discount**	**Quantity**	**Total**
6	Promaster Navihawk	265.00	50%		20%	5	
7	Ladies Citizen	200.00	60%		15%	4	
8	Solar Tech Chronograph	283.33	50%		20%	8	
9	Ladies Titanium	195.00	60%		15%	10	
10	Total						

Sheet1 Sheet2 Sheet3

2 Click in cell **D6**, where you will place the formula to calculate price.

3 Remember, the formula for determining price is cost plus markup; hence you must enter a formula that computes the markup and then adds it to the cost. Type the formula **= B6+(B6*C6)** into cell D6 and then press **[Enter]**. Note that B6 is the location of the cost and C6 is the location of the markup percentage. Note also that the cell has been preformatted so that two decimal places are always shown.

4 Click in cell **G6**, where you will place the formula to calculate the total sales of the Promaster Navihawk.

5 Recall that the formula for determining total sales is price less discount times the number sold; hence, you need to enter a formula that computes the net price and then multiplies it by the number sold. Type the formula **= (D6–(D6*E6))*F6** into cell G6, then press **[Enter]**. Note that D6 is the location of the price, E6 is the location of the discount percentage, and F6 is the location of the number sold. Note also that the cell has been preformatted so that two decimal places are always shown.

6 Keep this file open.

"Hold on a minute," Meagan says. "All of those parentheses are confusing me."

Kyle explains that the formula required those parentheses to specify the order of calculation. The formula (D6–(D6*E6))*F6 requires the innermost (here, bold) set of parentheses to be calculated first. This is the calculation of the discount (the price times the discount percentage). The outermost set of parentheses in the formula (D6–(D6*E6))*F6 is acted on next. This is the calculation of the discounted price (price less discount). Finally, the formula multiplies the newly calculated discounted price by the number sold to yield the total.

"Do we now have to type additional formulas for the other watches?" you ask.

"Thank goodness, no," Kyle replies. "Excel has an AutoFill feature that saves you the time and effort of reentering similar formulas."

Manipulating Data and Structuring Worksheets

The AutoFill feature is handy whenever you need formulas or data replicated down or across a worksheet. Kyle mentions that understanding this feature requires that you also understand the concept of relative and absolute references.

Using AutoFill

In the Weekly Watch Sales worksheet you created formulas to calculate price and total sales for the Promaster Navihawk watch. Now you want to use a similar formula to calculate the price and total sales for the other watches. Kyle suggests you try the AutoFill feature yourself.

To use the AutoFill feature:

1 Click in cell **D6** on the Weekly Watch Sales worksheet.

2 Note that, when selected, the cell is outlined and a small square appears in the lower right corner of the cell. Click and hold the mouse button down so the mouse pointer is over that square. Then drag the frame down to cell **D9** and release the mouse button.

3 Click in cell **G6.**

4 Click and hold the mouse button down so that the mouse pointer is over the square in the lower right corner of the cell. Drag the frame down to cell **G9** and then release the mouse button. Your revised worksheet should look like Figure 2.5.

Figure 2.5

Watch Sales with Price and Total Values

	A	B	C	D	E	F	G
1			*Coast Jewelers, Inc.*				
2			*Citizen Watch Sales*				
3			*Week of November 9, 2009*				
4							
5	**Product**	**Cost**	**Markup**	**Price**	**Discount**	**Quantity**	**Total**
6	Promaster Navihawk	265.00	50%	397.50	20%	5	1,590.00
7	Ladies Citizen	200.00	60%	320.00	15%	4	1,088.00
8	Solar Tech Chronograph	283.33	50%	425.00	20%	8	2,719.97
9	Ladies Titanium	195.00	60%	312.00	15%	10	2,652.00
10	Total						

H ◀ ▶ H   **Sheet1** / Sheet2 / Sheet3 /

5 Keep this file open.

"I see," you say. "By using the AutoFill feature we've copied the same formula down the worksheet."

"Not exactly," Kyle responds. "In fact, you've copied a similar formula down the worksheet, but it's not the same."

Kyle suggests that this is a good time to explain the worksheet concept of relative and absolute references.

Using Relative and Absolute References

The formula placed in cells D7, D8, and D9 after using the AutoFill feature is similar but not exactly like the formula you wrote in cell D6. If you look at the resulting formula created in cell D7 and compare it to the formula in cell D6 you will see relative referencing at work. Cell D6 contains the formula B6+(B6*C6). Cell D7 contains the formula B7+(B7*C7). In other words, using AutoFill changed the formula by increasing the row reference by 1, from row 6 to row 7. This will continue to occur as Autofill moves down relative to the original formula. Once again, looking at cell D8, you see the formula B8+(B8*C8) and at cell D9 the formula B9+(B9*C9).

"Do you always want AutoFill to change the references?" Nathan asks.

"Not necessarily," Kyle answers.

Kyle points out that relative referencing works well in this particular worksheet. An alternative scenario that would *not* use relative referencing is one where the discount is some specific percentage for all sales. If you locate that percentage in one cell, then relative referencing would not create proper formulas. He suggests you create a cell that specifies a discount percentage for that week, clear the discount part of the worksheet, and rewrite the total formula.

To use absolute references in the worksheet:

1 Before making the following changes, click **Microsoft Office** button, then **Save As** to save the Excel file.

2 Name the file **ch2-02_student_name.xls** (replacing student_name with your name as before), then click **Save.** You will now make changes to the file to illustrate absolute references.

3 Type **Discount %** in cell A13. This is a label for the value you will place in cell B13. Press [**Tab**] to move to the next cell.

4 Type **10%** in cell B13, then press [**Enter**].

5 Select cells E5 through E9 by clicking in cell **E5** and then, while holding down the Shift key, clicking cell **E9.** (This selects the five contiguous cells.) Alternatively, you could click in cell **E5** and, while holding the mouse button down, drag the mouse pointer down to cell E9.

6 Right-click the selected cells to reveal the Shortcut menu, then click **Clear Contents.** This removes values and text previously shown at E5 through E9.

7 Click cell **G6.**

8 Type a new formula = (**D6–(D6*B13))*F6** in cell G6. This results in replacing the cell reference E6 with the cell reference B13.

9 Using AutoFill, replicate the formula in cell G6 down to G9. This, however, causes a problem due to relative referencing: the formula in G7 now contains a reference to B14 instead of the discount specified in B13. What we should have done is changed the B13 reference from a relative reference to an absolute reference.

10 Change the formula at G6 to = (**D6–(D6*$B$13))*F6** by placing a $ in front of the B and the 13. The addition of the $ freezes the reference to an absolute cell, regardless of where the cell may be copied to or automatically filled using AutoFill. After you have edited the formula, press [**Enter**].

11 Using AutoFill, replicate the modified formula in cell G6 down through cell G9. Your worksheet should now look like Figure 2.6.

Figure 2.6

Using Absolute
Referencing

	A	B	C	D	E	F	G
1			*Coast Jewelers, Inc.*				
2			*Citizen Watch Sales*				
3			*Week of November 9, 2009*				
4							
5	**Product**	**Cost**	**Markup**	**Price**	**Discount**	**Quantity**	**Total**
6	Promaster Navihawk	265.00	50%	397.50		5	1,788.75
7	Ladies Citizen	200.00	60%	320.00		4	1,152.00
8	Solar Tech Chronograph	283.33	50%	425.00		8	3,059.96
9	Ladies Titanium	195.00	60%	312.00		10	2,808.00
10	Total						
11							
12							
13	Discount %		10%				
14							

Sheet1 / Sheet2 / Sheet3

12 Keep this file open.

"So what happens if I change the discount from 10 percent to 13 percent?" Nathan asks. Kyle demonstrates that the new formula creates new totals as a different discount percentage is entered into cell B13. He suggests you try some alternative percentages to see the effects on the total column. When you are finished experimenting, return the discount to 10 percent.

Inserting and Deleting Columns and Rows

To clean up the look of the worksheet, Kyle suggests you remove the old discount column and add a formula to sum total sales for the week in cell F10.

In addition, Nathan wants to know how to add a row if a different watch is sold.

To insert and delete columns and rows from the worksheet:

1 Click the **8** in row 8 to select the entire row.

2 Right-click the **8** in row 8 to reveal the Shortcut menu, then click **Insert** to add a new row.

3 Add the following watch sales information to the new row 8: product, **Men's Citizen**; cost, **300**; markup, **50%**; quantity, **1.**

4 Use AutoFill to fill down the proper formulas for cells D8 and G8.

5 Click the **E** in column E to select the entire column.

6 Right-click the **E** in column E to reveal the Shortcut menu, then click **Delete** to delete the column.

T r o u b l e ? Excel has an Undo command, which allows you to reverse any number of actions you have executed on a worksheet. If you accidentally delete the wrong column or too many columns, click the **Undo** button on the Quick Access toolbar.

7   Click cell **F11.**

8   Click the **AutoSum** tool from the Editing group, then press [**Enter**]. Note how Excel's AutoSum feature automatically selects cells adjacent to cell F11 that it thinks contain data you want to sum. This is a handy feature, but it doesn't always select the cell you want to sum. In this case it worked great!

9   To polish off your worksheet, click cell **F11** again and format it with a **Top and Double Bottom Border** by using the Borders tool from the Font group.

10   Click cell **B14.** Format the cell to make the label bold by clicking the **Bold** tool from the Font group. Your completed worksheet should look like Figure 2.7.

	A	B	C	D	E	F
1		*Coast Jewelers, Inc.*				
2		*Citizen Watch Sales*				
3		*Week of November 9, 2009*				
4						
5	Product	Cost	Markup	Price	Quantity	Total
6	Promaster Navihawk	265.00	50%	397.50	5	1,788.75
7	Ladies Citizen	200.00	60%	320.00	4	1,152.00
8	Men's Citizen	300.00	50%	450.00	1	405.00
9	Solar Tech Chronograph	283.33	50%	425.00	8	3,059.96
10	Ladies Titanium	195.00	60%	312.00	10	2,808.00
11	Total					9,213.71
12						
13						
14	Discount %	10%				
15						

Sheet1 / Sheet2 / Sheet3

Figure 2.7

Final Watch Sales Worksheet

11   Click the **Microsoft Office** button and then click **Save** to save your work.

12   Keep this file open.

Working with Multiple Worksheets

Meagan is pleased with the results of the completed Weekly Watch Sales worksheet, but now she would like the sales to be summarized in 4-week increments. Kyle replies that the best way to handle this would be to use multiple worksheets.

You can create a worksheet for every week and a summary sheet for every 4-week period.

At the bottom of the worksheet in Figure 1.9 you can see the three tabs labeling each worksheet: Sheet1, Sheet2, and Sheet3. Kyle suggests you first re-label Sheet1 as November 9, indicating the start of the week. Then he suggests you copy the November 6 worksheet and create a November 16 worksheet, then again for November 23, and so on until four worksheets have been created.

To work with multiple worksheets:

1 Double-click the tab **Sheet1**, change the name of the worksheet to **November 9**, and then press the [**Enter**] key.

2 Right-click the newly labeled tab **November 9** to reveal the Shortcut menu, then click **Move or Copy.**

3 Check the **Create a copy** checkbox, click **Sheet2**, then click **OK** in the Move or Copy window. A new worksheet labeled November 6 (2) appears in the workbook.

4 Double-click the tab **November 9 (2)**, change the name of the worksheet to **November 16**, and then press the [**Enter**] key. You now have two identical worksheets.

5 Repeat this process two more times to create a total of four worksheets, the last two labeled November 23 and November 30. To see all the worksheets, you may have to shrink the scroll box on the bottom of the worksheet.

6 Place the mouse pointer just to the left of the arrow on the horizontal scroll box. Click and drag the mouse pointer to the right until all four weekly worksheet tabs are visible.

7 Change the title of each worksheet to reflect the new dates by editing cell A3. Click cell **A3** on the worksheet November 13 and change the date to read November 13. Continue the same process for the last two worksheets. Remember: to change active worksheets, click the title of each worksheet on the bottom tabs.

8 Change the number of watches sold for the week of November 16 (located in cells E6 to E10) to **3,2,7,1,4** respectively. Also change the discount percentage of cell B14 to **0%.**

9 Change the number of watches sold for the week of November 23 (located in cells E6 to E10) to **4,1,8,2,5** respectively. Also change the discount percentage of cell B13 to **5%.**

10 Change the number of watches sold for the week of November 30 (located in cells E6 to E10) to **3,6,7,4,8** respectively. Also change the discount percentage of cell B13 to **15%.**

11 You now have four worksheets with different sales information for each period.

12 Save the updated worksheet.

13 Keep this file open.

Finally, a Summary worksheet can be created that summarizes sales from each week. Kyle suggests you change the name of Sheet2 to Summary, move that worksheet to the front of the workbook, and set up a Summary worksheet using the copy and paste features of Excel.

To set up a summary worksheet:

1 Double-click the tab **Sheet2**, change the name of the worksheet to **Summary** and press [**Enter**].

2 Click and hold the mouse button down over the **Summary** tab, then drag the tab to the left-most part of the workbook (just to the left of the November 9 tab). Release the mouse button.

3 Click the **November 9** worksheet tab.

4 Select cells **A1** to **A3**, right-click the mouse to activate the Shortcut menu, and click **Copy** to copy the worksheet title.

5 Click the **Summary** worksheet tab, click in cell **A1**, right-click the mouse button, and click **Paste** to paste the worksheet title. If the watch picture is captured as well, click to select it and then press [**Delete**].

6 Click cell **A3** and type **Summary.**

7 Resize the height of row **4** to **47** pixels.

8 Click the **November 9** worksheet tab.

9 Select cells **A5** to **A11**, right-click the mouse to activate the Shortcut menu and click **Copy** to copy the product title and names.

10 Click the **Summary** worksheet tab, click in cell **A5**, right-click the mouse button, and click **Paste** to paste the product title and names.

11 Resize column A to fit the product title and names (181 pixels).

12 In cells B5 to F5 type the various weekly dates: **Nov 9**, **Nov 16**, **Nov 23**, **Nov 30**, and **Total** respectively.

13 Format cells B5 to F5 using the **Bold**, **Center**, and **Bottom Border** tools on the Format toolbar. The resulting worksheet should look like Figure 2.8.

Figure 2.8

Creating a Summary Worksheet

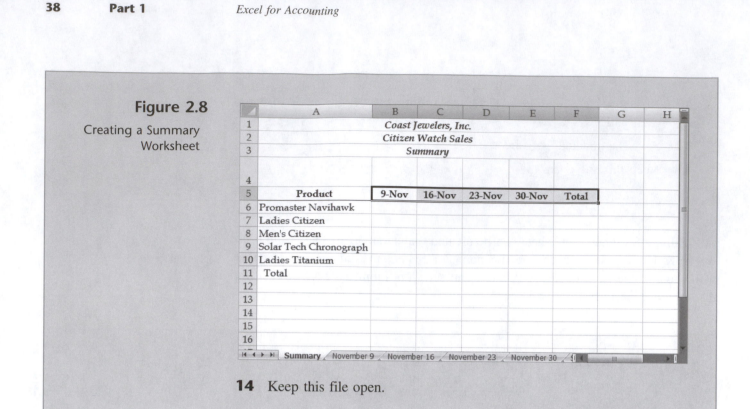

14 Keep this file open.

The Summary worksheet you've set up is now ready for weekly data. Rather than typing the totals from each product for each week, Excel enables you to link the Summary worksheet with the weekly worksheets.

To link the Summary worksheet to weekly worksheets:

1 Click in cell **B6** of the Summary worksheet.

2 Type = into cell B6.

3 Before pressing Enter, activate the November 9 worksheet and click in cell **F6**; then press **[Enter].** This automatically enters the reference 'November 9'!F6 into the Summary worksheet cell B6.

4 Use AutoFill to replicate the formula now entered in the Summary worksheet cell B6 down the worksheet to cell B10.

5 Click in cell **C6** of the Summary worksheet.

6 Type = into cell C6.

7 Before pressing Enter, activate the November 16 worksheet and click in cell **F6**; then press **[Enter].** This automatically enters the reference 'November 16'!F6 into the Summary worksheet cell C6.

8 Use AutoFill to replicate the formula now entered in the Summary worksheet cell C6 down the worksheet to cell C10.

9 Repeat this same process for November 23 and November 30.

10 Use the SUM function to total sales by product in cells F6 through F10 on the Summary worksheet.

11   Use the SUM function to total weekly sales in cells B11 through F11.

12   Format cells B11 to F11 with a Top and Double Bottom Border.

13   Increase the size of column F to remove the # signs in cell F11.

14   Reduce the size of the horizontal scroll box to reveal all worksheet tabs in your Watch Sales workbook. The completed summary worksheet should look like Figure 2.9.

Figure 2.9

Completed Summary Worksheet

	A	B	C	D	E	F	G
1		Coast Jewelers, Inc.					
2		Citizen Watch Sales					
3		Summary					
4							
5	Product	9-Nov	16-Nov	23-Nov	30-Nov	Total	
6	Promaster Navihawk	1,788.75	1,192.50	1,510.50	1,013.63	5,505.38	
7	Ladies Citizen	1,152.00	640.00	304.00	1,632.00	3,728.00	
8	Men's Citizen	405.00	3,150.00	3,420.00	2,677.50	9,652.50	
9	Solar Tech Chronograph	3,059.96	425.00	807.49	1,444.98	5,737.43	
10	Ladies Titanium	2,808.00	1,248.00	1,482.00	2,121.60	7,659.60	
11	Total	9,213.71	6,655.50	7,523.99	8,889.71	32,282.91	
12							

Summary | November 9 | November 16 | November 23 | November 30 | S...

15   Save your work.

16   Keep this file open.

Using Headers and Footers

Often you will create multiple versions of a worksheet and, when they are printed, you won't know which version is which. Thus, it's important to include a date and time stamp on each worksheet. Kyle indicates that Excel has a built-in function that will not only date and time-stamp your work but also indicate the file name on each worksheet when printed. Both of these functions can be placed in either the header or footer of a worksheet.

To use headers and footers in a worksheet:

1   Click the **View** tab on the Ribbon, then click **Page Layout** from the Workbook Views group.

2   Double-click **Click to add header**, and then click the **Design** tab on the Ribbon.

3   Click **Header** from the Header & Footer group on the Ribbon and then click **Summary.**

4   Press [**Tab**] to move to the right section of the header.

5 Click **Current Date** from the Header & Footer Elements group on the Ribbon. (This inserts &[Date] into the right header text box and will print the system date in the upper right corner of each worksheet; the *system date* is the current date you are printing your worksheet.)

6 Press [**Tab**]. Your screen should look like Figure 2.10 except for the current date, which will instead be the system date at the time you complete this work.

Figure 2.10

Adding a Header to Your Worksheet

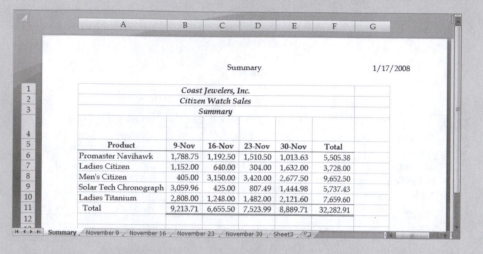

7 Scroll to the bottom of your worksheet.

8 Double-click **Click to add footer**, and then click **File Name** from the Header & Footer Elements group of the Design tab on the Ribbon. This inserts &[File] into the footer and will print the worksheet file name in the footer of each worksheet.

9 Click **OK** and note the file name (ch2-02_student_name.xls) in the Footer preview box.

10 Click **Normal** from the Workbook Views group on the View tab of the Ribbon.

11 Keep this file open.

Printing

Printing often requires three steps: previewing the print job, editing the page setup, and then finally printing the worksheet. Kyle suggests that, to save paper, these three steps should always be performed.

Using Print Preview and Page Setup

Previewing the print job will save you lots of paper and headaches, Kyle explains. A print preview is available from Microsoft Office button. In addition to previewing the print job, the Print window also gives you the option of zooming in on the print job, modifying margins, viewing page breaks, and printing the job.

Page Setup establishes the worksheet's page orientation and scaling, margin specifications, headers and footers (which we just addressed), and "sheet" provisions that include print area and print titles.

The Page section is the first tab, located on the far left of the Page Setup window. Here you can specify the page orientation (Portrait or Landscape). Kyle prefers the terms vertical and horizontal, which more accurately communicate the direction the worksheet will be printed on a standard 8½⬚ by 11⬚ piece of paper. If the worksheet is too big to print on just one sheet, the user can scale the printing by a percentage of its normal size or to fit on a specific number of pages.

The Margin section is the second tab. Here you can modify the header and footer depth as well as the top, bottom, right, and left margins. In addition, you can specify that the worksheet be centered on the page either horizontally, vertically, both, or neither.

The Sheet section allows you to restrict printing to a certain segment of the worksheet and to repeat titles at the top or left of the worksheet if your printing runs more than a single page. While editing worksheets, Kyle likes to print his work in process and take it on the road, where he doesn't have a computer. In this case he prints the gridlines and row and column headings so he can write additional formulas by hand.

Kyle decides to modify the page setup for the Summary worksheet by specifying a portrait orientation, centering the worksheet horizontally, and with gridlines and row and column headings.

To preview a print job and edit the page setup of a worksheet:

1 Click the **Microsoft Office** button and then click **Print** and then click **Print Preview.**

2 Click **Page Setup** to reveal the Page Setup window.

3 Click the **Page** tab and **Portrait** orientation option button if it is not already selected.

4 Click the **Margins** tab and click the **horizontally** checkbox on the **Center on page** section.

5 Click the **Sheet** tab and click the **Gridlines** and **Row and column headings** checkboxes.

6 Click the **Header/Footer** tab; note that your previous modifications to the header and footer (during the page layout) have been preserved here.

7 Click **OK.**

8 Click **Zoom** from the Print Preview tab to magnify the pending print job, then use the scroll bars to move around your view of the print job. You screen should look like Figure 2.11.

Figure 2.11

Print Preview with Mag-
nification

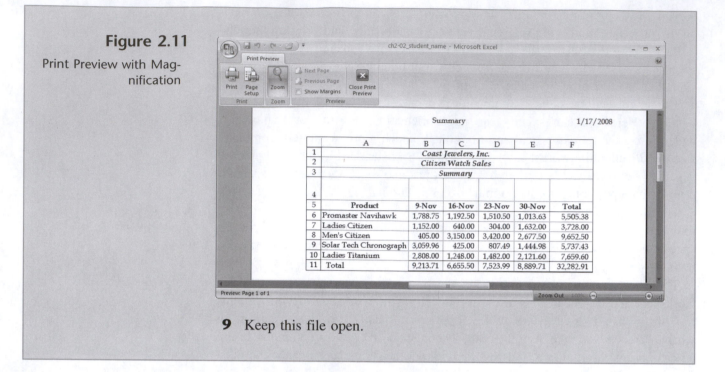

9 Keep this file open.

Printing a Worksheet

As already mentioned, you can print from the Print Preview window or print directly from the worksheet. Kyle once again suggests that you always preview your work before printing and thus that you get into the habit of printing from the Print Preview window.

The Print Preview window allows you to select a printer (assuming more than one printer is connected to your computer or network). In addition, you can specify the print range (which pages to print), what you wish to print (the entire workbook, the active sheet(s), or a specific selection you've already highlighted on the worksheet), and/or how many copies you want printed.

Meagan suggests you print one copy of the entire workbook with the gridlines and row and column headings specified previously as well as one copy of the summary worksheet without gridlines and row and column headings.

To print the workbook:

1 From the Print Preview window, click **Print.**

2 In the Print window click the **Entire workbook** option button in the Print what section, then click **OK.** This should print five pages.

> *Trouble?* You may have to specify which printer to print to in lab situations. Please see the lab consultant or your instructor for instructions.

3 Save your work.

Nathan notices that, when the workbook was printed in total, only the Summary worksheet had a header and footer. Kyle explains that this happened because you had set up the header and footer for the Summary worksheet only; thus, headers and footers for the remaining worksheets should not be expected.

Printing and Viewing Formulas

"Is there any way to look at a worksheet and see all the formulas in the worksheet without clicking on each cell?" Nathan asks.

"Yes," Kyle replies. "You can not only view the underlying formulas, but often you'll want to print them for later analysis."

Kyle offers to demonstrate this Excel feature and advises that, whenever you print a worksheet with formulas, you be sure to include gridlines and row and column headings for easy reference. He suggests you print the formulas found on the November 9 sheet.

To view and print formulas in a worksheet:

1 Click the **November 9** tab.

2 While holding the **Ctrl** key down, press the [`] key (located just above the Tab key). This reveals all cells as formulas, a feature known as the Formula view. Observe that the columns become larger when you press these keys.

3 While holding the **Ctrl** key down, press the [`] key again and the worksheet reverts back to values (known as the Value view). Simultaneously, the columns return to their original, smaller size.

4 Switch to the Formula view once again. (While holding the **Ctrl** key down, press the [`] key.)

5 Resize each column so that all formulas are viewable. (This will require some columns to be widened and others to be narrowed.)

6 Preview the print job. Note that printing this worksheet requires two pages, as indicated in the lower left corner of the Print Preview window.

7 Click **Page Setup** in the Print Preview window; then click the **Page** tab and change the page orientation to **Landscape.** This will tell the printer to print the worksheet horizontally instead of vertically.

8 Click the option button **Fit to 1 page wide by 1 page tall.**

9 Click the **Header/Footer** tab and then click **Custom Header.**

10 In the left section type **&[Date].** (Alternatively, you can just click the **Insert Date** button.)

11 Click **OK.**

12 Click the **Sheet** tab and check the **Gridlines** and **Row and column headings** checkboxes so that the worksheet, when printed, can help you decipher the formulas.

13 Click **OK** in the Page Setup window (note that printing now requires only one page, as specified in the lower left corner of the window). Your print Preview screen should look like Figure 2.12. Make sure the header and footer are visable. If not, you should click the **Show Margins** check box in Print Preview and adjust the margins accordingly.

Figure 2.12

Print Preview of Worksheet Formulas

14 Click **Print** in the Print Preview window.

15 Click **OK** in the Print window.

16 While holding the **Ctrl** key down, press the [`] key and so return to Value view.

17 Resize all columns so that all values are shown.

18 Close the worksheet and save your changes.

Kyle explains that printing the Formula view is an effective way of examining your worksheet logic and correcting any errors. It also allows you to view the formula logic when a computer is not available.

"That's a lot to grasp in one sitting," you complain.

"Oh there's a lot more to come, but let's take a break and start again tomorrow," Kyle says.

End Note

The three of you are somewhat overwhelmed by the capabilities of Excel but are pleased with what you've accomplished. You've learned some basics about Excel's help system, how to work with files, and how to enter information into a worksheet, use formulas, manipulate data, structure a worksheet, and print worksheets in both Value and Formula views.

In the next chapter, you will learn how to use Excel to create financial statements.

Chapter 2 Questions

1 Explain how information is entered into an Excel worksheet.

2 Identify the difference between labels and values.

3 What does it mean when a cell or cells in a worksheet include a series of # signs?

4 Explain the process for changing column width or row height.

5 How do you control the appearance of data in a worksheet?

✳ 6 What does the Format Painter tool do?

7 How are formulas written in Excel?

8 Explain the arguments used in the SUM function.

9 Explain the importance of parentheses in formulas.

10 How does the AutoFill feature of Excel help the worksheet user?

11 Why would you want to use absolute references instead of relative references?

✗ 12 How do you change a relative reference to an absolute reference?

✗ 13 Describe the procedure used to insert a column or row into a worksheet.

14 How do you change the name of a sheet in a workbook?

15 What is the recommended procedure for printing a workbook or worksheet?

Chapter 2 Assignments

1 Create Coast Jewelers' Trial Balance for March 31, 2009

You are to create Coast's trial balance in a format identical to that created in this chapter for December 31, 2009. Include a debit and credit column, totals for each column, and appropriate labels and formatting. Save the file as ch2-03_student_name.xls (replacing student_name with your name). An alphabetical listing of account information as of March 31, 2009, follows.

Accounts payable	85,124.25
Accounts receivable	95,125.15
Accumulated depreciation: Building	60,000.00
Accumulated depreciation: Equipment	8,000.00
Advertising expense	15,874.24

Building	315,000.00
Cash	28,335.14
Common stock	10,000.00
Cost of goods sold	275,135.54
Equipment	70,000.00
Inventory	130,541.87
Land	120,000.00
Long-term debt	380,000.00
Payroll expense	65,152.87
Prepaid expenses	10,544.27
Retained earnings	192,697.36
Sales revenue	410,325.17
Supplies	8,888.78
Utilities	11,548.92

a. Print the completed worksheet in Value view, with your name and date printed in the lower left footer and file name in the lower right footer.

b. Print the completed worksheet in Formula view, retaining gridlines and row and column headings, with your name and date printed in the lower left footer and file name in the lower right footer.

2 Modify Coast Jewelers' Diamond Ring Sales Worksheet

For this assignment use Ch2-04.xls. Add appropriate formulas to the existing Diamond Ring Sales worksheet to calculate price, total sales for each ring for the week, and total sales for all rings. Complete this worksheet in a manner consistent with the Weekly Watch Sales worksheet completed in this chapter. Prior to entering your formulas, the worksheet should look like Figure 2.13. Save the file as ch2-04_student_name.xls (replacing student_name with your name).

	A	B	C	D	E	F
1		Coast Jewelers, Inc.				
2		Diamond Ring Sales				
3		Week of December 4, 2009				
4						
5	Product	Cost	Markup	Price	Quantity	Total
6	18K 2 tone diamond set .70 ct	4,500.00	50%		2	
7	Diamond anniversary band	945.00	50%		1	
8	Emerald anniversary band	800.00	50%		1	
9	14K engagement ring .51 ct	1200.00	50%		3	
10	Total					
11						
12	Discount %		20%			

Figure 2.13

Partially Completed Diamond Ring Sales Worksheet

a. Print the completed worksheet in Value view, with your name and date printed in the lower left footer and file name in the lower right footer.

b. Print the completed worksheet in Formula view, retaining gridlines and row and column headings, with your name and date printed in the lower left footer and file name in the lower right footer.

Chapter 2 Case Problem 1:
KELLY'S BOUTIQUE

Kelly's Boutique, located in Pewaukee, Wisconsin, sells a unique combination of books and women's shoes. Customers love to peruse her book inventory while trying on the latest in shoe fashions, often buying both books and shoes even though they came in to buy only one type of merchandise. Casey, Kelly's youngest son, a college student studying accounting, is home for the holidays and can't wait to help his mom come in from the dark ages and use computers in her business. Throughout this text Casey will make every attempt to bring his mom up to speed by teaching her the use of Excel and Access as they apply to her accounting and business needs.

To begin, Casey suggests that Kelly use a worksheet to make a list of her book inventory. She doesn't maintain a large inventory, but she does carry books that she thinks moms in the community might be interested in reading or buying as gifts for their children or friends.

Start with worksheet ch2-05.xls. Format this worksheet using bold and italics formatting for the titles and bold and border formatting for the column names. Add formulas for column E to compute the sales price as list price less the discount specified. Add the following two books and related information to the list. (Be sure the list maintains its alphabetic organization by inserting rows in the correct place.)

Dept	Product	Author	List Price
Children	Make Way for Ducklings	McClosky	17.99
Adult	Snow Falling on Cedars	Guterson	21.95

Insert a new column D with the title "On Hand" in bold, centered, and center justified. Change the formatting of the column to no decimals. Add the following on hand values to column D.

Product	Author	On Hand
Angela's Ashes	McCourt	5
Betsy – Tacy	Lovelace	2
Blueberries for Sal	McCloskey	2
Caddie Woodlawn	Brink	1
Deep End of the Ocean	Mitchard	4
Divine Secrets of the YaYa Sisterhood	Wells	3
Green Eggs and Ham	Seuss	1
Harry Potter and the Chamber of Secrets	Rowling	4
Harry Potter and the Prisoner of Azkaban	Rowling	3
Harry Potter and the Sorcerer's Stone	Rowling	2

Product	Author	On Hand
Hop on Pop	Seuss	1
Horse Whisperer	Evans	2
Lentil	McCloskey	2
Make Way for Ducklings	McCloskey	2
Memoirs of a Geisha	Golden	4
Message in a Bottle	Sparks	2
One Morning in Maine	McCloskey	1
Snow Falling on Cedars	Guterson	2
The Cat in the Hat	Seuss	1
The Notebook	Sparks	3

Add a "Total" label in cell B27 and a SUM function in cell D27 to add up the quantity of books on hand. Change the name of Sheet1 to "15% Discount." Create a copy of this worksheet and place it before Sheet2. Change the name of the newly created worksheet to "20% Discount." Change the discount in cell F1 of this worksheet to 20 percent. Save the file as ch2-05_student_name.xls (replacing student_name with your name).

a. Print the completed 15% Discount worksheet in Value view, with your name and date printed in the lower left footer and file name in the lower right footer.

b. Print the completed 20% Discount worksheet in Value view, with your name and date printed in the lower left footer and file name in the lower right footer.

c. Print the completed 15% Discount worksheet in Formula view, with gridlines and row and column headings, landscape orientation, scaling to fit to 1 page wide by 1 page tall, and with your name and date printed in the lower left footer and file name in the lower right footer.

d. Print the completed 20% Discount worksheet in Formula view, with gridlines and row and column headings, landscape orientation, scaling to fit to 1 page wide by 1 page tall, and with your name and date printed in the lower left footer and file name in the lower right footer.

Chapter 2 Case Problem 2:
WINE DEPOT

The Wine Depot, located in Santa Barbara, California, imports and sells high-quality wine from around the world. Owner Barbara Fairfield is curious to see how Excel might help her manage the business and account for its inventory. Her husband, Bud, is the accountant in the family but hasn't had much experience with Excel. He's hired you to help him construct several worksheets to help the business better understand the financial and managerial aspects of the company.

To begin, you decide to create a worksheet of some of Barbara's wine inventory. Start with worksheet ch2-06.xls. Format the company name and worksheet title bold and italics. Format the title of each column of data bold with a bottom border. Format all values for the column Price as Accounting Number Format. Add two column labels, Quantity and Value, to the right of the existing data and then insert quantity amounts as shown below [Note: SKU (Stock Keeping Unit) is a unique identifier for each of the distinct products and services that can be ordered from a supplier.]:

SKU	Quantity
17521	4
16716	10
16528	12
16739	5
15347	7
17539	3
11599	1
14539	5
17840	12
13883	12
15966	24
17454	24
17024	10
16554	8
17425	7
17549	3
17578	2
17275	1

Insert a formula to calculate value as quantity times price in cell I9, then fill-down this formula for all cells in the table. Insert a text label "Total" in cell H28 and a formula to calculate the total value in cell I28. Insert two additional rows after row 27. Add two American Syrah wines in those two rows: Carhatt, $34 (750 ml, year 2000, SKU 16769), quantity 10; and Cafaro, $35 (750 ml, year 2000, SKU 16874), quantity 15. Delete the row containing the American Merlot from Wildhorse. Change the formatting of the Price and Value columns to include no decimals. After using Excel's Help function to learn how to sort items in a worksheet, sort the information on your worksheet by location and then by type, in ascending order. Change the name of Sheet1 to "Pricing". Create a copy of this worksheet and place it before Sheet2, then change the name of this sheet to "Cost". Add a label at cell C4 of the Cost sheet called Cost % in Bold, Italics. Type 60% as the cost percentage in cell D4 of the Cost sheet. Change the name of the column "Value" to "Cost". Create a new formula in cell I9 to calculate cost as Price times Cost % times Quantity. (Be sure to use absolute or relative references where appropriate.) Fill the formula in cell I9 down to all items. Save the file as ch2-06_student_name.xls (replacing student_name with your name).

    a.   Print the completed Pricing worksheet in Value view, with portrait orientation, scaling to fit to 1 page wide by 1 page tall, and with your name and date printed in the lower left footer and file name in the lower right footer.

b. Print the completed Cost worksheet in Value view, with portrait orientation, scaling to fit to 1 page wide by 1 page tall, and with your name and date printed in the lower left footer and file name in the lower right footer.

c. Print the completed Pricing worksheet in Formula view, with gridlines and row and column headings, portrait orientation, scaling to fit to 1 page wide by 1 page tall, and with your name and date printed in the lower left footer and file name in the lower right footer.

d. Print the completed Cost worksheet in Formula view, with gridlines and row and column headings, portrait orientation, scaling to fit to 1 page wide by 1 page tall, and with your name and date printed in the lower left footer and file name in the lower right footer.

Financial Statement Analysis

In this chapter you will learn:

- How to perform a vertical financial analysis
- How to create a pie chart of expenses
- How to perform a horizontal financial analysis
- How to create a column chart of expenses
- How to calculate financial ratios

Case: **Coast Jewelers, Inc.**

Nathan and Meagan are ready to evaluate the company's performance, examine trends and relationships, and assess liquidity and solvency. Kyle suggests three forms of analysis that can provide information to Nathan and Meagan for business decision making: vertical, horizontal, and ratio analysis.

You recall learning about these three methods of analysis while studying financial accounting. Kyle reminds you that Excel is a great tool for preparing these analyses and suggests that you take the lead in explaining the formulas used in creating these types of worksheets.

"Can Excel also help us prepare charts? We have to prepare some information for our bankers, and they seem to prefer both numbers and charts," Nathan asks. "Most definitely!" Kyle answers. "We'll use Excel to look at the financial information we recently created, and then we'll compute vertical, horizontal, and ratio analyses as well as prepare charts to describe important relationships and trends."

Vertical Analysis

Vertical analysis, often referred to as *component* analysis, is used to express each item on a particular financial statement as a percentage of a single base amount. In an income statement, the base is sales revenue. Each expense is expressed as a percentage of sales revenue. Meagan seems very interested in comparing what percentages of revenues are spent on various expenses and how that compares from one period to the next.

To create a vertical analysis on an income statement:

1 Click the **Microsoft Office** button and then click **Open**.

2 Navigate the Open window to the location of this text's student files. (The location would be the CD provided with the text or from your computer lab's server.)

3 Double-click the file **ch3-01**, which should be located in a Ch 03 folder.

4 Click the **Income Statement** tab.

5 Right-click column **C** and click **Insert** to insert a new column.

6 Click cell **C4** and type **%** as a label to the new column.

7 Click cell **C5** and type the formula **=B5/$B$5**; then press [**Enter**]. (*Note:* use an absolute reference in the denominator so you can fill down the formula later.)

8 Click cell **C5** again and reformat the cell by clicking the **%** tool in the Number group of the Home tab.

9 Resize column C to 61 pixels.

10 Fill down the formula in C5 to C16 by dragging the handle in the lower right corner of cell C5 to C16. (*Note:* this will also copy down the formatting from cell C5, removing border formats that you can fix later.)

11 Eliminate the formula from cell C8 by clicking the cell and pressing [**Delete**], then [**Enter**].

12 Add appropriate border formats to cells C6, C13, and C16.

13 Repeat Steps 6 to 11 in column E, substituting E for C in all column references. Substitute D for B in the formulas. Your worksheet should look like Figure 3.1.

Figure 3.1

Income Statement
Vertical Analysis

	A	B	C	D	E
1	*Coast Jewelers, Inc.*				
2	*Income Statement*				
3	*For the Year Ended*				
4		**12/31/08**	**%**	**12/31/09**	**%**
5	Sales Revenue	$ 850,511.65	100%	$ 825,974.15	100%
6	Less: Cost of Goods Sold	442,619.87	52%	489,547.25	59%
7	Gross Margin	407,891.78	48%	336,426.90	41%
8	Expenses:				
9	Advertising	20,654.21	2%	26,548.55	3%
10	Depreciation	22,000.00	3%	22,000.00	3%
11	Interest	40,846.24	5%	32,338.94	4%
12	Payroll	115,365.11	14%	129,547.97	16%
13	Utilities	23,541.25	3%	27,546.16	3%
14	Net income before taxes	185,484.97	22%	98,445.28	12%
15	Income taxes	65,218.98	8%	31,600.00	4%
16	Net income	$ 120,265.99	14%	$ 66,845.28	8%

Income Statement / Balance Sheet

14 Click the **Microsoft Office** button again and then click **Save As.** (This preserves your original student and provides a unique name for your file.)

15 Change the file name to reflect the vertical analysis just performed and your name by using the underscore key as before. In this example, the file will be saved as ch3-01_Vertical_Analysis_student_name (replace student_name with your name). Save your file to a location (e.g., a USB drive) from which you can retrieve it later.

16 Switch to a Page Layout view. Place your name in the left section of the footer. Note that the file name is already in the right section of the footer.

17 Switch back to a Normal view.

18 Click **Print** and then **Print Preview** from the Microsoft Office Button to make sure the worksheet will print the way you want.

19 Click **Print** and then click **OK** to print your analysis.

20 Save your file once again but do not close it.

Meagan is pleased that Excel can produce these amounts so quickly. She notes that the firm's gross profit percentage is down from the previous year and that the cost of goods sold as a percentage of sales is higher. This, coupled with an increase in payroll costs relative to sales, helps explain the reduction in net income as a percentage of sales.

"Is the balance sheet used for vertical analysis as well?" Nathan asks. "Yes," you respond.

In a balance sheet the base is total assets. Each asset, liability, and equity component is expressed as a percentage of total assets.

To create a vertical analysis on a balance sheet:

1 Click the **Balance Sheet** tab.

2 Right-click column **C** and click **Insert** to insert a new column.

3 Click cell **C5** and type % as a label to the new column.

4 Click cell **C7** and type the formula **=B7/$B$17**, then press [**Enter**]. (*Note:* Once again, use an absolute reference in the denominator so you can fill down the formula later.)

5 Click cell **C7** again and reformat the cell by clicking the % tool in the Number group of the Home tab.

6 Resize column C to 61 pixels.

7 Fill down the formula in C7 to C17 by dragging the handle in the lower right corner of cell C7 to C17. (*Note:* This will also copy down the formatting from cell C7, removing border formats that you can fix later.)

8 Eliminate the formula from cell C12 by clicking the cell and pressing [**Delete**], then [**Enter**].

9 Add appropriate border formats to cell C17.

10 Repeat Steps 3 to 9 in column E, substituting E for C in all column references. The asset part of your worksheet should look like Figure 3.2.

Figure 3.2

Balance Sheet Assets
Vertical Analysis

	A	B	C	D	E
1	Coast Jewelers, Inc.				
2	Balance Sheet				
3	as of				
4					
5	Assets	12/31/08	%	12/31/09	%
6	Current Assets:				
7	Cash	$ 25,412.35	4%	$ 20,182.15	3%
8	Accounts Receivable	84,245.25	12%	102,544.24	14%
9	Inventory	125,351.45	18%	152,154.21	21%
10	Prepaid Expenses	15,625.26	2%	15,241.75	2%
11	Supplies	10,245.15	2%	6,578.24	1%
12	Property, Plant, and Equipment:				
13	Land	120,000.00	18%	120,000.00	17%
14	Building	300,000.00	44%	315,000.00	44%
15	Equipment	65,000.00	10%	70,000.00	10%
16	Less: Accumulated Depreciation	(68,000.00)	-10%	(90,000.00)	-13%
17	Total	$ 677,879.46	100%	$ 711,700.59	100%

◄ ◄ ► ►│ Income Statement **Balance Sheet**

11 Save your work.

12 Click cell **C22** and type the formula **=B22/$B$28**; then press [**Enter**]. (*Note:* Again, use an absolute reference in the denominator.)

13 Click cell **C22** again and reformat the cell by clicking the **%** tool in the Number group of the Home tab.

14 Fill down the formula in C22 to C28 by dragging the handle in the lower right corner of cell C22 to C28. (*Note:* This will also copy down the formatting from cell C7, removing border formats that you can fix later.)

15 Eliminate the formula from cell C25 by clicking the cell and pressing [**Delete**], then [**Enter**].

16 Add appropriate border formats to cell C28.

17 Repeat Steps 12 to 16 in column E, substituting E for C in all column references. The liability and equity part of your worksheet should look like Figure 3.3.

18 Switch to a Page Layout view. Place your name in the left section of the footer. Note that the file name is already in the right section of the footer.

19 Switch back to a Normal view.

20 Click **Print** and then **Print Preview** from the Microsoft Office Button to make sure the worksheet will print the way you want.

	A	B	C	D	E
19	**Liabilities and Stockholders' Equity**				
20	Liabilities				
21	Current Liabilities:				
22	Accounts Payable	$ 75,182.10	11%	$ 84,005.70	12%
23	Payroll Liabilities		0%	8,152.25	1%
24	Long-Term Debt	400,000.00	59%	350,000.00	49%
25	Stockholders' Equity				
26	Common Stock	10,000.00	1%	10,000.00	1%
27	Retained Earnings	192,697.36	28%	259,542.64	36%
28	Total	$ 677,879.46	100%	$ 711,700.59	100%

Income Statement | Balance Sheet

Figure 3.3

Balance Sheet Liabilities & Equities Vertical Analysis

21 Click **Print** and then click **OK** to print your analysis.

22 Save your file but do not close it.

Once again Meagan notes some interesting facts from the vertical analysis of the balance sheet. A larger percentage of total assets are invested in accounts receivable and inventory than in the prior year. Yet long-term debt is down, offset by an increase in retained earnings as a percentage of total assets.

To complete the vertical analysis, you offer to demonstrate Excel's charting capability by creating a pie chart of expenses for the year ended December 31, 2009.

Pie Charts

"Excel's chart wizard makes creating a chart from a worksheet a breeze," you remark. "This will give you a graphical picture of the firm's expenses as a percentage of revenues."

To create a pie chart of expenses:

1 Click on **Income Statement** tab and select cells **D9** through **D13**.

2 Click the **Insert** tab on the Ribbon and then click the **Pie Chart** tool on the Charts group.

3 Select **Pie in 3D** from the list of Standard Pie Chart types.

4 Click the picture of a pie chart with **3-D visual effect.**

5 Click the **Quick Layout** tool in the Chart Layouts group and then select **Layout 6.** See Figure 3.4.

6 Select the text **Chart Title** and then type **2009 Expenses** as the new chart title.

7 Click the **Select Data** tool in the Data group.

Figure 3.4

Creating a New Pie Chart

Quick Layout

Layout 6

8 Click **Edit** under the text Horizontal (Category) Axis Labels as shown in Figure 3.5.

Figure 3.5

Editing the Pie Chart Axis Labels

Click here to edit

9 Type **='Income Statement'!$A$9:$A$13** as the Axis label range and then click **OK.** (Alternatively, you could click the button on the right-hand side of the window and then select the range A9:A13 instead of typing the cell location.)

10 Click **OK** to close the Select Data Source window.

11 Click anywhere in the chart and, holding the mouse button down, drag the new chart so that it appears below the data.

12 Click in the lower right-hand corner of the chart and, holding the mouse button down, resize the chart so that it fits in the window; see Figure 3.6.

13 With the chart still selected, click **Print** and then click **Print Preview** to make sure the chart will print the way you want.

14 Click **Print** to then print the chart.

15 Save your work and then close the file.

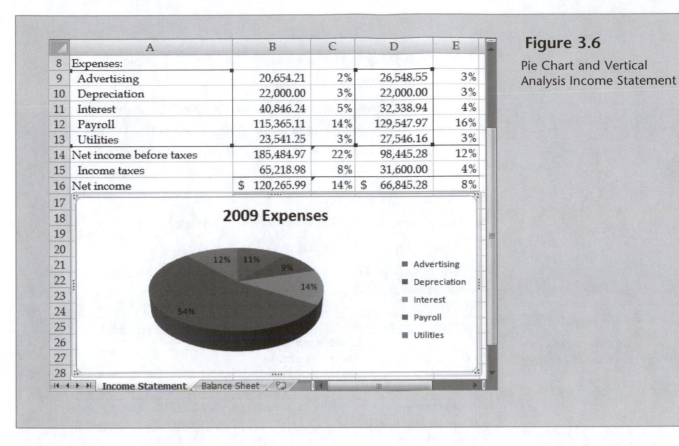

Figure 3.6

Pie Chart and Vertical Analysis Income Statement

You have now completed the vertical analysis. Nathan and Meagan are eager to examine the percentages and the chart more carefully, but not until they see how horizontal and ratio analyses can be created in Excel.

Horizontal Analysis

Horizontal analysis examines trends over time. This can include comparisons of months, quarters, or years for both the income statement and the balance sheet. Income statements and balance sheets for two or more periods are compared side by side, and a percentage increase or decrease is computed between periods.

"Isn't that what we just did in vertical analysis?" Meagan asks. Kyle replies: "The percentages computed in vertical analysis are usually done for just one period, although they are often compared period to period. Remember, vertical analysis compares each statement element with a single base amount, such as sales or total assets, whereas horizontal analysis compares elements side by side with other periods."

To create a horizontal analysis on an income statement:

1 Open ch3-01.xls (This is the same file you opened for vertical analysis. It should still look the same, because the changes you made were saved under another file name.)

2   Click the **Income Statement** tab.

3   Click cell **D4** and type **% Change** as a label to the column.

4   Format cell D4 bold, center, bottom align, and with a bottom border.

5   Click cell **D5** and type the formula **=(C5–B5)/B5**; then press [**Enter**].

6   Format cell D5 as Percent Style by clicking cell **D5** and selecting the **Percent Style** tool on the Number group on the Home tab.

7   Use the fill-down procedure to copy the formula from D5 to D16.

8   Delete the formula in cell D8.

9   Format cells D6 and D13 with a bottom border.

10 Format cell D16 with a top and double bottom border.

11 Resize column D to 96 pixels. Your completed income statement with horizontal analysis should look like Figure 3.7.

Figure 3.7

Income Statement Horizontal Analysis

	A	B	C	D
1	*Coast Jewelers, Inc.*			
2	*Income Statement*			
3	*For the Year Ended*			
4		**12/31/08**	**12/31/09**	**% Change**
5	Sales Revenue	$ 850,511.65	$ 825,974.15	-3%
6	Less: Cost of Goods Sold	442,619.87	489,547.25	11%
7	Gross Margin	407,891.78	336,426.90	-18%
8	Expenses:			
9	Advertising	20,654.21	26,548.55	29%
10	Depreciation	22,000.00	22,000.00	0%
11	Interest	40,846.24	32,338.94	-21%
12	Payroll	115,365.11	129,547.97	12%
13	Utilities	23,541.25	27,546.16	17%
14	Net income before taxes	185,484.97	98,445.28	-47%
15	Income taxes	65,218.98	31,600.00	-52%
16	Net income	$ 120,265.99	$ 66,845.28	-44%

Income Statement / Balance Sheet

12 Click the **Microsoft Office** button again and then click **Save As.** (Again, this preserves the original file by giving a unique name to your file.)

13 Change the file name to include a reference to your horizontal analysis, and then add your name to the file name using the underscore key as before. In this example the file will be saved as ch3-01_Horizontal_Analysis_student_name (replace student_name with your name). Save your file to a location from which it can be retrieved later.

14 Switch to a Page Layout view. Place your name in the left section of the footer. Note that the file name is already in the right section of the footer.

15 Switch back to a Normal view.

16 Click **Print** and then **Print Preview** from the Microsoft Office Button to make sure the worksheet will print the way you want.

17 Click **Print** and then click **OK** to print your analysis.

18 Save your file but do not close it.

"The trends shown here are not very good," Nathan says. "The analysis reveals a decline in sales of 3 percent but an 11 percent increase in the costs of goods sold."

Kyle explains that the income statement analysis reveals operational and profitability performance and trends while the balance sheet reflects financial stability and solvency trends. The horizontal analysis on the balance sheet compares current balances for each asset, liability, and equity element with the same element in the prior period.

To create a horizontal analysis on a balance sheet:

1 Click the **Balance Sheet** tab.

2 Click in cell D5 and type **% Change** as a label to the column.

3 Format cell D5 bold, center, bottom align, and with a bottom border.

4 Click in cell D7 and type the formula **=(C7–B7)/B7**; then press **[Enter]**.

5 Format cell D7 as Percent Style.

6 Use the fill-down procedure to copy the formula from D7 to D28.

7 Delete the formula in cells D12, D18–D21, D23, and D25.

8 Format cells D17 and D28 with a top and double bottom border.

9 Resize column D to 93 pixels. Your completed balance sheet horizontal analysis should look like Figure 3.8.

10 Switch to a Page Layout view. Place your name in the left section of the footer. Note that the file name is already in the right section of the footer.

11 Switch back to a Normal view.

12 Click **Print** and then **Print Preview** from the Microsoft Office Button to make sure the worksheet will print the way you want.

13 Click **Print** and then click **OK** to print your analysis.

14 Save your file once again and then close it.

Figure 3.8

Balance Sheet
Horizontal Analysis

	A	B	C	D
1	Coast Jewelers, Inc.			
2	Balance Sheet			
3	as of			
4				
5	Assets	12/31/08	12/31/09	% Change
6	Current Assets:			
7	Cash	$ 25,412.35	$ 20,182.15	-21%
8	Accounts Receivable	84,245.25	102,544.24	22%
9	Inventory	125,351.45	152,154.21	21%
10	Prepaid Expenses	15,625.26	15,241.75	-2%
11	Supplies	10,245.15	6,578.24	-36%
12	Property, Plant, and Equipment:			
13	Land	120,000.00	120,000.00	0%
14	Building	300,000.00	315,000.00	5%
15	Equipment	65,000.00	70,000.00	8%
16	Less: Accumulated Depreciatior	(68,000.00)	(90,000.00)	32%
17	Total	$ 677,879.46	$ 711,700.59	5%
18				
19	Liabilities and Stockholders' Equity			
20	Liabilities			
21	Current Liabilities:			
22	Accounts Payable	$ 75,182.10	$ 84,005.70	12%
23	Payroll Liabilities		8,152.25	
24	Long-Term Debt	400,000.00	350,000.00	-13%
25	Stockholders' Equity			
26	Common Stock	10,000.00	10,000.00	0%
27	Retained Earnings	192,697.36	259,542.64	35%
28	Total	$ 677,879.46	$ 711,700.59	5%

Income Statement   **Balance Sheet**

"I'm a little concerned about the 22 percent growth in accounts receivable, the 21 percent growth in inventory, and the 21 percent decrease in cash," Meagan says. Kyle reminds her that, when those events occurred, long-term debt decreased 13 percent and retained earnings increased 35 percent. "Excel can also provide some graphical evidence of these trends by creating column charts using the chart wizard," Kyle says.

Column Charts

Previously you created a pie chart of expenses using Excel's Chart Wizard. Now it is time to create a column chart comparing expenses from one period to the next. This column chart will illustrate expenses side by side for the two years ended December 31, 2008 and December, 31, 2009.

To create a column chart comparing expenses:

1 Click the **Income Statement** tab.

2 Select cells **A9** through **C13** (expenses for both periods).

3 Click the **Insert** tab on the Ribbon and then click the **Column** chart tool from the Charts group.

4 Select **3-D Cone** as the chart type.

5 Click and hold down the mouse on the top border of the chart created; then move the chart to a location below the data.

6 Scroll down the worksheet so that row 8 is at the top of your screen and the chart is fully visible, as shown in Figure 3.9.

Click here to change series name   **Click here to change chart layout**

	A	B	C	D	E	F	G
8	Expenses:						
9	Advertising	20,654.21	26,548.55	29%			
10	Depreciation	22,000.00	22,000.00	0%			
11	Interest	40,846.24	32,338.94	-21%			
12	Payroll	115,365.11	129,547.97	12%			
13	Utilities	23,541.25	27,546.16	17%			
14	Net income before taxes	185,484.97	98,445.28	-47%			
15	Income taxes	65,218.98	31,600.00	-52%			
16	Net income	$ 120,265.99	$ 66,845.28	-44%			

Figure 3.9

Creating a Column Chart

7 Note that the Design tab is now selected and Chart Tools are visible in the Ribbon.

8 Click **Select Data** from the Data group.

9 Click **Series1** from the Legend Entries (Series) section (see Figure 3.10).

Figure 3.10

Editing a Data Source

Click here to edit series name

Select Data Source

Chart data range: ='Income Statement'!$A$9:$C$13

Switch Row/Column

Legend Entries (Series)   Horizontal (Category) Axis Labels

Add   Edit   Remove   Edit

Series1   Advertising
Series2   Depreciation
                                           Interest
                                           Payroll
                                           Utilities

Hidden and Empty Cells   OK   Cancel

10 Click **Edit.**

11 Click inside the **Series name** text box and the click in cell **B4.** This should enter the formula ="Income Statement"!$B$4 the Series name text box. Click **OK.**

12 Click **Series2** from the Legend Entries (Series) section.

13 Click **Edit.**

14 Click inside the **Series name** text box and the click in cell **C4.** This should enter the formula ="Income Statement"!$C$4 into the Series name text box. Click **OK.**

15 Click **OK** again in the Select Data Source window.

16 From the Chart Layouts group click **Layout 1.**

17 Double-click the text **Chart Title** in the chart, select the text Chart Title, and then type **Expense Comparison** as the new chart title.

18 Click the **Microsoft Office** button again and then click **Save As.**

19 Change the file name to include a reference to column charts, and add your name to the file name using the underscore key as you have done previously. In this example, the file will be saved as ch3-01_Column_Chart_student_name (replace student_name with your name). Be sure to save your file to a location that you can access later.

20 Click **Print** and then click **Print Preview** from the Microsoft Office button, then click **Print** to print the worksheet with the chart. Your printout should look like Figure 3.11

Figure 3.11

Printed Income Statement with Expense Comparison Chart

Coast Jewelers, Inc.
Income Statement
For the Year Ended

	12/31/08	12/31/09	% Change
Sales Revenue	$ 850,511.65	$ 825,974.15	-3%
Less: Cost of Goods Sold	442,619.87	489,547.25	11%
Gross Margin	407,891.78	336,426.90	-18%
Expenses:			
Advertising	20,654.21	26,548.55	29%
Depreciation	22,000.00	22,000.00	0%
Interest	40,846.24	32,338.94	-21%
Payroll	115,365.11	129,547.97	12%
Utilities	23,541.25	27,546.16	17%
Net income before taxes	185,484.97	98,445.28	-47%
Income taxes	65,218.98	31,600.00	-52%
Net income	$ 120,265.99	$ 66,845.28	-44%

21 Save your work again.

"All of this is very interesting," says Nathan. "I'll bet there's more. Am I right?"

"Yes, we still need to do a ratio analysis in order to complete our financial statement analyses portfolio," Kyle responds.

Ratio Analysis

Kyle explains that several standard ratios are often used to assess a company's profitability, liquidity, and solvency. Profitability represents the company's ability to generate a profit to investors. Liquidity represents the company's ability to pay its bills currently. Solvency represents the company's ability to stay in business given its debt structure. A chart of each ratio's formula follows.

Profitability

Return on owners' investment	Net income ÷ Average stockholders' equity
Return on total investment	Net income before interest expense ÷ Average total assets
Profit margin	Net income ÷ Sales
Gross margin	Gross margin ÷ Sales

Liquidity

Current ratio	Current assets ÷ Current liabilities
Quick ratio	(Cash + Accounts Receivable) ÷ Current liabilities
Receivable turnover	Sales ÷ Average accounts receivable
Inventory turnover	Cost of goods sold ÷ Average inventory

Solvency

| Debt-to-equity | Total liabilities ÷ Total equity |
| Liability | Total liabilities ÷ Total assets |

In Excel, each of these amounts is a part of a given financial statement or can easily be computed. Therefore, you can create a new worksheet that has formulas referencing these amounts. Kyle suggests you create a new worksheet to compute these ratios.

To calculate the first financial ratio on a new worksheet (refer to preceding ratio table for the *return on owners' investment* formula):

1 Right-click the **Income Statement** tab of your workbook and click **Insert …**; then click **Worksheet** and then **OK** to insert a new worksheet.

2 Double-click the **Sheet1** tab and rename the worksheet **Ratio Analysis.**

3 Format the Ratio Analysis worksheet like Figure 3.12 with a heading and listing of ratios as shown. To center and merge the title, select the range of cells **A1:B1** and then click the **Merge and Center** button from the Alignment group on the Home tab of the Ribbon. Repeat these steps for the ranges A2:B2 and A3:B3.

4 Click in cell **B6** and type the following =‘Income Statement’!C16/ ((‘Balance Sheet’!B26+‘Balance Sheet’!B27+‘Balance Sheet’!C26+ ‘Balance Sheet’!C27)/2) to compute return on owners' investment.

5 Alternatively, you could utilize multiple worksheet referencing. Type = in cell B6, then activate the income statement worksheet and click cell **C16.**

6 Type **/((** (the forward slash and two left parentheses, which determine the all-important *order* of calculation).

7 Activate the balance sheet worksheet and click cell **B26.**

8 Type +, then click cell **B27.**

9 Type +, then click cell **C26.**

10 Type +, then click cell **C27.**

11 Type **)/2)** to end the summation of equity accounts and divide the result by 2 to derive an average.

Figure 3.12

Format for Ratio Analysis

	A	B
1	Coast Jewelers, Inc.	
2	Ratio Analysis	
3	Dec-09	
4		
5	**Profitability**	
6	Return on owners' investment	
7	Return on total investment	
8	Profit margin	
9	Gross margin	
10	**Liquidity**	
11	Current ratio	
12	Quick ratio	
13	Receivable turnover	
14	Inventory turnover	
15	**Solvency**	
16	Debt-to-equity	
17	Liability	

12 Press [**Enter**] to end your formula.

13 Format cell **B6** in a percent style.

Trouble? If you choose to type the formula as written here and forget an apostrophe or exclamation point or misspell a word, then Excel will give you an error message and you'll have to debug your formula. Also, if you don't have the correct number of parentheses, Excel will give you an error message. Note that when you edit the formula, Excel changes the color of each set of parentheses so that you can clearly see which is which. Also be careful when typing formulas to use the apostrophe and not the accent key to create formulas. The apostrophe key is usually located next to the Enter key on your keyboard, and the accent key is usually located above the Tab key.

"The point-and-click method of cell referencing on multiple worksheets is sure easier than typing the references themselves," you comment. "Otherwise I would have to type all of those apostrophes and exclamation points. With my typing skills, I would probably forget one of them and create an error in the formula."

"Good point," Kyle says. "Let's finish the profitability ratios next."

To enter remaining formulas for profitability analysis (refer to the ratio table for these formulas):

1 Click cell **B7** and type =.

2 Use the values at cells C16 and C11 on the income statement to compute net income before interest expense, which is the numerator of the *return on total investment* ratio.

3 Use the values at cells B17 and C17 on the balance sheet to add total assets, and then divide the result by 2 to obtain average total assets.

4 Once your formula is typed, press [**Enter**] to compute the ratio. Your formula should look like this: =('**Income Statement**'!**C16**+'**Income Statement**'!**C11**)/(('**Balance Sheet**'!**B17**+'**Balance Sheet**'!**C17**)/2). Be careful to use the correct parentheses.

5 Format the cell in percent style.

6 In cell B8, use the values at cells C16 and C5 on the income statement to compute the *profit margin*. (Use the ratio table to enter the appropriate formula.) Your formula should look like this: ='**Income Statement**'! **C16**/'**Income Statement**'!**C5.**

7 Format the cell in percent style.

8 In cell B9, use the values at cells C7 and C5 on the income statement to compute the *gross margin*. (Use the ratio table to enter the appropriate formula.) Your formula should look like this: = '**Income Statement**'!**C7**/ '**Income Statement**'!**C5.**

9 Format the cell in percent style. Your window should look like Figure 3.13.

Figure 3.13

Ratio Analysis Completed

	A	B
1	Coast Jewelers, Inc.	
2	Ratio Analysis	
3	Dec-09	
4		
5	**Profitability**	
6	Return on owners' investment	28%
7	Return on total investment	14%
8	Profit margin	8%
9	Gross margin	41%
10	**Liquidity**	
11	Current ratio	3.22
12	Quick ratio	1.33
13	Receivable turnover	8.84
14	Inventory turnover	3.53
15	**Solvency**	
16	Debt-to-equity	164%
17	Liability	62%

Ratio Analysis / Income

10 Click the **Microsoft Office** button again and then click **Save As.**

11 Change the file name to include a reference to ratios, and then add your name to the file name using the underscore key as before. In this example, the file will be saved as ch3-01_Ratios_student_name (replace student_name with your name). Be sure to save your file to a safe location.

Remember, profitability ratios measure the company's ability to generate a profit to investors. In this case, Nathan and Meagan are fairly satisfied with their profitability in comparison to other companies of their size and type of business. They are eager to see if their liquidity ratios are equally as positive.

Kyle encourages you to continue with your ratio analysis.

To compute the liquidity ratios:

1   In cell B11, use the values in cells C7 through C11 (current assets) and C22 through C23 (current liabilities) on the balance sheet to compute the *current ratio*. (Use the ratio table to find the appropriate formula.) Your formula could be **=('Balance Sheet'!C7+'Balance Sheet'!C8 +'Balance Sheet'!C9+'Balance Sheet'!C10+'Balance Sheet'!C11)/ ('Balance Sheet'!C22+'Balance Sheet'!C23)**, where current assets and current liabilities are added up separately; or you could use the SUM function and write the formula as **=SUM('Balance Sheet'!C7: C11)/SUM('Balance Sheet'!C22:C23)**.

2   Format the cell in comma style.

3   In cell B12, use the values in cells C7–C8 (cash and accounts receivable) and C22–C23 (current liabilities) on the balance sheet to compute the *quick ratio*. (Refer to the ratio table for the appropriate formula.) Your formula could be either **=('Balance Sheet'!C7+'Balance Sheet'!C8)/('Balance Sheet'!C22+'Balance Sheet'!C23)** or **=SUM ('Balance Sheet'!C7:C8)/SUM('Balance Sheet'!C22:C23)**.

4   Format the cell in comma style.

5   In cell B13, use the values in cell C5 (sales revenue) on the income statement and cells B8 and C8 (accounts receivable) on the balance sheet to compute the *receivable turnover* ratio. (Use the ratio table to find the appropriate formula.) Your formula should look like this: **='Income Statement'!C5/(('Balance Sheet'!B8+'Balance Sheet'! C8)/2)**.

6   Format the cell in comma style.

7   In cell B14, use the values in cell C6 (cost of goods sold) on the income statement and cells B9 and C9 (inventory) on the balance sheet to compute the *inventory turnover* ratio. (Use the ratio table to find the appropriate formula.) Your formula should look like this: **='Income Statement'!C6/(('Balance Sheet'!B9+'Balance Sheet'!C9)/2)**.

8   Format the cell in comma style.

9   Save your work.

Remember, the liquidity ratios measure the company's ability to pay its bills currently. In this case, Nathan and Meagan are surprised at how good their current and quick ratios are. Usually, their current ratio is around 2:1, which is normal. The 3.22 current ratio and the 1.33 quick ratio indicate they have plenty of resources to meet their current liabilities. Receivable turnover is a little low, given they have 30-day credit terms, but this is still a healthy report. Inventory turnover is a little slow at 3.53, but this is fairly common in their business. They are eager to see if the solvency ratios continue the favorable trend.

To compute the solvency ratios:

1 In cell B16, use the values in cells C22 through C24 (accounts payable, payroll liabilities, and long-term debt) and C26 and C27 (common stock and retained earnings) on the balance sheet to compute the *debt-to-equity* ratio. (Refer to the ratio table for the appropriate formula.) Your formula should look like this: **=SUM('Balance Sheet'!C22:C24)/SUM('Balance Sheet'!C26:C27).**

2 Format the cell in percent style.

3 In cell B17, use the values in cells C22 through C24 (accounts payable, payroll liabilities, and long-term debt) and C17 (total assets) on the balance sheet to compute the *liability* ratio. (Refer to the ratio table for the appropriate formula.) Your formula should look like this: **=SUM('Balance Sheet'!C22:C24)/'Balance Sheet'!C17.**

4 Format the cell in percent style.

5 Save your work.

Now the news is not as good. It turns out the positive liquidity ratio is somewhat offset by the solvency ratios, which indicate that debt is 164 percent of equity. The company is financed heavily with debt, and this can lead to problems if the return on investment doesn't exceed the cost of the debt. The liability ratio reflects the same problem in that 62 percent of the company's assets are financed with debt versus equity. Nathan's business plan calls for a reduction in debt over the next several years as profits provide the necessary cash.

"This is great," Meagan says. "Although the solvency ratios are high, they do reflect our business plan. As long as we continue to generate profits and cash flow, we should be able to improve the solvency ratios."

End Note

You've applied some of what you learned in the first two chapters to create a set of useful worksheets that identify trends and relationships. Plus you've created them in a reusable format for future periods.

In the next chapter you will learn how to use Excel to perform depreciation calculations and prepare depreciation schedules.

Chapter 3 Questions

1 What is another term for vertical analysis?

2 What base amount is used for vertical analysis of an income statement?

3 What base amount is used for vertical analysis of a balance sheet?

4 What base amount is used for horizontal analysis of both income statements and balance sheets? Give an example.

5 What do profitability ratios represent?

6 What do liquidity ratios represent?

7 What do solvency ratios represent?

8 Why is the point-and-click method of cell referencing easier than typing references directly into worksheet cells?

9 Which ratios are usually formatted as percentages?

10 Which ratios are usually formatted as numbers?

Chapter 3 Assignments

1 Create Coast Jewelers' Financial Analysis for December 31, 2010

You are to create Coast's financial analysis as of December 31, 2010, from the information found on file ch3-02.xls. This file contains three worksheets, which are labeled Income Statement, Balance Sheet, and Ratios.

2 Following the Chapter 3 examples, create a vertical analysis of both the income statement and balance sheet for December 31, 2010, only. Then create a horizontal analysis of both the income statement and balance sheet. (*Note:* The horizontal analysis will compare December 31, 2009, with December 31, 2010.) In addition, create a pie chart of expenses for the year ended December 31, 2010; a column chart (in a format of your choice) of expenses for the years ended December 31, 2009, and 2010; and a ratio analysis as of December 31, 2010. Save the file as ch3-02_student_name.xls (replacing student_name with your name).

a. Print each completed worksheet in Value view, with your name and date printed in the lower left footer and the file name in the lower right footer.

b. Print each completed worksheet in Formula view, with your name and date printed in the lower left footer and the file name in the lower right footer.

3   Create Coast Jewelers' Financial Analysis for December 31, 2011

You are to create Coast's financial analysis as of December 31, 2011, from the information found on file ch3-03.xls. This file contains three worksheets, which are labeled Income Statement, Balance Sheet, and Ratios.

Following the Chapter 3 examples, create a vertical analysis of both the income statement and balance sheet for December 31, 2011, only. Then create a horizontal analysis of both the income statement and balance sheet. (*Note:* The horizontal analysis will compare December 31, 2010, with December 31, 2011.) In addition, create a pie chart of expenses for the year ended December 31, 2010; a column chart (in a format of your choice) of expenses for the years ended December 31, 2010, and 2011; and a ratio analysis as of December 31, 2011. Save the file as ch3-03_student_name.xls (replacing student_name with your name).

a. Print each completed worksheet in Value view, with your name and date printed in the lower left footer and the file name in the lower right footer.

b. Print each completed worksheet in Formula view, with your name and date printed in the lower left footer and the file name in the lower right footer.

Chapter 3 Case Problem 1:
KELLY'S BOUTIQUE

You are to create Kelly's Boutique's financial analyses as of December 31, 2009, and as of December 31, 2010. Following the Chapter 3 examples, use the student file ch3-04.xls to create a vertical analysis of the balance sheet and income statement as of December 31, 2009, as well as a horizontal analysis of both the income statement and balance sheet. (*Note:* The horizontal analysis will compare December 31, 2009, with December 31, 2010.) Also create a pie chart of expenses for the year ended December 31, 2010; a column chart of expenses for the years ended December 31, 2009, and December 31, 2010; and a ratio analysis as of December 31, 2010. Save the file as ch3-04_student_name.xls (replacing student_name with your name).

a. Print each completed worksheet in Value view, with your name and date printed in the lower left footer and the file name in the lower right footer.

b. Print each completed worksheet in Formula view, with gridlines and row and column headings, portrait orientation, scaling to fit to 1 page wide by 1 page tall, and with your name and date printed in the lower left footer and the file name in the lower right footer.

Chapter 3 Case Problem 2:
WINE DEPOT

You are to create Wine Depot's financial analyses as of December 31, 2008, and as of December 31, 2009. Following the Chapter 3 examples, use the student file ch3-05.xls to create a vertical analysis of the balance sheet and income statement as of December 31, 2008, and December 31, 2009—as well as a horizontal analysis of both the income statement and balance sheet—in the columns provided. (*Note:* The horizontal analysis will compare December 31, 2008 with December 31, 2009.) Also create a pie chart of expenses for the year ended December 31, 2009; a column chart of expenses for the years ended December 31, 2008, and December 31, 2009; and a ratio analysis as of December 31, 2009. Save the file as ch3-05_student_name.xls (replacing student_name with your name). *Note*: You will have to use Excel's help feature to create the column chart, because the columns are not adjacent to one another as in the chapter example. Use whatever chart layout you prefer.

a. Print each completed worksheet in Value view, with landscape orientation, scaling to fit to 1 page wide by 1 page tall, and with your name and date printed in the lower left footer and the file name in the lower right footer. Use Excel's help feature to move charts on your worksheet so that they print on a separate page.

b. Print each completed worksheet in Formula view, with gridlines and row and column headings, landscape orientation, scaling to fit to 1 page wide by 1 page tall, and with your name and date printed in the lower left footer and the file name in the lower right footer.

Depreciation

In this chapter you will learn:

- How to calculate straight-line depreciation using Excel's built-in function
- How to use what-if analysis with the depreciation function
- How to create a depreciation summary for many assets
- How to calculate depreciation using double declining balance and sum-of-the-year's digits methods using Excel's built-in functions
- How to create charts to illustrate depreciation expense

Case: Coast Jewelers, Inc.

Worksheets are used for more than financial statement preparation and analysis. For the accountant, worksheets serve a useful supporting schedule role. Nathan and Meagan want to make sure that you are fully trained on all aspects of Excel's use in accounting for their business.

Depreciation Calculations

The financial statements you analyzed in the preceding chapter didn't just appear. They were created using the company's trial balance, which in turn was prepared from the accounts in the general ledger. Prior to financial statement preparation, accounts in the general ledger needed adjustment to properly present accrual accounting. One of those adjustments, of course, is the depreciation of a company's fixed assets.

You recall learning that depreciation is the allocation of a firm's investment in fixed assets in a systematic and rational manner. The easiest of several generally accepted methods of depreciating these assets is called the straight-line method.

"How can Excel help us with depreciation?" Nathan asks.

"Excel has some built-in functions that, when given the appropriate information, can calculate depreciation for you." Kyle responds.

"What about salvage value, useful life, et cetera?" you ask. "Aren't those important factors in determining depreciation?"

"Indeed they are," Kyle says. "That's the appropriate information that I am referring to. In order to calculate depreciation, the Excel function requires information about the asset's cost, estimated salvage value, and economic useful life."

Kyle explains that Excel's built-in function for calculating straight-line depreciation is written as follows: =SLN(Cost, Salvage Value, Useful Life), where SLN stands for straight-line depreciation. Inside the parentheses are three arguments separated by commas. The first argument identifies the asset's cost, the second its salvage value, the third its useful life. You can type the dollar cost, salvage value, and number of years into the function or you can point the function to the cell locations where the cost, salvage value, and useful life are located. This second alternative is much more effective because the cell references can then be duplicated across several cells.

Kyle suggests that you use a template he's created to compute depreciation for one asset. You are up to the challenge and proceed with the task. The asset you'll depreciate—number 1001, Display Cases—was acquired January 1, 2009, for $15,000. It has no salvage value and has an economic useful life of 5 years.

To calculate depreciation using Excel's built-in function:

1 Start Excel and open file ch4-01.xls.

2 Activate the Asset 1001 worksheet; it should look like Figure 4.1. (*Note:* You'll use the summary worksheet later.)

Figure 4.1

Depreciation Calculation Worksheet

	A	B	C
1	**Coast Jewelers, Inc. Depreciation Schedule**		
2			
3	**Asset #**		
4	**Asset**		
5	**Date acquired**		
6	**Cost**		
7	**Depreciation method**		
8	**Salvage value**		
9	**Estimated useful life**		
10			
11	**Year**	**Depreciation Expense**	**Accumulated Depreciation**
12	2009		
13	2010		
14	2011		
15	2012		
16	2013		

Summary | Asset 1001

3 Enter the appropriate information on the worksheet: the asset number, date acquired, depreciation method (use S/L for straight-line), salvage value, and estimated useful life.

4 Enter the formula =**SLN($B$6,$B$8,$B$9)** in cell B12, and then press the [**Enter**] key. B6 is the location of the asset's cost, B8 is the location of its salvage value, and B9 is the location of its useful life. (*Note:* Entering these references as absolute values using the $ will help later as we replicate the formula for each year.)

5 Fill the formula in cell B12 down to cells B13 through B16.

6 Enter the formula **=B12** into cell C12.

7 Enter the formula **=C12+B13** into cell C13 and fill this formula down to cells C14 through C16. These formulas create a running total of deprecation over the years. Your worksheet should now look like Figure 4.2.

	A	B	C
1	Coast Jewelers, Inc. Depreciation Schedule		
2			
3	Asset #	1001	
4	Asset	Display Cases	
5	Date acquired	1/1/2009	
6	Cost	$ 15,000.00	
7	Depreciation method	S/L	
8	Salvage value	$ -	
9	Estimated useful life	5	
10			
11	Year	Depreciation Expense	Accumulated Depreciation
12	2009	$3,000.00	$3,000.00
13	2010	$3,000.00	$6,000.00
14	2011	$3,000.00	$9,000.00
15	2012	$3,000.00	$12,000.00
16	2013	$3,000.00	$15,000.00

Summary | Asset 1001

Figure 4.2

Completed Depreciation Calculation Worksheet for Asset 1001

8 Save your work to ch4-01_SLN_student_name.xls (replacing student_name with your name).

Meagan offers to create another depreciation worksheet. The company purchased chairs on January 1, 2009, for $5,000. These assets were designated as asset #1002, have a $500 salvage value, and were estimated to have a 5-year useful life.

To create another deprecation worksheet:

1 Right-click the **Asset 1001** tab to reveal the Shortcut menu.

2 Click **Move or Copy.**

3 Check the **Create a Copy checkbox**, and then click **OK.**

4 Change the name of the newly created worksheet to Asset 1002.

5 Modify the appropriate information on the worksheet to reflect the new asset: the asset number, date acquired, depreciation method (use S/L for straight-line), salvage value, and estimated useful life. Your completed worksheet should look like Figure 4.3.

Figure 4.3

Depreciation Worksheet
for Asset 1002

	A	B	C	D
1	Coast Jewelers, Inc. Depreciation Schedule			
2				
3	Asset #	1002		
4	Asset	Chairs		
5	Date acquired	1/1/2009		
6	Cost	$ 5,000.00		
7	Depreciation method	S/L		
8	Salvage value	$ 500.00		
9	Estimated useful life	5		
10				
11	Year	Depreciation Expense	Accumulated Depreciation	
12	2009	$900.00	$900.00	
13	2010	$900.00	$1,800.00	
14	2011	$900.00	$2,700.00	
15	2012	$900.00	$3,600.00	
16	2013	$900.00	$4,500.00	

◄ ◄ ► ►◄   Summary / Asset 1001 / **Asset 1002** ◄

6 Save your work.

Meagan asks: "How is using the SLN function and all the cell references different from using a calculator or just typing the values into the function?" Kyle responds that Excel's power is in its sensitivity or *what-if* analysis capability, which he offers to illustrate next.

Conducting a What-If Analysis with the Depreciation Function

What-if analysis helps you determine the consequences of changes in your assumptions or variables. For instance, what if Asset 1001 did have some salvage value. How would that change the depreciation calculation each year?

To utilize the what-if capabilities of Excel:

1 Activate the worksheet for Asset 1001.

2 Change the salvage value in your deprecation worksheet by entering **1000** into cell B8. Note the change in depreciation expense each period and the resulting change in accumulated depreciation.

3 Now change the cost of the asset from $15,000 to $20,000. Note the change in depreciation expense each period and the resulting change in accumulated depreciation.

4 Now change the cost back to $15,000 and the salvage value back to 0; then save your file again.

Figure 4.4

Depreciation Summary
Worksheet

Kyle explains that the only thing missing is a way for collecting similar asset cost, depreciation, and accumulated depreciation to support the financial statement.

Creating a Depreciation Summary

A depreciation summary is designed to capture all the costs, depreciation, and accumulated depreciation from similar assets and thus facilitate preparation of financial statements on an annual basis. Kyle sketches out a worksheet design (shown in Figure 4.4) that he suggests could be used for this purpose.

Using Excel, Kyle demonstrates how multiple worksheets can be summarized.

To create a depreciation summary worksheet:

1 Activate the Summary worksheet. (*Note:* This worksheet is pre-formatted for you without formulas. Observe also that your workbook should contain three worksheets: Summary, Asset 1001, and Asset 1002.)

2 In cell A5 enter the formula =**'Asset 1001'!B4.** (Remember from previous chapters that you can either type this formula or type = and then click in the Asset 1001 worksheet at cell **B4** and press [**Enter**].)

3 Using either method, continue the same process to include the date acquired, cost, and depreciation method in cells B5, C5, and D5, respectively. Adjust column widths as needed and format without decimal places.

4 In cell E5, enter the formula =**'Asset 1001'!B12.** This enters the depreciation for 2009 on Asset 1001.

5 In cell F5 enter the formula =**'Asset 1001'!C12.** This enters the accumulated depreciation for Asset 1001 as of the end of 2009.

6 Continue the same process for cells G5, H5, I5, and J5, referencing depreciation and accumulated depreciation for years 2010 and 2011.

7 In cell A6 enter the formula **='Asset 1002'!B4.** (Note that this closely resembles the formula used in cell A5 except now you are referencing a different asset, Asset 1002.)

8 Continue referencing formulas from Asset 1002 to the summary worksheet. Your completed worksheet should look like Figure 4.5.

Figure 4.5

Completed Depreciation Summary Worksheet

	A	B	C	D	E	F	G	H	I	J
1	Coast Jewelers, Inc.									
2	Equipment Depreciation Summary									
3										
4	Asset	Date Acquired	Cost	Deprec. Method	2009 Deprec.	2009 Acc. Deprec.	2010 Deprec.	2010 Acc. Deprec.	2011 Deprec.	2011 Acc. Deprec.
5	Display Cases	1/1/2009	$ 15,000	S/L	$3,000	$3,000	$3,000	$6,000	$3,000	$9,000
6	Chairs	1/1/2009	$ 5,000	S/L	$900	$900	$900	$1,800	$900	$2,700
7										
8										
9										
10										
11	Total		$ 20,000		$3,900	$3,900	$3,900	$7,800	$3,900	$11,700

H ◀ ▶ H   Summary   Asset 1001   Asset 1002   Sheet2   Sheet3

9 Save your work again.

Coast Jewelers uses the straight-line method of depreciation, but Kyle explains that there are alternative methods, such as declining balance and sum-of-the-year's digits.

Calculating Depreciation Using Other Methods

You inform Nathan and Meagan that, even though you are familiar with the declining balance and sum-of-the-year's digits methods, you've never used a worksheet to calculate depreciation.

Kyle explains how easy it is, given that you've already invested the time and energy creating the worksheet itself. He suggests you make a copy of one of the depreciation worksheets and just change the depreciation formula to include the new depreciation function.

To create depreciation worksheets using the declining balance method:

1 Click the **Microsoft Office** button and select **Save As.**

2 Type **ch4-01_DDB_student_name** as the file name (replacing student_name with your name).

3 Click the **Asset 1001** tab.

4 Change cell B7 to read **DDB** (for double declining balance)

5 Change cell B12 to read **=DDB($B$6,$B$8,$B$9,1).** Once again, the depreciation function DDB takes arguments located within the parentheses. The first three arguments are the same as the SLN function: cost, salvage value, and useful life. All three of these arguments have been set for absolute referencing so that later, when you copy them down the worksheet, they will continue to reference the appropriate cells. The fourth argument is the period for which the asset is being depreciated (e.g., the first, second, or third period).

6 Change cell B13 to read **=DDB($B$6,$B$8,$B$9,2).** Note that the only difference between B13 and B12 is the fourth argument.

7 Continue to place the DDB formula in cells B14, B15, and B16, changing only the last argument. This is best accomplished by filling down the formula and then going back to edit each cell individually. Upon completion, your worksheet should look like Figure 4.6.

	A	B	C
1	**Coast Jewelers, Inc. Depreciation Schedule**		
2			
3	**Asset #**	1001	
4	**Asset**	Display Cases	
5	**Date acquired**	1/1/2009	
6	**Cost**	$ 15,000.00	
7	**Depreciation method**	DDB	
8	**Salvage value**	$ -	
9	**Estimated useful life**	5	
10			
11	**Year**	**Depreciation Expense**	**Accumulated Depreciation**
12	2009	$6,000.00	$6,000.00
13	2010	$3,600.00	$9,600.00
14	2011	$2,160.00	$11,760.00
15	2012	$1,296.00	$13,056.00
16	2013	$777.60	$13,833.60

⏮ ◀ ▶ ⏭ Summary / Asset 1001 / Asset 1...

Figure 4.6

Initial Calculation of Declining Balance Depreciation for Asset 1001

8 Save your work.

You, however, raise a question. "I remember that when using the double declining balance depreciation method we ignore the salvage value, but in this case shouldn't your accumulated depreciation at the end of 5 years be equal to the cost, since your salvage value was zero?"

"Right you are," Kyle responds. "Generally accepted accounting principles for this method of depreciation require that we switch to straight-line depreciation once that method would calculate depreciation expense greater than that calculated by the double declining balance method. That then assures us that the asset is fully depreciated to its salvage value."

Kyle explains that he'll have to modify the existing worksheet to include a calculation of what the straight-line deprecation would be for each year based on the asset's cost (less salvage value) divided by its remaining useful life. Then he will create a "switch" column that will test to see if the straight-line depreciation method produces a higher depreciation amount than the double declining balance method. Then he will create a new depreciation expense column that will establish if the previous period required a switch or not. If it did, then the depreciation expense will be that previously calculated by the straight-line method. If not, the formula will indicate if a switch should take place in the current period. If a switch is appropriate, then the straight-line depreciation amount will be entered; otherwise, the double declining balance depreciation amounts previously calculated will be used. Kyle will then add a new accumulated depreciation column based on the new depreciation expense calculations.

To do all this, Kyle will need to use a built-in Excel function called IF. The IF function tests a condition and returns a value of "true" if the test is true or a value if "false" if the test is not true. The formula is written =IF(condition, value if true, value if false) where the three arguments result in some value. For example =IF (10>4,5A,6A) would return 5A since 10 is greater than 4.

Kyle points out that he can use the basic IF function to determine if a switch is necessary by comparing calculated depreciation amounts. To determine which amount to use will depend on two things. First, he will have to determine whether the switch was made in the previous period or not. Second, he will have to determine whether it is appropriate to switch in the current period. This will require the use of what are known as *nested* IF statements.

"This is getting pretty complicated!" you comment.

"I agree, but it's well worth the trouble once we're finished," Kyle responds.

Kyle offers to show you how to modify this worksheet to calculate the proper depreciation method using the double declining balance method.

To modify this worksheet to properly calculate double declining depreciation:

1   Change the width of column D to 18 pixels.

2   Type **Straight-Line Test** in cell E11.

3   Type **Switch** in cell F11.

4   Type **Depreciation Expense** in cell G11.

5   Type **Accumulated Depreciation** in cell H11.

6   Change the column width of columns E, F, G, and H to 105 pixels.

7   Type **=SLN($B$6,$B$8,$B$9)** into cell E12. (Note that this is the same calculation we performed before to calculate straight-line depreciation expense.)

8   Type **=SLN($B$6-C12,$B$8,$B$9-1)** into cell E13. (This is the same calculation we performed before to calculate straight-line depreciation expense minus the previous period's accumulated depreciation and with one less year of useful life.)

9 Type **=SLN($B$6-C13,$B$8,$B$9-2)** into cell E14. (Again, this is the same calculation as for straight-line depreciation expense minus the previous period's accumulated depreciation and with one less year of useful life.)

10 Type **=SLN($B$6-C14,$B$8,$B$9-3)** into cell E15.

11 Type **=SLN($B$6-C15,$B$8,$B$9-4)** into cell E16. Your window should look like Figure 4.7.

Figure 4.7

DDB Depreciation Schedule with Straight-Line Test

	A	B	C	D	E	F	G	H
1	Coast Jewelers, Inc. Depreciation Schedule							
2								
3	Asset #	1001						
4	Asset	Display Cases						
5	Date acquired	1/1/2009						
6	Cost	$ 15,000.00						
7	Depreciation method	DDB						
8	Salvage value	$ -						
9	Estimated useful life	5						
10								
11	Year	Depreciation Expense	Accumulated Depreciation		Straight-Line Test	Switch	Depreciation Expense	Accumulated Depreciation
12	2009	$6,000.00	$6,000.00		$3,000.00			
13	2010	$3,600.00	$9,600.00		$2,250.00			
14	2011	$2,160.00	$11,760.00		$1,800.00			
15	2012	$1,296.00	$13,056.00		$1,620.00			
16	2013	$777.60	$13,833.60		$1,944.00			

H ◀ ▶ H   Summary   Asset 1001   Asset 1002   Sheet2   Sheet3

12 Observe that straight-line depreciation is greater than the calculated double declining balance depreciation in 2012. Type **= IF(E12>B12, "X","-")** in cell F12 to determine if the straight-line depreciation method produces an expense greater than from the double declining balance depreciation method. (*Note:* Kyle has chosen to place an X in the Switch column if this is true and dash (hyphen) in the Switch column if the condition is not true. The quotes indicate that the entry is text, not a number.)

13 Format cell F12 to center the text by clicking the **Center text** button in the Alignment group of the Ribbon.

14 Fill that formula down from cell F12 to cell F16. (*Note:* Kyle points out that an X appears in the 2012 and 2013 rows.)

15 Type **=IF(F12="X",E12,B12)** in cell G12. (This will test to see if a switch to straight-line depreciation method is appropriate for the current period.)

16 Fill that formula down from cell G12 to G13.

17 Edit the formula in G13 so that it reads exactly as follows: **=IF (F12="X",G12,IF(F13="X",E13,B13))**. (*Note:* Here we test to see if we used straight-line deprecation in the previous year. If we did then we'll use that same amount for the current year; otherwise, we'll use the amount calculated by testing to see if a switch is necessary for the current year.)

18   Fill this new formula down from cell G13 to G16.

19   Type **=G12** in cell H12, and then type **=H12+G13** into cell H13.

20   Fill down the formula in H13 to cell H16. Your screen should look like Figure 4.8.

Figure 4.8

DDB Depreciation Schedule with New Depreciation Amounts

	A	B	C	D	E	F	G	H
1	Coast Jewelers, Inc. Depreciation Schedule							
2								
3	Asset #	1001						
4	Asset	Display Cases						
5	Date acquired	1/1/2009						
6	Cost	$ 15,000.00						
7	Depreciation method	DDB						
8	Salvage value	$ -						
9	Estimated useful life	5						
10								
11	Year	Depreciation Expense	Accumulated Depreciation		Straight-Line Test	Switch	Depreciation Expense	Accumulated Depreciation
12	2009	$6,000.00	$6,000.00		$3,000.00	-	$6,000.00	$6,000.00
13	2010	$3,600.00	$9,600.00		$2,250.00	-	$3,600.00	$9,600.00
14	2011	$2,160.00	$11,760.00		$1,800.00	-	$2,160.00	$11,760.00
15	2012	$1,296.00	$13,056.00		$1,620.00	X	$1,620.00	$13,380.00
16	2013	$777.60	$13,833.60		$1,944.00	X	$1,620.00	$15,000.00

Summary | Asset 1001 | Asset 1002 | Sheet2 | Sheet3

21   Follow the same steps to modify Asset 1002 for double declining balance depreciation. Your completed screen for Asset 1002 should look like Figure 4.9. (Observe that no switch was necessary in this case.)

Figure 4.9

DDB Depreciation Schedule for Asset 1002

	A	B	C	D	E	F	G	H
1	Coast Jewelers, Inc. Depreciation Schedule							
2								
3	Asset #	1002						
4	Asset	Chairs						
5	Date acquired	1/1/2009						
6	Cost	$ 5,000.00						
7	Depreciation method	DDB						
8	Salvage value	$ 500.00						
9	Estimated useful life	5						
10								
11	Year	Depreciation Expense	Accumulated Depreciation		Straight-Line Test	Switch	Depreciation Expense	Accumulated Depreciation
12	2009	$2,000.00	$2,000.00		$900.00	-	$2,000.00	$2,000.00
13	2010	$1,200.00	$3,200.00		$625.00	-	$1,200.00	$3,200.00
14	2011	$720.00	$3,920.00		$433.33	-	$720.00	$3,920.00
15	2012	$432.00	$4,352.00		$290.00	-	$432.00	$4,352.00
16	2013	$148.00	$4,500.00		$148.00	-	$148.00	$4,500.00

Summary | Asset 1001 | Asset 1002 | Sheet2 | Sheet3

22   Save your work and then close the workbook.

A third common depreciation method is called *sum-of-the-year's digits*. Like the double declining balance method, this is an accelerated method that places more depreciation expense in the first few years of use than in later years. For a 5-year asset, the method sums up the years: $1 + 2 + 3 + 4 + 5 = 15$. In the first year of depreciation, 5/15 of the depreciable cost is recorded as depreciation expense; in the next year, 4/15 of the depreciable cost is recorded; and so forth. Kyle offers to show you how to create a worksheet to calculate the depreciation using the sum-of-the-year's digits method built into Excel.

To create a sum-of-the-year's digits depreciation schedule:

1 Open the straight-line depreciation workbook you created earlier in the chapter named ch4-01_SLN_student_name.xls.

2 Save this workbook with a new name: **ch4-01_SYD_student_name.xls** (replacing student_name with your name).

3 Activate the Asset 1001 worksheet.

4 Type **SYD** in cell B7.

5 Change cell B12 to read **=SYD($B$6,$B$8,$B$9,1)**. Once again, the depreciation function SYD takes arguments located within the parentheses. The first three arguments are the same as the SLN function: cost, salvage value, and useful life. All three of these arguments have been set for absolute referencing so that later, when you copy them down the worksheet, they will continue to reference the appropriate cells. The fourth argument is the period for which the asset is being depreciated: the first, second, third, etc.

6 Change cell B13 to read **=SYD($B$6,$B$8,$B$9,2)**. Note that the only difference between B13 and B12 is the fourth argument.

7 Continue to place the SYD formula in cells B14, B15, and B16, changing only the last argument. This is best accomplished by filling down the formula and then going back to edit each cell individually. Upon completion, your worksheet should look like Figure 4.10.

	A	B	C	D
1	Coast Jewelers, Inc. Depreciation Schedule			
2				
3	Asset #	1001		
4	Asset	Display Cases		
5	Date acquired	1/1/2009		
6	Cost	$ 15,000.00		
7	Depreciation method	SYD		
8	Salvage value	$ -		
9	Estimated useful life	5		
10				
11	Year	Depreciation Expense	Accumulated Depreciation	
12	2009	$5,000.00	$5,000.00	
13	2010	$4,000.00	$9,000.00	
14	2011	$3,000.00	$12,000.00	
15	2012	$2,000.00	$14,000.00	
16	2013	$1,000.00	$15,000.00	

Summary / Asset 1001 / Asset 1002

Figure 4.10

SYD Depreciation Schedule for Asset 1001

8 Save your work.

9 Follow the same steps for Asset 1002. When complete, your worksheet should look like Figure 4.11.

Figure 4.11

SYD Depreciation
Schedule for Asset 1002

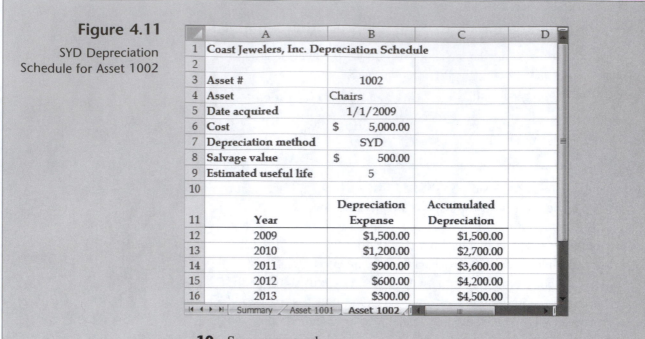

10 Save your work.

"This makes calculating depreciation fairly easy!" you say.

"That's the idea," Kyle responds.

Kyle points out that the charting feature you've used previously can also be used to help illustrate the effects of different depreciation methods.

Charting Depreciation Expense

You have created three files calculating depreciation expense for Asset 1001. Kyle states that, by using the charting feature of Excel, you can easily see the accounting impacts of the three different methods: straight-line, double declining balance, and sum-of-the-year's digits. First he suggests you create a simple chart illustrating the straight-line depreciation of Asset 1001.

To create a chart illustrating the straight-line depreciation of Asset 1001:

1 Open all three workbooks: ch4-01_SLN_student_name.xls, ch4-01_DDB_student_name.xls, and ch4-01_SYD_student_name.xls.

2 Click the **Microsoft Office** button and then select **New.**

3 Press the [**Enter**] key to create a new workbook.

4 Save the workbook as ch4-01_Chart_student_name.xls (replacing student_name with your name).

5 Click the **Insert** tab and then click the **Line** icon from the Charts group.

6 Click the **3-D** chart.

7 Click **Select Data** from the Data group.

8 Click **Add** from the Legend Entries (Series) section.

9 Type **SL** (to represent straight-line depreciation) in the Series name: text box.

10 Select whatever text appears in the Series values: text box.

11 Press and hold the [**Alt**] key, then press the [**Tab**] key as many times as necessary until the ch4-01_SLN_student_name.xls file is active.

12 Select cells **B12** through **B16** from the Asset 1001 worksheet located in the ch4-01_SLN_student_name.xls workbook. Your screen should look like Figure 4.12.

	A	B	C	D	E
1	Coast Jewelers, Inc. Depreciation Schedule				
2					
3	Asset #	1001			
4	Asset	Display Cases			
5	Date acquired	1/1/2009			
6	Cost	$ 15,000.00			
7	Depreciation method	S/L			
8	Salvage value	$ -			
9	Estimated useful life	5			
10					
11	Year	Depreciation Expense	Accumulated Depreciation		
12	2009	$3,000.00	$3,000.00		
13	2010	$3,000.00	$6,000.00		
14	2011	$3,000.00	$9,000.00		
15	2012	$3,000.00	$12,000.00		
16	2013	$3,000.00	$15,000.00		
17					

Edit Series dialog box:
Series name: SL = SL
Series values:]Asset 1001'!$B$12:$B$16 = $3,000.00 , $3...
OK   Cancel

Figure 4.12

Creating a Line Chart

13 Click **OK** in the Edit Series window.

14 Click **Edit** in the Horizontal (Category) Axis Labels section of the Select Data Source window.

15 Press and hold the [**Alt**] key, then press the [**Tab**] key as many times as necessary until the ch4-01_SLN_student_name.xls file is active.

16 Select cells **A12** through **A16** from the Asset 1001 worksheet located in the ch4-01_SLN_student_name.xls workbook.

17 Click **OK** in the Axis Labels window and then click **OK** in the Select Data Source window.

18 Move the chart to fit in the upper left-hand corner of the worksheet.

19 Click and hold the mouse in the lower right-hand corner of the chart, and then drag it down and to the right until it covers the range from cell A1 to H16.

20 With the chart still selected, click **Layout 3** from the Chart Layouts group.

21 Select the chart title and type **Asset 1001 Depreciation Comparison.** Your chart should look like Figure 4.13.

Figure 4.13

Asset 1001 Straight-Line Depreciation Chart

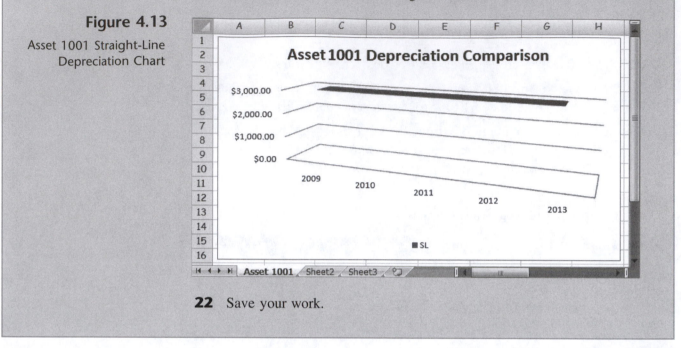

22 Save your work.

Kyle then explains how to make the depreciation chart comparative. Once the original chart is created, all that is needed is to add lines that depict depreciation based on the double declining balance and sum-of-the-year's digits methods. Adding a new series of data to an existing chart is simple: first you select the chart and then, using Chart Tools, you add data from existing workbooks you've already created.

Kyle suggests that you now add data from the double declining and sum-of-the-year's digits files that you saved before.

To modify an existing chart to show comparative depreciation methods:

1 Click and select the chart you created previously.

2 From the Design tab, click **Select Data** from the Data Group as you did before.

3 Click **Add** from the Legend Entries (Series) section.

4 Type **DDB** (for double declining balance depreciation) in the Series name: text box.

5 Select whatever text appears in the Series values: text box.

6 Press and hold the [**Alt**] key, then press the [**Tab**] key as many times as necessary until the ch4-01_DDB_student_name.xls file is active.

7 Select cells **G12** through **G16** from the Asset 1001 worksheet located in the ch4-01_DDB_student_name.xls workbook.

8 Click **OK** in the Edit Series window.

9 Click **Add** from the Legend Entries (Series) section.

10 Type **SYD** (for sum-of-the-year's digits depreciation) in the Series name: text box.

11 Select whatever text appears in the Series values: text box.

12 Press and hold the [**Alt**] key, then press the [**Tab**] key as many times as necessary until the ch4-01_SYD_student_name.xls file is active.

13 Select cells **B12** through **B16** from the Asset 1001 worksheet located in the ch4-01_SYD_student_name.xls workbook.

14 Click **OK** in the Edit Series window.

15 Click **OK** in the Select Data Source window.

16 Click and hold the mouse in the lower right-hand corner of the chart, and then drag it down and to the right until it covers the range from cell A1 to H21. Your new comparative depreciation chart should look like Figure 4.14.

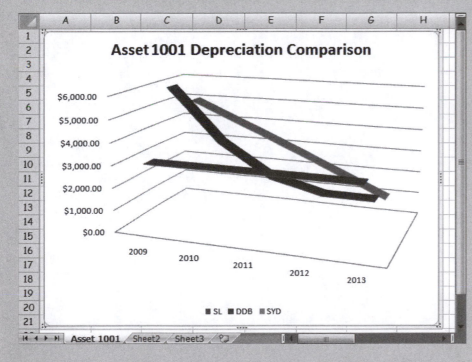

Figure 4.14

Asset 1001 Comparative Depreciation Chart

17 With the chart still selected, click the **Microsoft Office** button.

18 Click **Print.**

19 Make sure that the **Selected Chart** option button is selected, and then click **OK** to print the chart.

20 Save your work and close all windows.

"That's just like I remember from my college classes," you comment.

Kyle points out that straight-line depreciation will always produce a horizontal line, reflecting a constant depreciation expense. The double declining balance method will always produce a curved line, reflecting larger depreciation in the first years with declines thereafter. Finally, sum-of-the-year's digits always produces a straight line that goes down from left to right, reflecting larger depreciation in the first years with a constant decline each year thereafter.

End Note

You've applied some of what you learned in the first three chapters to a specific accounting problem, the depreciation of fixed assets. In the next chapter you will learn how to use Excel to create loan amortization schedules.

Chapter 4 Questions

1   What function is built-into Excel to help you calculate straight-line depreciation?

2   What arguments does the SLN function take?

3   Should the arguments in the SLN function be values or references?

4   Why?

5   Should references used as arguments to the SLN function be absolute or relative?

6   What is the purpose of a depreciation summary?

7   What other depreciation functions are built into Excel?

8   What additional argument is added for these depreciation functions?

9   How do you add a new series of data to an existing chart?

10 Describe the shape of the three lines in a depreciation comparison chart depicting straight-line, double declining balance, and sum-of-the-year's digits depreciation.

Chapter 4 Assignments

1   Modify Coast Jewelers' Straight- Line Depreciation Schedule

You are to add another depreciation schedule for Coast Jewelers. Use the ch4-01_SLN_student_name.xls worksheet you created in this chapter. Add a new depreciation worksheet, labeled Asset 1003, using the Move or Copy Shortcut menu. The asset to be depreciated is a forge purchased on January 1, 2010, for $45,000. It has an estimated salvage value of $5,000 and is to be depreciated over 4 years using the straight-line method. Update the summary worksheet to include information on this new asset. (Be careful to note the date this asset was acquired.) Save the file as ch4-02_SLN_ student_name.xls (replacing student_name with your name).

a. Print the newly completed worksheet for Asset 1003 and the modified Summary worksheet in Value view, with your name and date printed in the lower left footer and the file name in the lower right footer.

b. Print each worksheet from part a (above) in Formula view, with your name and date printed in the lower left footer and the file name in the lower right footer.

2   Modify Coast Jewelers' Double Declining Balance Depreciation Schedule

You are to add another depreciation schedule for Coast Jewelers. Use the ch4-01_DDB_student_name.xls worksheet you created in this chapter. Add a new depreciation worksheet, labeled Asset 1003, using the Move or Copy Shortcut menu. The asset to be depreciated is the forge purchased on January 1, 2010, for $45,000 (again, its estimated salvage value is $5,000). The forge is to be depreciated (over 4 years) using the double declining balance method. Update the summary worksheet to include information on this asset. (Be careful to note the date this asset was acquired.) Save the file as ch4-02_DDB_student_name.xls (replacing student_name with your name).

a.   Print the newly completed worksheet for Asset 1003 and the modified Summary worksheet in Value view, with your name and date printed in the lower left footer and the file name in the lower right footer.

b.   Print each worksheet from part a (above) in Formula view, with your name and date printed in the lower left footer and the file name in the lower right footer.

3   Modify Coast Jewelers' Sum-of-the-Year's Digits Depreciation Schedule

You are to add another depreciation schedule for Coast Jewelers. Use the ch4-01_SYD_student_name.xls worksheet you created in this chapter. Add a new depreciation worksheet, labeled Asset 1003, using the Move or Copy Shortcut menu. The asset to be depreciated is the forge purchased on January 1, 2010, for $45,000 (again, itsestimated salvage value is $5,000). The forge is to be depreciated (over 4 years) using the sum-of-the-year's digits method. Update the summary worksheet to include information on this asset. (Be careful to note the date this asset was acquired.) Save the file as ch4-02_SYD_student_name.xls (replacing student_name with your name).

a.   Print the newly completed worksheet for Asset 1003 and the modified Summary worksheet in Value view, with your name and date printed in the lower left footer and the file name in the lower right footer.

b.   Print each worksheet from part a (above) in Formula view, with your name and date printed in the lower left footer and the file name in the lower right footer.

4   Coast Jewelers' Depreciation Comparison Chart for Asset 1002

You are to add another depreciation chart for Coast Jewelers. Use the ch4-01_Chart_student_name.xls workbook you created in this chapter. Add a new depreciation chart by changing the name of Sheet2 to Asset 1002. Following the steps shown in the chapter, create a new chart comparing straight-line, double declining balance, and sum-of-the-year digit's depreciation amounts for Asset 1002. Save the workbook as ch4-02_Chart_student_name.xls (replacing student_name with your name). Print then newly created chart.

5 Coast Jewelers' Depreciation Comparison Chart for Asset 1003

You are to create a depreciation chart for Coast Jewelers for Asset 1003. After completing assignments 1, 2, and 3, and following the steps shown in the chapter, create a new chart comparing straight-line, double-declining balance, and sum-of-the-year digits depreciation amount for Asset 1003. Save the workbook as ch4-02_Asset 1003_Chart_student_name.xls (replacing student_name with your name). Then print the newly created chart.

Chapter 4 Case Problem 1:
KELLY'S BOUTIQUE

Kelly's Boutique's owned the following fixed assets as of December 31, 2010:

Description

Asset #	101	102	103
Asset	Building	Computer System	Phone System
Date acquired	1/1/07	1/1/09	1/1/09
Cost	$500,000	$65,000	$46,500
Salvage value	$50,000	$1,000	$1,000
Estimated useful life	20 years	5 years	5 years

You are to create Kelly's Boutique's fixed asset depreciation summary and individual depreciation worksheets using the straight-line depreciation method based on the information tabulated above. Be sure to pay close attention to the date of purchase for each asset so that your summary sheet is correct. The summary sheet need only include depreciation from 2007 through 2010. Individual assets must show depreciation over their entire useful life. Follow the text examples for formatting. Label your worksheets as follows: Summary SL, Asset 101 SL, Asset 102 SL, and Asset 103 SL.

In the same workbook, create Kelly's Boutique's fixed asset depreciation summary and individual depreciation worksheets using the double declining balance method and based on the tabulated information. Again, pay close attention to the date of purchase for each asset so that your summary sheet is correct. Label your worksheets: Summary DDB, Asset 101 DDB, Asset 102 DDB, and Asset 103 DDB.

In the same workbook, next create Kelly's Boutique's fixed asset depreciation summary and individual depreciation worksheets using the sum-of-the-year's digits method and based on the tabulated information. Pay close attention to the date of purchase for each asset so that your summary sheet is correct. Label your worksheets: Summary SYD, Asset 101 SYD, Asset 102 SYD, and Asset 103 SYD.

In the same workbook, you should now create a chart of Asset 101's depreciation (over its 20-year estimated useful life) that compares the straight-line, double declining balance, and sum-of-the-year's digits methods of calculating depreciation. Label this worksheet: Chart. Choose any 2D line chart and chart layout that you like.

Save the workbook as ch4-03_student_name.xls (replacing student_name with your name). Print all worksheets in Value view, with your name and date printed in the lower left footer and the file name in the lower right footer.

Chapter 4 Case Problem 2:
WINE DEPOT

The Wine Depot owned the following fixed assets as of December 31, 2010:

Description

Asset #	101	102	103
Asset	Equipment	Truck	Portable
Date acquired	1/1/07	1/1/08	1/1/09
Cost	$485,000	$75,200	$188,642
Salvage value	$25,000	$6,000	$16,800
Estimated useful life	6 years	7 years	15 years

You are to create Wine Depot's fixed asset depreciation summary and individual depreciation worksheets using the straight-line depreciation method and based on the information in the preceding table. Be sure to pay close attention to the date of purchase for each asset so that your summary sheet is correct. The summary sheet need only include depreciation from 2007 through 2010. Individual assets must show depreciation over their entire useful life. Follow the text examples for formatting. Label your worksheets as follows: Summary SL, Asset 101 SL, Asset 102 SL, and Asset 103 SL.

In the same workbook, create Wine Depot's fixed asset depreciation summary and individual depreciation worksheets using the double declining balance method and based on the same tabulated information. Again, pay close attention to the date of purchase for each asset so that your summary sheet is correct. Label your worksheets: Summary DDB, Asset 101 DDB, Asset 102 DDB, and Asset 103 DDB.

In the same workbook, next create Wine Depot's fixed asset depreciation summary and individual depreciation worksheets using the sum-of-the-year's digits method and based on the tabulated information. Be sure to pay close attention to the date of purchase for each asset so that your summary sheet is correct. Label your worksheets: Summary SYD, Asset 101 SYD, Asset 102 SYD, and Asset 103 SYD.

In the same workbook, you should now create a chart of Asset 103's depreciation (over its 15-year estimated useful life) that compares the straight-line, double declining balance, and sum-of-the-year's digits methods of calculating depreciation. Label this worksheet: Chart. Choose any 2D line chart and chart layout that you like.

Save the workbook as ch4-04_student_name.xls (replacing student_name with your name). Print all worksheets in Value view, with your name and date printed in the lower left footer and the file name in the lower right footer.

Loan and Bond Amortization

In this chapter you will learn:

- How to use the payment function to calculate payments to retire a loan
- How to create a loan amortization schedule
- How to use a what-if analysis with the payment function
- How to use names in a worksheet
- How to use the present value function to calculate the proceeds of a bond
- How to create a bond amortization schedule
- How to use Excel's what-if analysis and goal-seeking capabilities with the present value function
- How to use Excel's Scenario Manager
- How to integrate monthly periods into loan or bond amortization analyses

Case: Coast Jewelers, Inc.

Nathan and Meagan have been contemplating the prospect of opening several new locations. They are somewhat strapped for cash and are interested in looking into their financing alternatives. On one hand, they could borrow funds from their local banker. Alternatively, they could borrow money by issuing bonds to local investors. They are curious whether Excel could help them analyze the alternatives or at least help them determine the payments required to pay back a loan or bond.

"Can Excel perform these types of loan calculations?" Meagan asks.

"Yes," Kyle responds, "not only can Excel help you with the calculations. it can also help you with what-if sensitivity analyses to determine interest costs, loan payments, and balances."

Loan Calculations

Kyle explains that loans usually involve some constant periodic payment that pays both interest and principal over a specified period of time. Banks usually want to see some principal payment rather than the interest-only payments often associated with bonds. Excel has a built-in function that calculates the payment on a loan given three variables: interest rate, period, and loan amount. The PMT function takes three arguments and is written =PMT (rate, nper, pv), where rate is the periodic interest rate, nper is the number of periods, and pv is the present value (usually the loan amount). Kyle suggests that you create a worksheet to calculate the annual payment necessary on a 3-year, $100,000 loan at an interest rate of 10 percent.

To calculate a loan payment using Excel's built-in function:

1 Start Excel and open file ch5-01.xls. The worksheet should look like Figure 5.1.

Figure 5.1

Loan Worksheet

	A	B	C	D	E
1	Coast Jewelers, Inc.				
2	Loan Amortization Schedule				
3					
4	Amount				
5	Rate				
6	Term				
7	Payment				
8					
9					
10	Payment #	Payment	Interest	Principal	Balance
11					
12	1				
13	2				
14	3				

Sheet1 / Sheet2 / Sheet3

2 Type **100000** in cell B4, **10%** in cell B5, and **3** in cell B6.

3 Type **=PMT(B5,B6,B4)** in cell B7, and then press [**Enter**]. Note that the resulting amount is a negative number. This is Excel's way of indicating that cash must be paid out to repay the loan proceeds received.

4 Place a negative sign in front of the function PMT so that the formula reads as follows: =–PMT(B5,B6,B4). This has the effect of making the payment a positive number.

5 Save your work to ch5-01_student_name.xls (replacing student_name with your name).

Thus, a payment of $40,211.48, when made at the end of each year for 3 years, will repay the loan and interest charges.

"How much of those payments is interest and how much principal?" Nathan asks.

"Good question." Kyle responds. "That's why it is helpful to create a loan amortization schedule with each worksheet."

Loan Amortization Schedule

Kyle explains how a loan amortization schedule answers Nathan's question. The schedule breaks down each payment into the components of interest and principal. You remind Kyle that interest expense, based on the accrual accounting principal, is calculated as the balance owed multiplied by the periodic interest rate. The amount of payment that exceeds the interest owed is applied to the principal and so reduces the loan amount.

"I can do that." you say.

To add a loan amortization schedule to your worksheet:

1 Type **=B4** in cell E11. This places the loan amount at the beginning of the schedule.

2 Type **=$B$7** in cell B12. This places the loan payment in the schedule. (This reference is absolute so that it can be replicated later.)

3 Type **=E11*$B$5** in cell C12. This formula calculates interest expense as the loan amount multiplied by the interest rate. (The reference to the interest rate is absolute so that it can be replicated later.)

4 Type **=B12–C12** in cell D12. This formula calculates the amount of the payment that reduces the loan amount, otherwise known as principal.

5 Type **=E11–D12** in cell E12. This formula calculates the new loan balance after the loan payment as the previous loan balance less principal reduction.

6 Replicate formulas located at cells B12 through E12 down through row 14.

7 The resulting worksheet should look like Figure 5.2.

8 Save your work.

	A	B	C	D	E
1	Coast Jewelers, Inc.				
2	Loan Amortization Schedule				
3					
4	Amount	$ 100,000.00			
5	Rate	10%			
6	Term	3			
7	Payment	$40,211.48			
8					
9					
10	Payment #	Payment	Interest	Principal	Balance
11					$100,000.00
12	1	$40,211.48	$10,000.00	$30,211.48	$ 69,788.52
13	2	$40,211.48	$ 6,978.85	$33,232.63	$ 36,555.89
14	3	$40,211.48	$ 3,655.59	$36,555.89	$ 0.00

Sheet1 / Sheet2 / Sheet3

Figure 5.2

Loan Amortization Schedule for a $100,000 Loan at 10%

Kyle points out that, at the end of the loan period, the balance should (of course) be zero, which it is in the worksheet.

"What is the payment if the interest rate is higher or lower?" Meagan asks.

"Another good question," Kyle comments. "That leads us into the sensitivity features of Excel that we've worked on previously."

What-If Analysis and the Payment Function

Kyle explains that, because you built the loan amortization worksheet with cell references, a what-if analysis is easy. To investigate the effects of changing interest rates or different loan balances, Kyle suggests he determine the effect on the loan payment of interest rates of 11 percent and 9 percent as well as loan balances of $150,000 or $75,000.

Using Excel, Kyle demonstrates how these variable changes affect the loan payment.

To perform a what-if analysis using the payment function:

1 Type **11%** in cell B5, and then press [**Enter**]. Note the change in payment.

2 Type **9%** in cell B5, and then press [**Enter**]. Again, note the change in payment. Your worksheet should look like Figure 5.3.

Figure 5.3

Loan Amortization Schedule for a $100,000 Loan at 9%

	A	B	C	D	E
1	Coast Jewelers, Inc.				
2	Loan Amortization Schedule				
3					
4	Amount	$ 100,000.00			
5	Rate	9%			
6	Term	3			
7	Payment	$39,505.48			
8					
9					
10	Payment #	Payment	Interest	Principal	Balance
11					$100,000.00
12	1	$39,505.48	$ 9,000.00	$30,505.48	$ 69,494.52
13	2	$39,505.48	$ 6,254.51	$33,250.97	$ 36,243.56
14	3	$39,505.48	$ 3,261.92	$36,243.56	$ 0.00

Sheet1 / Sheet2 / Sheet3

3 Type **10%** in cell B5, and then press [**Enter**].

4 Type **150000** in cell B4, then press [**Enter**]. Note the change in payment.

5 Type **75000** in cell B4, then press [**Enter**]. Note the change in payment. Your worksheet should look like Figure 5.4.

Figure 5.4

Loan Amortization Schedule for a $75,000 Loan at 10%

	A	B	C	D	E
1	Coast Jewelers, Inc.				
2	Loan Amortization Schedule				
3					
4	Amount	$ 75,000.00			
5	Rate	10%			
6	Term	3			
7	Payment	$30,158.61			
8					
9					
10	Payment #	Payment	Interest	Principal	Balance
11					$ 75,000.00
12	1	$30,158.61	$ 7,500.00	$22,658.61	$ 52,341.39
13	2	$30,158.61	$ 5,234.14	$24,924.47	$ 27,416.92
14	3	$30,158.61	$ 2,741.69	$27,416.92	$ 0.00

Sheet1 / Sheet2 / Sheet3

6 Type **100000** in cell B4.

"Fascinating" Meagan exclaims. "This is a great tool!"

"Yes, but these formulas get a bit confusing," Nathan comments. "I have trouble understanding what the payment function is doing with B5, B6, and B4. Isn't there a better way of describing the arguments to functions or what these cell references mean?"

Kyle decides to introduce the concept of named ranges to you, Nathan, and Meagan. He explains that cell references can also be named for clearer analysis.

Names in a Worksheet

Excel provides a naming feature in every worksheet that allows you to define a cell or cells with a name that can then be used elsewhere in the worksheet. There are two steps involved in changing an existing worksheet from cell references to named references. Step 1 is defining cell names; Step 2 is applying those names throughout the worksheet. Kyle suggests that you first name the variables Amount, Rate, Term, and Payment and then apply those names throughout the loan amortization worksheet.

To use names in the loan amortization worksheet:

1 Select the cell range **A4** through **B7.**

2 Click **Create from Selection** from the Defined Names group of the Formula tab.

3 Click in the check box next to Left column as shown in Figure 5.5. (*Note:* This will name the cells in B4 through B7 with the corresponding name in the left column.)

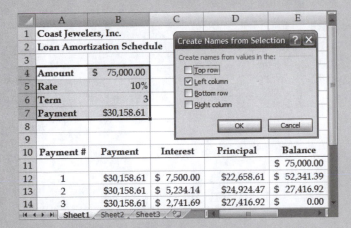

Figure 5.5

Creating Names

4 Click **OK.**

5 Click in cell **E11.**

6 Click **Use in Formula** from the Defined Names group on the Formula tab.

7 Click **Amount** and then press **[Enter]**. (*Note:* This action only replaces the reference to B4 in cell E11 with the newly defined name Amount.)

8 Click the drop-down arrow next to Define Name from the Defined Names group on the Formula tab.

9 Click **Apply Names** and then click **OK** from the Apply Names window. (*Note:* This action replaces all references to B4, B5, B6, and B7 with the respective new names of Amount, Rate, Term, and Payment.)

10 Click in cell **B7.** Observe that the new argument references the payment function: =−PMT(Rate,Term,Amount).

11 Save your work.

Kyle explains that not all cell references will be replaced, since you defined only four cells. However, all references to those cells will now refer to the names instead of specific cells such as B4 and B5.

"This looks much better," Nathan says. "Now I can clearly see that the payment function takes three arguments: Rate, Term, and Amount."

Kyle further explains that these named cells can be used in other ways as well. For example, Excel provides you with a Name Box that lists all the named cells and ranges on the worksheet. He suggests that you explore the use of names further.

To explore the use of named cells and ranges:

1 Click on the drop-down arrow of the Name box located next to the formula text box to reveal the named cells on the worksheet. Then highlight Rate but don't click; see Figure 5.6.

Figure 5.6

Name Box

2 Now click **Rate.** (Note how Excel now positions the active cell as B5, the location of the name Rate.)

3 Save and close this file.

Once names have been created, they can be used throughout the worksheet as you'll see in the next section. Kyle suggests that you now explore the use of worksheets as tools for bond calculations.

Present Value and Bonds

You recall having lots of trouble with present value and bonds while in school and are leery of using them in a worksheet. However, Kyle calms your fears by explaining how the use of a worksheet actually helped him better understand bonds and the concept of present value.

"Whoa now!" Meagan comments. "Why should I learn about present values?"

"Present values are very helpful to an accountant and businessperson," Kyle explains. "In fact, you were using present value concepts when you computed the loan payment above!"

Kyle reminds you that bonds are financial instruments that usually require constant interest payments to the bondholder and then a lump-sum payment equal to the bond's face value at the end of a specified term. The proceeds from a bond's sale, however, depend on the market interest rate at the time of sale.

Kyle explains that Excel's present value function can compute those proceeds based on the following variables: market interest rate, term, periodic interest payment, and lump-sum face value payment. The present value function is written: PV(rate,nper,pmt,fv), where rate is the market rate of interest, nper is the number of periods, pmt is the periodic interest payment, and fv is the future value that is paid at the end of the bond term.

You recall that, if the stated rate of interest on a bond differs from the market rate of interest, then the bond's proceeds won't match its face value. If the stated rate is lower than the market rate then buyers will pay less than the face value, resulting in a discount; if the stated rate is higher than the market rate then buyers will pay more than the face value, resulting in a premium.

Kyle suggests you use Excel to calculate proceeds of a $100,000 bond paying 10 percent per year for 5 years, given an 11 percent market interest rate at the time of the bond's issuance.

To calculate bond proceeds:

1 Open file ch5-02.xls. The worksheet should look like Figure 5.7.

2 Type **100000** in cell B4 to identify the bond face value.

3 Type **10%** in cell B5 to identify the bond's stated interest rate.

4 Type **11%** in cell B6 to identify the market interest rate.

Figure 5.7

Bond Worksheet

	A	B	C	D	E	F
1	Coast Jewelers, Inc.					
2	Bond Amortization Schedule					
3						
4	Amount					
5	Stated Rate					
6	Market Rate					
7	Term					
8	Interest Payment					
9	Proceeds					
10	(Discount) / Premium					
11						
12	Payment #	Interest Payment	Interest Expense	Amortization	(Discount) Premium	Carrying Value
13						
14	1					
15	2					
16	3					
17	4					
18	5					

Sheet1 / Sheet2 / Sheet3

5 Type **5** in cell B7 to identify the bond term.

6 Type **=B4*B5** in cell B8 to calculate annual interest payment.

7 Type **=–PV(B6,B7,B8,B4)** in cell B9 to calculate bond proceeds. (Don't forget the minus sign in front of PV to make the proceeds positive.)

8 Type **=B9–B4** in cell B10 to calculate the bond discount or premium. Your worksheet should look like Figure 5.8.

Figure 5.8

Calculating Bond Proceeds

	A	B
1	Coast Jewelers, Inc.	
2	Bond Amortization Schedule	
3		
4	Amount	$ 100,000.00
5	Stated Rate	10.00%
6	Market Rate	11.00%
7	Term	5
8	Interest Payment	$10,000.00
9	Proceeds	$96,304.10
10	(Discount) / Premium	($3,695.90)

Sheet1 / Sheet2

9 Name the cells located at B4 through B10.

10 Apply the names you just defined. (*Hint:* If you need help doing this, review the Names in a Worksheet section of this chapter.)

11 Click on cell **B9**. The new formula should read as follows: =–PV (Market_Rate,Term,Interest_Payment,Amount).

12 Save the file as ch5-02_student_name.xls (replacing student_name with your name).

Next you need to create a bond amortization schedule to summarize interest payments, interest expense, bond amortization, and remaining carrying value.

Bond Amortization Schedule

A bond amortization schedule is, in essence, a reconciliation of interest payments and bond accounting. Interest expense, usually recorded using the "effective interest" method, is based on the market rate of interest and the carrying value of the debt.

Kyle suggests that you complete the bond amortization table using the named cell ranges that you've already created. In addition to the effective interest formula described previously, you'll need to compute the bond discount/premium amortization as the difference between the interest expense recorded and the interest payment. The ending carrying value for each period will then be the previous period carrying value plus or minus the remaining discount or premium amortization.

To create the bond amortization schedule:

1 Select cell **E13.**

2 Click **Use in Formula** from the Defined Names group of the Formula tab.

3 Click **Discount_Premium** from the drop-down list of names and then press [**Enter**]. (*Note:* This is one way to use previously defined names.)

4 Type **=Amount+E13** in cell F13. Then replicate this formula down to cell F18. This calculation represents the sum of the discount or premium left to be amortized plus the face value of the note. (*Note:* Typing a name is another way of using previously defined names.)

5 Type **=Interest_Payment** in cell B14. Replicate this formula down to cell B18.

6 Type **=F13*Market_Rate** in cell C14. Replicate this formula down to cell C18. These cells will calculate interest expense as the previous period carrying value multiplied by the market rate of interest.

7 Type **=B14−C14** in cell D14. Replicate this formula down to cell D18. These cells will calculate the amortization for the period as the amount by which interest expense differs from the interest payment.

8 Type **=E13–D14** in cell E14. Replicate this formula down to cell E18. These cells will calculate the remaining amount of bond discount or premium to be amortized in future periods.

9 Type **=SUM(B14:B18)** in cell B19 to sum interest payments.

10 Format the cell with a top and double bottom border.

11 Replicate the formula to cell D19 to sum interest expense and amortization.

12 Select cell **B19**, then click **Define Name** from the Defined Names group on the Formulas tab of the Ribbon.

13 Type **Total_Interest_Payments** in the Name: text box and then click **OK.**

14 Select cell **C19**, then click **Define Name** from the Defined Names group on the Formulas tab of the Ribbon.

15 Type **Total_Interest_Expense** in the Name: text box and then click **OK.** (*Note:* You'll use this name later.)

16 The resulting amortization table should look like Figure 5.9.

Figure 5.9

Bond Amortization at a Market Rate of 11%

	A	B	C	D	E	F
1	Coast Jewelers, Inc.					
2	Bond Amortization Schedule					
3						
4	Amount	$ 100,000.00				
5	Stated Rate	10.00%				
6	Market Rate	11.00%				
7	Term	5				
8	Interest Payment	$10,000.00				
9	Proceeds	$96,304.10				
10	(Discount) / Premium	($3,695.90)				
11						
12	Payment #	Interest Payment	Interest Expense	Amortization	(Discount) Premium	Carrying Value
13					($3,695.90)	$96,304.10
14	1	$10,000.00	$10,593.45	($593.45)	($3,102.45)	$96,897.55
15	2	$10,000.00	$10,658.73	($658.73)	($2,443.71)	$97,556.29
16	3	$10,000.00	$10,731.19	($731.19)	($1,712.52)	$98,287.48
17	4	$10,000.00	$10,811.62	($811.62)	($900.90)	$99,099.10
18	5	$10,000.00	$10,900.90	($900.90)	$0.00	$100,000.00
19		$50,000.00	$53,695.90	($3,695.90)		

Sheet1 / Sheet2 / Sheet3

17 Save the file.

"I'll bet we can use this schedule to do some what-if analyses like we did with the loan amortization schedule," you suggest.

"Exactly!" Kyle responds. "Let's see the impact of changing the effective interest rate on bond proceeds and interest expense."

What-If Analysis and Goal Seeking

Nathan is curious about the impact that different market interest rates will have on the proceeds from a bond issuance and on the company's interest expense. He suggests you try interest rates of 9 percent and 12 percent.

To assess the effect of different market rates:

1 Type **9%** into cell B6. Note the effect on bond proceeds and total interest expenses, as shown in Figure 5.10.

	A	B	C	D	E	F
1	Coast Jewelers, Inc.					
2	Bond Amortization Schedule					
3						
4	Amount	$ 100,000.00				
5	Stated Rate	10.00%				
6	Market Rate	9.00%				
7	Term	5				
8	Interest Payment	$10,000.00				
9	Proceeds	$103,889.65				
10	(Discount) / Premium	$3,889.65				
11						
12	Payment #	Interest Payment	Interest Expense	Amortization	(Discount) Premium	Carrying Value
13					$3,889.65	$103,889.65
14	1	$10,000.00	$9,350.07	$649.93	$3,239.72	$103,239.72
15	2	$10,000.00	$9,291.57	$708.43	$2,531.29	$102,531.29
16	3	$10,000.00	$9,227.82	$772.18	$1,759.11	$101,759.11
17	4	$10,000.00	$9,158.32	$841.68	$917.43	$100,917.43
18	5	$10,000.00	$9,082.57	$917.43	$0.00	$100,000.00
19		$50,000.00	$46,110.35	$3,889.65		

 Sheet1 / Sheet2 / Sheet3

Figure 5.10

Bond Amortization at a Market Rate of 9%

2 Type **12%** into cell B6. Note the effect on bond proceeds and total interest expenses.

"Wow, that sure is useful." Nathan says. "We can use this information for our accounting record keeping as well as for financial planning."

"Quite true," Kyle responds. "Excel also has a goal seek feature to help determine a stated rate given needed bond proceeds. Let's assume the company wants to issue a 5-year, $100,000 bond when the market interest rate is 8 percent. If the company needs at least $95,000 from the proceeds, what must be the bond's stated rate of interest?"

"I'll use the existing worksheet and try different stated rates to see how close I can get to $95,000," you comment.

"Not necessary," Kyle explains. "We can use the existing worksheet formulas and simply use Excel's goal seek feature. First you change the variable information, such as the market rate of interest. Then you invoke the goal seek command, set the location of the desired value (B9), specify the desired value (95,000), and identify the location of the variable that should be changed to achieve the desired value (B5). In this case, that location is the cell containing the stated interest rate."

"I'll try that," Meagan says.

To use the goal seek feature:

1 Type **8%** into cell B6. Observe the effect on bond proceeds (the old stated rate of 10% implied payment of a bond premium).

2 Now click **What-If Analysis** from the Data Tools group of the Data tab of the Ribbon.

3 Select **Goal Seek** from the drop-down menu.

4 Type **Proceeds** in the Set cell: edit box. (Alternatively, you could click in the **Set cell: edit** box and then click cell **B9.**)

5 Type **95000** in the To value: edit box.

6 Type **Stated_Rate** in the By changing cell: edit box, as shown in Figure 5.11.

Figure 5.11

Goal Seek Window

7 Click **OK.** The Goal Seek Status window should appear as shown in Figure 5.12, indicating that a solution has been found.

8 Click **OK** in the Goal Seek Status window.

9 Save your work.

Figure 5.12

Goal Seek Status Window and Goal Seek Solution

Kyle remarks that the goal seek solution indicates that a stated rate of 6.75 percent yields the $95,000 proceeds needed, given an 8 percent market rate for a 5-year, $100,000 bond. In reality, the stated rate necessary to produce exactly $95,000 in proceeds is slightly smaller than 6.75. The B5 cell is formatted to show only two decimal places. If you formatted the cell to read additional decimal places it would have shown 6.74771772716582%. However, Kyle contends that 6.75 percent is close enough!

"This is very cool," Nathan comments, "but I wish I could see the effects of the different market rates on the bond proceeds in one worksheet at one time."

Kyle responds: "Sounds like I need to demonstrate the Scenario Manager to you."

Scenario Manager

Scenarios are part of a suite of commands called *what-if analysis tools*. When you use scenarios, you are performing what-if analysis. As we've seen, what-if analysis is the process of changing the values in cells to see how those changes will affect the outcome of formulas on the worksheet. The values in cells are independent variables but formulas, by their very nature, yield dependent variables. That is, the value generated by a formula is dependent on the values in the worksheet's cells that are specified in that formula. You can use scenarios to create and save different sets of independent variable values and switch between them. You can also create a scenario summary report, which combines all the scenarios into one worksheet.

Kyle suggests you use the Scenario Manager to create a scenario describing the effects a change in the market interest rate (an independent variable) on the proceeds from issuing a bond (a dependent variable) and the related total interest expense (another dependent variable) over the term of the bond.

To use the Scenario Manager:

1 Type **100000** in cell B4, **10%** in cell B5, and **11%** in cell B6 to return to the original bond proposal.

2 Click **What-If-Analysis** from the Data Tools group of the Data tab on the Ribbon.

3 Click **Scenario Manager.**

4 Click **Add** to add a new scenario.

5 Type **1** in the Scenario name: text box.

6 Type **Market_Rate** in the Changing cells: text box. Your window should look like Figure 5.13.

Figure 5.13

Adding a Scenario

7 Click **OK.**

8 Type **0.12** for the Market_Rate, as shown in Figure 5.14. (*Note:* 0.12 represents interest at 12 percent.)

Figure 5.14

Entering Scenario Values

9 Click **OK.**

10 Continue the same process by adding scenarios 2, 3, and 4, which change the Market_Rate cell to 0.10, 0.09, and 0.08 respectively. Your window should now look like Figure 5.15.

11 Click **Summary.**

12 Select the Scenario summary option button and then type **Proceeds, Total_Interest_Expense** in the Result cells text box. (*Note:* This action specifies the target variables affected by the change in interest rate— namely, bond proceeds, located in cell B9, and total interest expense, located in cell C19.) See Figure 5.16.

Figure 5.15

Scenario Manager with 4 Scenarios

Figure 5.16

Scenario Summary Options

13 Click **OK.**

14 A new worksheet should appear, entitled Scenario Summary, that looks like Figure 5.17.

Figure 5.17

Scenario Summary

15 Save your work.

You explain to Nathan and Meagan how the Scenario Manager is just an extension of the what-if analysis capabilities of Excel. The ability to compare alternative outcomes based on variations in market rates should prove most helpful in planning and future decision making.

Monthly Periods

So far you have created annual loan and bond amortization schedules and have determined loan payments and bond proceeds based on annual payments. Nathan is curious how this analysis would change if you were confronted with a monthly payment situation.

Kyle offers to help you modify your worksheets for monthly payments. He suggests you take the previous loan workbook you created—a 3-year loan of $75,000 with interest at 10 percent and payments due every year—and convert it to a 3-year loan at 10 percent with 36 monthly payments. Kyle explains that the PMT function was used to determine annual payments; converting to monthly payments requires that the arguments in the payment function be changed from annual to monthly. The first argument is the periodic interest rate. The annual rate is 10 percent, so we need only divide by 12 to obtain the monthly interest rate. The second argument is the term. Since the term is 3 years, we simply multiply 3 by 12 to obtain the number of monthly periods: 36.

To modify your worksheets from annual to monthly:

1 Open your previously saved workbook, ch5-01_student_name.

2 Change the name of Sheet1 to **Annual.**

3 Right-click the **Annual** sheet tab and then click **Move or Copy.**

4 Select the **Create a copy** check box and then select **Sheet2** to insert a copy of your worksheet before Sheet2; then click **OK.**

5 Change the name of Annual (2) to **Monthly.**

6 Type **=−PMT(Rate/12,Term*12,Amount)** as the formula for cell B7.

7 Select cells A13 and A14, then fill down the column so that payment numbers 1 through 36 show.

8 Type **=E11*Rate/12** as the new formula in cell C12

9 Fill that formula down to cell C14.

10 Select cells B14 through E14.

11 Fill the formulas in those cells down through B47 through E47.

12 Click the **Microsoft Office** button and place your mouse over the word **Print**; then click **Print Preview.**

13 Click **Page Setup** and then chose the **Fit to:** option to scale the worksheet to 1 page wide by 1 page tall.

14 Click **OK** and then click **Print.** Your printout should look like Figure 5.18.

15 Save your work.

Coast Jewelers, Inc.
Loan Amortization Schedule

Amount	$	75,000.00
Rate		10%
Term		3
Payment		$2,420.04

Payment #	Payment	Interest	Principal	Balance
				$ 75,000.00
1	$2,420.04	$ 625.00	$1,795.04	$ 73,204.96
2	$2,420.04	$ 610.04	$1,810.00	$ 71,394.96
3	$2,420.04	$ 594.96	$1,825.08	$ 69,569.88
4	$2,420.04	$ 579.75	$1,840.29	$ 67,729.59
5	$2,420.04	$ 564.41	$1,855.63	$ 65,873.97
6	$2,420.04	$ 548.95	$1,871.09	$ 64,002.88
7	$2,420.04	$ 533.36	$1,886.68	$ 62,116.20
8	$2,420.04	$ 517.63	$1,902.40	$ 60,213.79
9	$2,420.04	$ 501.78	$1,918.26	$ 58,295.53
10	$2,420.04	$ 485.80	$1,934.24	$ 56,361.29
11	$2,420.04	$ 469.68	$1,950.36	$ 54,410.93
12	$2,420.04	$ 453.42	$1,966.61	$ 52,444.31
13	$2,420.04	$ 437.04	$1,983.00	$ 50,461.31
14	$2,420.04	$ 420.51	$1,999.53	$ 48,461.78
15	$2,420.04	$ 403.85	$2,016.19	$ 46,445.59
16	$2,420.04	$ 387.05	$2,032.99	$ 44,412.60
17	$2,420.04	$ 370.11	$2,049.93	$ 42,362.67
18	$2,420.04	$ 353.02	$2,067.02	$ 40,295.65
19	$2,420.04	$ 335.80	$2,084.24	$ 38,211.41
20	$2,420.04	$ 318.43	$2,101.61	$ 36,109.80
21	$2,420.04	$ 300.91	$2,119.12	$ 33,990.67
22	$2,420.04	$ 283.26	$2,136.78	$ 31,853.89
23	$2,420.04	$ 265.45	$2,154.59	$ 29,699.30
24	$2,420.04	$ 247.49	$2,172.54	$ 27,526.75
25	$2,420.04	$ 229.39	$2,190.65	$ 25,336.11
26	$2,420.04	$ 211.13	$2,208.90	$ 23,127.20
27	$2,420.04	$ 192.73	$2,227.31	$ 20,899.89
28	$2,420.04	$ 174.17	$2,245.87	$ 18,654.01
29	$2,420.04	$ 155.45	$2,264.59	$ 16,389.43
30	$2,420.04	$ 136.58	$2,283.46	$ 14,105.97
31	$2,420.04	$ 117.55	$2,302.49	$ 11,803.48
32	$2,420.04	$ 98.36	$2,321.68	$ 9,481.80
33	$2,420.04	$ 79.01	$2,341.02	$ 7,140.77
34	$2,420.04	$ 59.51	$2,360.53	$ 4,780.24
35	$2,420.04	$ 39.84	$2,380.20	$ 2,400.04
36	$2,420.04	$ 20.00	$2,400.04	$ (0.00)

Figure 5.18

Printed Monthly Loan
Amortization Worksheet

"I see," Nathan says. "Not only is the payment reduced, but the loan is fully amortized after the 36th payment."

"Exactly," responds Kyle. "Note how the interest portion of each payment diminishes with each payment while the principal portion increases."

Meagan and Nathan are impressed with Excel's robust features and functionality. Kyle and you point out that you've barely scratched the surface and that more is to come.

End Note

You've applied some of what you learned in the first four chapters to better understand how Excel can be used to analyze loans and bonds. In addition, you've learned some new functions—conditional (IF), payment (PMT) and present value (PV)—as well as two new features, goal seeking and Scenario Manager. In the next chapter you'll explore cash flow budgets.

Chapter 5 Questions

✗ **1** Explain the difference between a loan and a bond.

2 What function is used to calculate a loan payment?

3 What arguments does the loan payment function take?

4 Why does the payment function result in a negative number?

5 What does a loan amortization schedule do?

6 Describe the formula for computing interest expense each period for a loan.

7 What function is used to calculate bond proceeds, and what arguments does that function take?

8 Describe the formula computing interest expense each period for a bond.

✗ **9** Describe the goal seek process.

✗ **10** Describe the Scenario Manager.

Chapter 5 Assignments

1 Create a new Coast Jewelers' Loan Amortization Schedule   ✗ *Disregard*

Using the ch5-03 file to start your work, create a worksheet (similar to the one created in this chapter) that calculates the required annual payment for a $350,000, 10-year loan at 8 percent and includes a loan amortization schedule. (Be sure to use names in the worksheet, as illustrated in the chapter.) Save your file as ch5-03_student_name (replacing student_name with your name).

a. Print the newly completed worksheet in Value view, with your name and date printed in the lower left footer and the file name in the lower right footer.

b. Print the worksheet from part a (above) in Formula view, with your name and date printed in the lower left footer and the file name in the lower right footer.

c. Use the Scenario Manager to create a scenario using rates of 10, 9, 7, and 6 percent to calculate alternative payments. Print the resulting summary worksheet.

d. Use Excel's goal seek feature to calculate the amount the company could borrow if it could afford a payment of $50,000 per year. Print the resulting worksheet in Value view, with your name and date printed in the lower left footer and the file name in the lower right footer.

2   Create a new Coast Jewelers' Bond Amortization Schedule

Using the ch5-04 file to start your work, create a worksheet (similar to the one created in this chapter) that calculates the bond proceeds for a $700,000, 15-year, 6 percent stated interest bond issued when the market interest rate is 6.5 percent. Include a bond amortization schedule and use names in the worksheet, as illustrated in the chapter. Save your file as ch5-04_student_name (replacing student_name with your name).

a. Print the newly completed worksheet in Value view, with your name and date printed in the lower left footer and the file name in the lower right footer.

b. Print the worksheet from part a (above) in Formula view, with your name and date printed in the lower left footer and the file name in the lower right footer.

c. Use the Scenario Manager to create a scenario using stated rates of 8, 7, 5, and 4 percent to calculate alternative annual interest payments and bond proceeds. Print the resulting summary worksheet.

d. Use Excel's goal seek feature to calculate the interest rate it would have to pay under the original bond analysis (in part a) to achieve bond proceeds of $725,000. Print the resulting worksheet in Value view, with your name and date printed in the lower left footer and the file name in the lower right footer.

Chapter 5 Case Problem 1:
KELLY'S BOUTIQUE

Kelly's Boutique is contemplating several alternative means of financing an expansion. One alternative is to borrow $500,000 from a local bank; another alternative is to borrow this amount from investors by issuing bonds. Both alternatives involve a 5-year debt period. Modify the workbook file ch5-05 to compute a loan and bond analysis. Name cell ranges as appropriate. Assume an initial loan rate of 6 percent, an initial bond stated rate of 6 percent, and a market interest rate of 7.5 percent.

a. Print the newly completed loan and bond worksheets in Value view, with your name and date printed in the lower left footer and the file name in the lower right footer.

b. Print the worksheets from part a (above) in Formula view, with your name and date printed in the lower left footer and the file name in the lower right footer.

c. Use the Scenario Manager to create two loan scenarios called Best Case and Worst Case. In the Best Case, the rate would be 5 percent and the loan amount would be $750,000; in the Worst Case, the rate would be 7 percent and the loan amount would be $400,000. (*Hint:* You'll need to place two cell references, separated by a comma, in the Changing cells: text box.) The resulting comparison values you're trying to predict are Payment, Total Payments, and Total Interest. Print the resulting summary worksheet.

d.   Use the Scenario Manager to create two bond scenarios called Best Case and Worst Case. In the Best Case, the market rate would be 7 percent and the stated rate would be 5 percent; in the Worst Case, the market rate would be 8 percent and the stated rate would be 6.5 percent. (Again, you'll need to place two cell references, separated by a comma, in the Changing cells: text box.) The resulting comparison values you're trying to predict are Proceeds, Total Interest Payments, and Total Interest Expense. Print the resulting summary worksheet.

e.   Use Excel's goal seek feature to calculate the interest rate that the company would have to negotiate under the original loan analysis (in part a) to achieve a payment of $115,000. Round the interest rate to two decimal places. Print the resulting worksheet in Value view, with your name and date printed in the lower left footer and the file name in the lower right footer.

f.   Use Excel's goal seek feature to calculate the market rate necessary to achieve bond proceeds of $475,000. Round the interest rate to two decimal places. Print the resulting worksheet in Value view, with your name and date printed in the lower left footer and the file name in the lower right footer.

Chapter 5 Case Problem 2:
WINE DEPOT

Wine Depot is considering several alternative means of financing an expansion. One alternative is to borrow $300,000 from a local bank, but another alternative is to borrow this amount from investors by issuing bonds. Both alternatives involve a 3-year debt period with monthly payments. Modify the workbook ch5-06 to compute a loan and bond analysis, naming cell ranges as appropriate. Assume an initial loan rate of 4percent, an initial bond stated rate of 4 percent, and a market interest rate of 3.5 percent.

a.   Print the newly completed loan and bond worksheets in Value view, with your name and date printed in the lower left footer and the file name in the lower right footer.

b.   Print the worksheets from part a (above) in Formula view, with your name and date printed in the lower left footer and the file name in the lower right footer.

c.   Use the Scenario Manager to create two loan scenarios called Best Case and Worst Case. In the Best Case, the rate would be 3 percent and the loan amount would be $350,000; in the Worst Case, the rate would be 5 percent and the loan amount would be $200,000. (*Hint:* You'll need to place two cell references, separated by a comma, in the Changing cells: text box.) The resulting comparison values you're trying to predict are Payment, Total Payments, and Total Interest. Print the resulting summary worksheet.

d. Use the Scenario Manager to create two bond scenarios called Best Case and Worst Case. In the Best Case, the market rate would be 3.75 percent and the stated rate would be 5 percent. In the Worst Case, the market rate would be 4.5 percent and the stated rate would be 3.25 percent. (Again, you'll need to place two cell references, separated by a comma, in the Changing cells: text box.) The resulting comparison values you're trying to predict are Proceeds, Total Interest Payments, and Total Interest Expense. Print the resulting summary worksheet.

e. Use Excel's goal seek feature to calculate the interest rate the company would have to negotiate under the original loan analysis (in part a) to achieve a monthly payment of $8,600. Round the interest rate to two decimal places. Print the resulting worksheet in Value view, with your name and date printed in the lower left footer and the file name in the lower right footer.

f. Use Excel's goal seek feature to calculate the market rate necessary to achieve bond proceeds of $490,000. Round the interest rate to two decimal places. Print the resulting worksheet in Value view, with your name and date printed in the lower left footer and the file name in the lower right footer.

Cash Budgeting

Case: **Coast Jewelers, Inc.**

Nathan and Meagan have been contemplating an expansion of their business to include jewelry repair, which will require some new equipment. Nathan is certain they don't have the cash resources necessary to pull it off. Meagan believes that, with the right financing, they'll be okay. At Kyle's suggestion, they have contacted their bankers, who recommended that they prepare a budget for the next year that specifically addresses their cash needs.

"You'll need to complete an operating activities budget that includes forecasts of sales, purchases, selling and administrative expenses, operating cash receipts, and operating cash payments for the year," Kyle informs them. "In addition, you'll need to budget for investing activities such as equipment purchases and sales as well as a budget for financing activities such as loan proceeds and repayments."

"I'll bet we could use Excel to help us!" Meagan responds. "However, since I'm not much of an accountant, I'll need help."

"I did some budgeting in my accounting classes," you comment. "If Kyle can help me get started I'm sure this can be done on Excel."

"The first place to start is with the operating activities budget," Kyle says.

Operating Activities Budget

Kyle explains that the operating activities budget will include an operating cash receipts budget and an operating activities cash payments budget. However, before you can complete either, you must first determine your sales and purchases budgets.

"What is the difference between operating cash receipts and sales?" Meagan asks.

"The sales budget will estimate the service revenues we expect to earn and the products you expect to sell during the year; however, not all of those revenues will be collected in cash during the year. Also, some of the sales you made on account in the previous year will be collected in the current year," Kyle answers. "So the first thing we need to do is create a sales budget."

Sales Budget

Kyle explains that most budgets are broken into periods smaller than a year. He suggests that you prepare a quarterly budget with an annual summary column. He reminds you that you'll need to plan for both product and repair revenue and that no cost of goods sold or expenses will appear on this part of the sales budget.

Nathan estimates product sales revenue to be $425,000, $400,000, $375,000, and $450,000 for the first through fourth quarters, respectively. During these periods, Nathan thinks he'll bill 1,500, 1,600, 1,700, and 1,800 hours of jewelry repair (respectively) at $50 per hour.

Kyle suggests that you place most of your assumptions that you might consider changing at a later date in a special section of the worksheet called Assumptions. This makes it easy to locate these assumptions in case you want to do some what-if analysis after the budget is created.

To prepare a sales budget:

1 Start Excel and open file ch6-01. The worksheet should look like Figure 6.1.

Figure 6.1

Cash Budget Worksheet

2 Type **Estimated repair hours** into cell A6. (*Note:* Don't worry about the cells above it, since we'll be putting additional labels there momentarily.)

3 Type **1500** into cell B6, **1600** into cell C6, **1700** into cell D6, and **1800** into cell E6.

4 Type **=SUM(B6:E6)** into cell F6 and then press [**Enter**] to sum estimated repair hours.

5 Format cells B6 to F6 with commas and no decimals. (*Hint:* Use the comma style and decimal tools.)

6   Format cells B6 to F6 with a bottom border by selecting those cells, clicking the **Border** tool located in the Font group of the Home tab of the Ribbon, and then selecting the **Bottom Border** tool. (*Note:* This is done to indicate that the number is not summed in later formulas.)

7   Type **Assumptions** in cell A41, format this cell to be bold, and then type **Hourly repair rate** in cell A42.

8   Type **50** into cell B42 and format that cell with commas and no decimals.

9   Define cell B42 as the Hourly repair rate by selecting cells **A42** to **B42.** From the Defined Names group in the Formula tab of the Ribbon, click **Create from Selection.** With the Left column check box checked, click **OK.**

10   Type **Professional services revenue** in cell A7.

11   Type **=B6*** into cell B7 but do *not* press the [Enter] key.

12   From the Defined Names group in the Formulas tab of the Ribbon, click **Use in Formula**, select **Hourly_repair_rate**, and then press [**Enter**] to compute professional services revenue. (Observe how the formatting from B6 is transferred to cell B6.) Fill the formula across to cells B7 through E7.

13   Type **=SUM(B7:E7)** into cell F7 and then press [**Enter**] to sum estimated repair hours.

14   Type **Product sales revenue** into cell A8.

15   Type the product sales revenue estimates **425000, 400000, 375000,** and **450000** into cells B8 through E8, respectively.

16   Type **=SUM(B8:E8)** into cell F8 and then press [**Enter**] to sum Professional services revenues.

17   Format cells B8 to F8 with commas and no decimals and a bottom border.

18   Type **Total revenue** into cell A9.

19   Type the formula **=B7+B8** into cell B9 to calculate total revenue. Fill the formula across to cells C9 through E9.

20   Type **=SUM(B9:E9)** into cell F9 and then press [**Enter**] to sum revenues.

21   Format cells B9 to F9 with commas and no decimals and a bottom border.

22   The completed worksheet should look like Figure 6.2.

23   Save your work to ch6-01_student_name (replacing student_name with your name as before).

Figure 6.2

Sales Budget

	A	B	C	D	E	F
1	Coast Jewelers	1st	2nd	3rd	4th	
2	Cash Budget	Quarter	Quarter	Quarter	Quarter	Year
3						
4						
5						
6	Estimated repair hours	1,500	1,600	1,700	1,800	6,600
7	Professional services revenue	75,000	80,000	85,000	90,000	330,000
8	Product sales revenue	425,000	400,000	375,000	450,000	1,650,000
9	Total revenue	500,000	480,000	460,000	540,000	1,980,000

Cash Budget / Sheet2 / Sheet3

Now that you have created the sales budget, you can create the operating cash receipts budget.

Operating Cash Receipts Budget

Kyle explains that the operating cash receipts budget must account for the timing of revenue collection. Whenever a company offers terms to customers (i.e., payment at other than the time of sale, such as "net 30"), the budget must take into consideration when revenue will actually be collected.

"Based on the last two years, our customers usually pay 80 percent of what we've invoiced them in the quarter when sales were earned and 20 percent in the next quarter" says Nathan. "At the end of last year we had a balance of $81,000 in accounts receivable."

Kyle suggests that you use that information, along with the data provided in the sales budget, to calculate an operating cash receipts budget.

To create the operating cash receipts budget:

1 Type **Operating activities** in cell A4 and format this cell bold.

2 Type **Operating cash receipts** in cell A5.

3 To add the new assumptions just discussed, type **Pct. collections in current quarter** in cell A43.

4 Type **80%** in cell B43.

5 Type **Pct. collections in subsequent quarter** in cell A44.

6 Type **20%** in cell B44.

7 Type **Beginning accounts receivable** in cell A45.

8 Type **81000** in cell B45 and then format the cell in comma format with no decimals.

9 Define names for cells B43 through B45 as you have done before.

10 Type **Current quarter collections** in cell A10.

11 Type **Subsequent quarter collections** in cell A11.

12 Type **Operating cash receipts** in cell A12.

13   Type **=B9*** into cell B10 but do *not* press the [Enter] key.

14   From the Defined Names group in the Formulas tab of the Ribbon, click **Use in Formula**, select **Pct._collections_in_current_quarter**, and then press [**Enter**] to compute current quarter collections. Fill the formula across to cells C10 through E10.

15   Type **=SUM(B10:E10)** into cell F10 and then press [**Enter**] to sum current quarter collections.

16   Type **=** into cell B11 but do *not* press the [Enter] key.

17   From the Defined Names group in the Formulas tab of the Ribbon, click **Use in Formula**, select **Beginning_accounts_receivable**, and then press [**Enter**]. Format the cell in comma format with no decimals.

18   Type **=B9*** into cell C11 but do *not* press the [Enter] key.

19   From the Defined Names group in the Formulas tab of the Ribbon, click **Use in Formula**, select **Pct._collections_in_subsequent_quarter**, and then press [**Enter**] to compute subsequent quarter collections. Fill the formula across to cells C11 through E11.

20   Type **=SUM(B11:E11)** into cell F11 and then press [**Enter**] to sum subsequent quarter collections.

21   Place a bottom border in cells B11 through F11.

22   Type **=B10+B11** into cell B12 and then fill this formula across to cells C12 through E12.

23   Type **=SUM(B12:E12)** into cell F12 and then press [**Enter**] to sum operating cash receipts.

24   Place a bottom border in cells B12 through F12. Your cash budget so far should look like Figure 6.3.

	A	B	C	D	E	F
1	Coast Jewelers	1st	2nd	3rd	4th	
2	Cash Budget	Quarter	Quarter	Quarter	Quarter	Year
3						
4	Operating activities					
5	Operating cash receipts					
6	Estimated repair hours	1,500	1,600	1,700	1,800	6,600
7	Professional services revenue	75,000	80,000	85,000	90,000	330,000
8	Product sales revenue	425,000	400,000	375,000	450,000	1,650,000
9	Total revenue	500,000	480,000	460,000	540,000	1,980,000
10	Current quarter collections	400,000	384,000	368,000	432,000	1,584,000
11	Subsequent quarter collections	81,000	100,000	96,000	92,000	369,000
12	Operating cash receipts	481,000	484,000	464,000	524,000	1,953,000

Cash Budget / Sheet2 / Sheet3

Figure 6.3

Cash Budget of Operating Cash Receipts

25   Save your work.

Kyle explains that now it is time to move on to budgeting operating cash payments. It is important first to budget purchases to meet sales demand and then to contemplate when those purchases will be paid for and then to consider what other operating cash payments must be made, such as selling and administrative expenses.

Purchase Budget

Nathan and Meagan explain that quarterly purchases are dependent on beginning inventory, the cost of expected sales, and the desired amount of ending inventory. They give the following example. Assume a beginning inventory of $500 and expected merchandise sales of $1,500 (that cost them $900). Further, assume they would like to keep an inventory of $400 on hand for next month's sales. Hence they will need to purchase $800 of inventory during the quarter. This is computed using the following formula: cost of expected sales (900) + desired ending inventory (400) – beginning inventory (500) = required purchases (800).

Nathan estimates that the cost of most of his inventory is 60 percent of sales. For example, a necklace Coast sells for $100 cost them $60. Further, he would like to maintain an inventory on hand each month of 80 percent of expected sales in the following month. Inventory at the beginning of the year was $125,000, and product sales in the first quarter of the next year are expected to be $500,000.

Kyle recommends that you take a shot at producing the desired purchases budget while explaining the process to Meagan and Nathan.

To create a purchases budget:

1 Type **Operating cash payments** in cell A13 and format this cell bold.

2 Type **Purchases** in cell A14.

3 To add the new assumptions discussed above, type **Cost of expected sales** in cell A46.

4 Type **60%** in cell B46.

5 Type **Required ending inventory** in cell A47.

6 Type **80%** in cell B47.

7 Type **Beginning inventory** in cell A48.

8 Type **125000** in cell B48

9 Type **Product sales 1st quarter of next year** in cell A49.

10 Type **500000** in cell B49.

11 Define names for cells B46 through B49 as you have done before.

12 Type **Cost of expected sales** in cell A15.

13 Type **Required ending inventory** in cell A16.

14 Type **Beginning inventory** in cell A17.

15 Type **Purchases** in cell A18.

16 Type **=B8*** into cell B15 but do *not* press the [Enter] key. (*Note:* This is not total revenue but just product sales revenue.)

17 From the Defined Names group in the Formulas tab of the Ribbon, click **Use in Formula**, select **Cost_of_expected_sales**, and then press [**Enter**] to compute the cost of expected sales for the quarter.

18 Format the cell in comma format with no decimals, and then fill the formula across to cells C15 through E15.

19 Type **=SUM(B15:E15)** into cell F15 and then press [**Enter**] to sum the cost of expected sales for the year.

20 Type **=C15*** into cell B16 but do *not* press the [Enter] key.

21 From the Defined Names group in the Formulas tab of the Ribbon, click **Use in Formula**, select **Required_ending_inventory**, and then press [**Enter**] to compute the required ending inventory for the quarter. Format the cell in comma format with no decimals, and then fill the formula across to cells C16 through D16.

22 Type **=** into cell E16 but do *not* press the [Enter] key.

23 From the Defined Names group in the Formulas tab of the Ribbon, click **Use in Formula.** Then select **Cost_of_expected_sales**, **Required_ending_inventory**, and **Product_sales_1st_quarter_of_next_year** to create a formula where there terms are multiplied together. Your completed formula should read as follows. =Cost_of_expected_sales*Required_ending_inventory* Product_sales_1st_quarter_of_next_year

24 If it does, press [**Enter**]. Format the cell in comma format with no decimals.

25 Type **=E16** in cell F16 to indicate that the required ending inventory for the year is the same as the required ending inventory for the fourth quarter.

26 Type **=–** in cell B17, and then click **Use in Formula** from the Defined Names group on the Formulas tab of the Ribbon. (*Note:* Be sure you type the equals sign *and* the minus sign here to indicate you are going to make this value negative.)

27 Select **Beginning_inventory** and then press [**Enter**].

28 Type **=–B16** in cell C17 and then press [**Enter**] to indicate that the current quarter's beginning inventory is equal to the previous quarter's ending inventory. Fill this formula across from cell D17 to E17.

29 Type **=B17** in cell F17 to indicate that the beginning inventory for the year was the same as the beginning inventory for the first quarter.

30 Place a bottom border in cells B17 through F17.

31 Type **=SUM(B15:B17)** in cell B18 to calculate the first quarter's purchases. Fill this formula across to cell C18 to F18.

32 Place a bottom border in cells B18 through F18. Your completed cash budget, including purchases, should look like Figure 6.4.

Figure 6.4

Cash Budget of Operating Cash Receipts through Purchases

	A	B	C	D	E	F
1	Coast Jewelers	1st	2nd	3rd	4th	
2	Cash Budget	Quarter	Quarter	Quarter	Quarter	Year
3						
4	Operating activities					
5	Operating cash receipts					
6	Estimated repair hours	1,500	1,600	1,700	1,800	6,600
7	Professional services revenue	75,000	80,000	85,000	90,000	330,000
8	Product sales revenue	425,000	400,000	375,000	450,000	1,650,000
9	Total revenue	500,000	480,000	460,000	540,000	1,980,000
10	Current quarter collections	400,000	384,000	368,000	432,000	1,584,000
11	Subsequent quarter collections	81,000	100,000	96,000	92,000	369,000
12	Operating cash receipts	481,000	484,000	464,000	524,000	1,953,000
13	Operating cash payments					
14	Purchases					
15	Cost of expected sales	255,000	240,000	225,000	270,000	990,000
16	Required ending inventory	192,000	180,000	216,000	240,000	240,000
17	Beginning inventory	(125,000)	(192,000)	(180,000)	(216,000)	(125,000)
18	Purchases	322,000	228,000	261,000	294,000	1,105,000

◄ ► ►│ Cash Budget / Sheet2 / Sheet3 / ♀/

33 Save your work.

"As you can see, the purchases budget is based on the sales budget we had previously created and some additional facts and assumptions, such as the relationship between sales and costs of goods sold," Kyle notes.

"How does all this relate to cash flow?" you ask.

"We must now factor in the relationship between when we purchase merchandise and when we actually pay for it," Kyle answers. "Thus, we have to adjust purchases for our payment expectations."

Operating Cash Payments for Purchases

Kyle explains that, whenever a vendor or supplier does not require immediate payment, the budget must take into consideration when payment is actually paid. In this case, it is expected that 75 percent of purchases are paid in the month of purchase and 25 percent are paid in the month following purchases. He also points out that, at the beginning of the year, the company's accounts payable amount to $16,000, which must be paid in the first quarter. He suggests you add the assumptions he just made to your cash budget and incorporate them into your calculation of cash payments for purchases.

To create a cash payments for purchases budget:

1 Type **Current quarter payments** in cell A19.

2 Type **Subsequent quarter payments** in cell A20.

3 Type **Cash payments for purchases** in cell A21.

4 To add the new assumptions just discussed, type **Beginning accounts payable** in cell A50.

5 Type **16000** in cell B50.

6 Type **Pct. of purchases paid in current quarter** in cell A51.

7 Type **75%** in cell B51.

8 Type **Pct. of purchases paid in subsequent quarter** in cell A52.

9 Type **25%** in cell B52.

10 Define names for cells B50 through B52 as you have done before.

11 Type **=B18*** into cell B19 but do *not* press the [Enter] key.

12 From the Defined Names group in the Formulas tab of the Ribbon, click **Use in Formula**, select **Pct._of_purchases_paid_in_current_quarter**, and then press [**Enter**].

13 Format the cell in comma format with no decimals, and then fill the formula across to cells C19 through E19.

14 Type **=SUM(B19:E19)** into cell F19 and then press [**Enter**] to sum the current quarter payments for the year.

15 Type **=** into cell B20 but do *not* press the [Enter] key.

16 From the Defined Names group in the Formulas tab of the Ribbon, click **Use in Formula**, select **Beginning_accounts_payable**, and then press [**Enter**].

17 Format the cell in comma format with no decimals.

18 Type **=B18*** into cell C20 but do *not* press the [Enter] key.

19 From the Defined Names group in the Formulas tab of the Ribbon, click **Use in Formula**, select **Pct._of_purchases_paid_in_subsequent_quarter**, and then press [**Enter**].

20 Format the cell in comma format with no decimals, and then fill the formula across to cells D20 through E20.

21 Type **=SUM(B20:E20)** into cell F20 and then press [**Enter**] to sum the subsequent quarter payments for the year.

22 Place a bottom border in cells B20 through F20.

23 Type **=B19+B20** in cell B21 to sum payments made in the quarter, and then fill the formula across to cells C21 through F21.

24 Place a bottom border in cells B21 through F21. Your modified cash budget should look like Figure 6.5.

Figure 6.5

Cash Budget with Cash
Payments for Purchases

	A	B	C	D	E	F
1	Coast Jewelers	1st	2nd	3rd	4th	
2	Cash Budget	Quarter	Quarter	Quarter	Quarter	Year
3						
4	Operating activities					
5	Operating cash receipts					
6	Estimated repair hours	1,500	1,600	1,700	1,800	6,600
7	Professional services revenue	75,000	80,000	85,000	90,000	330,000
8	Product sales revenue	425,000	400,000	375,000	450,000	1,650,000
9	Total revenue	500,000	480,000	460,000	540,000	1,980,000
10	Current quarter collections	400,000	384,000	368,000	432,000	1,584,000
11	Subsequent quarter collections	81,000	100,000	96,000	92,000	369,000
12	Operating cash receipts	481,000	484,000	464,000	524,000	1,953,000
13	Operating cash payments					
14	Purchases					
15	Cost of expected sales	255,000	240,000	225,000	270,000	990,000
16	Required ending inventory	192,000	180,000	216,000	240,000	240,000
17	Beginning inventory	(125,000)	(192,000)	(180,000)	(216,000)	(125,000)
18	Purchases	322,000	228,000	261,000	294,000	1,105,000
19	Current quarter payments	241,500	171,000	195,750	220,500	828,750
20	Subsequent quarter payments	16,000	80,500	57,000	65,250	218,750
21	Cash payments for purchases	257,500	251,500	252,750	285,750	1,047,500

Cash Budget / Sheet2 / Sheet3 / ♫

25 Save your work.

"Operating cash flow encompasses cash inflow from sales as well as cash outflow for purchases and expenses," Kyle explains. "Next up is budget for sales and administrative expenses. The nice thing about these expenses is that they are usually paid in the same period they are incurred."

Sales and Administrative Expense Budget

Kyle explains to you, Nathan, and Meagan that the sales and administrative expense budget won't be linked to either sales or purchases. Instead, the budget will be based on expected costs to be incurred for advertising, depreciation, payroll, and utilities. Nathan thinks that advertising expense will be $25,000 in the first quarter and then increase $5,000 per quarter over the year. Depreciation will be $8,000 in the first quarter and then increase $1,000 per quarter over the year based on new equipment purchases. Payroll will vary based on the expected expansion of business and seasonal sales but is expected to be $125,000 the first quarter, $150,000 in the first and second quarter, and then $185,000 in the fourth quarter. Utilities will be based on the prior year's actual results, which were $15,000, $18,000, $17,500, and $19,000 in the first through fourth quarters, respectively.

"How does depreciation affect our cash budget?" you ask. "Isn't depreciation a noncash outlay?"

"As a matter of fact, it is," Kyle answers. "It is still an expense, but we won't include it in our selling and administrative expense budget."

Kyle suggests that you prepare the sales and administrative expense budget based on the data provided—excluding depreciation, as you so aptly pointed out.

To create the selling and administrative expense portion of your cash budget:

1 Type **Selling and administrative expenses** in cell A22.

2 Type **Advertising expense** in cell A23.

3 Type **Payroll expense** in cell A24.

4 Type **Utilities expense** in cell A25.

5 Type **Selling and administrative expenses** in cell A26.

6 Enter the expense information provided by Nathan into cells B23 through E25.

7 Enter formulas to sum quarterly expenses in cells B26 through E26.

8 Enter formulas to sum expenses in cells F23 through F26.

9 Place a bottom border in cells B24 through F24.

10 Place a bottom border in cells B25 through F25. Your modified cash budget should look like Figure 6.6.

	A	B	C	D	E	F
1	Coast Jewelers	1st	2nd	3rd	4th	
2	Cash Budget	Quarter	Quarter	Quarter	Quarter	Year
3						
4	**Operating activities**					
5	Operating cash receipts					
6	Estimated repair hours	1,500	1,600	1,700	1,800	6,600
7	Professional services revenue	75,000	80,000	85,000	90,000	330,000
8	Product sales revenue	425,000	400,000	375,000	450,000	1,650,000
9	Total revenue	500,000	480,000	460,000	540,000	1,980,000
10	Current quarter collections	400,000	384,000	368,000	432,000	1,584,000
11	Subsequent quarter collections	81,000	100,000	96,000	92,000	369,000
12	Operating cash receipts	481,000	484,000	464,000	524,000	1,953,000
13	Operating cash payments					
14	Purchases					
15	Cost of expected sales	255,000	240,000	225,000	270,000	990,000
16	Required ending inventory	192,000	180,000	216,000	240,000	240,000
17	Beginning inventory	(125,000)	(192,000)	(180,000)	(216,000)	(125,000)
18	Purchases	322,000	228,000	261,000	294,000	1,105,000
19	Current quarter payments	241,500	171,000	195,750	220,500	828,750
20	Subsequent quarter payments	16,000	80,500	57,000	65,250	218,750
21	Cash payments for purchases	257,500	251,500	252,750	285,750	1,047,500
22	Selling and administrative expenses					
23	Advertising expense	25,000	30,000	35,000	40,000	130,000
24	Payroll expense	125,000	150,000	150,000	185,000	610,000
25	Utilities expense	15,000	18,000	17,500	19,000	69,500
26	Selling and administrative expenses	165,000	198,000	202,500	244,000	809,500

Cash Budget / Sheet2 / Sheet3

Figure 6.6

Cash Budget with Cash Payments for Expenses

11 Save your work.

Operating Cash Payments Budget

Kyle remarks that you must now put all the pieces together in order to complete the operating cash payments budget. The budget will consist of the sum of payments made for purchases and payments made for selling and administrative expenses.

To finalize the operating cash payments budget:

1 Type **Operating cash payments** in cell A27.

2 Type **=B21+B26** in cell B27 to add the first-quarter cash payments for purchases to the first-quarter cash payments for selling and administrative expenses together.

3 Fill this formula across to cell C27 through F27.

4 Place a bottom border in cells B27 through F27.

To finalize the operating portion of the cash budget, all that is left is to subtract the operating cash payments from the operating cash receipts.

To finalize the operating cash budget:

1 Type **Cash from (to) operating activities** in cell A28.

2 Type **=B12−B27** in cell B28 to subtract the first-quarter cash payments from the first-quarter cash receipts.

3 Fill this formula across to cell C28 through F28.

4 Place a bottom border in cells B28 through F28. Your completed cash budget for operating activities is shown in Figure 6.7.

Figure 6.7

Completed Cash Budget from Operating Activities

	A	B	C	D	E	F
1	Coast Jewelers	1st	2nd	3rd	4th	
2	Cash Budget	Quarter	Quarter	Quarter	Quarter	Year
3						
4	Operating activities					
5	Operating cash receipts					
6	Estimated repair hours	1,500	1,600	1,700	1,800	6,600
7	Professional services revenue	75,000	80,000	85,000	90,000	330,000
8	Product sales revenue	425,000	400,000	375,000	450,000	1,650,000
9	Total revenue	500,000	480,000	460,000	540,000	1,980,000
10	Current quarter collections	400,000	384,000	368,000	432,000	1,584,000
11	Subsequent quarter collections	81,000	100,000	96,000	92,000	369,000
12	Operating cash receipts	481,000	484,000	464,000	524,000	1,953,000
13	Operating cash payments					
14	Purchases					
15	Cost of expected sales	255,000	240,000	225,000	270,000	990,000
16	Required ending inventory	192,000	180,000	216,000	240,000	240,000
17	Beginning inventory	(125,000)	(192,000)	(180,000)	(216,000)	(125,000)
18	Purchases	322,000	228,000	261,000	294,000	1,105,000
19	Current quarter payments	241,500	171,000	195,750	220,500	828,750
20	Subsequent quarter payments	16,000	80,500	57,000	65,250	218,750
21	Cash payments for purchases	257,500	251,500	252,750	285,750	1,047,500
22	Selling and administrative expenses					
23	Advertising expense	25,000	30,000	35,000	40,000	130,000
24	Payroll expense	125,000	150,000	150,000	185,000	610,000
25	Utilities expense	15,000	18,000	17,500	19,000	69,500
26	Selling and administrative expenses	165,000	198,000	202,500	244,000	809,500
27	Operating cash payments	422,500	449,500	455,250	529,750	1,857,000
28	Cash from (to) operating activities	58,500	34,500	8,750	(5,750)	96,000

H ◀ ▶ H   Cash Budget / Sheet2 / Sheet3 / ℃

5 Save your work.

"That was interesting," you comment. "I have prepared a statement of cash flows before but never a budget that looked like a statement of cash flows!"

"Ah, but there is more," Kyle responds. "Remember, the other two components of cash flow are investing and financing activities."

Investing and Financing Activities Budgets

You recall that investing activities usually involve not only the purchase or sale of such long-term assets as land, buildings, and equipment but also the purchase or sale of long-term investments. You also know that financing activities usually involve borrowings or repayment of borrowings, the sale or repurchase of stock, and/or the payment of dividends.

"What are your plans for the coming year?" Kyle asks.

"Well, I'd like to purchase some new equipment in the second quarter for about $300,000," Nathan says. "The bank is willing to lend me $250,000, provided these budgets support the stories I've been telling them about the business. The quarterly payment on the loan, which includes interest, is about $20,000 starting in the third quarter."

"That's all the information we need to create the investing and financing portion of our cash budget," Kyle says. "Let's have our student here finalize the budget."

To create the investing and financing portion of our cash budget:

1 Type **Investing activities** in cell A29.

2 Format this cell's font bold.

3 Type **Equipment purchases** in cell A30.

4 Type **Equipment sales** in cell A31.

5 Type **Cash from (to) investing activities** in cell A32.

6 Type **Financing activities** in cell A33.

7 Format this cell's font bold.

8 Type **Loan proceeds** in cell A34.

9 Type **Loan payments** in cell A35.

10 Type **Cash from (to) financing activities** in cell A36.

11 Type **−300000** in cell C30 to reflect the equipment purchase in the second quarter.

12 Type **250000** in cell C34 to reflect the proceeds from the loan in the second quarter.

13 Type **−20000** in cells D35 and E35 to reflect payments on the loan made in the third and fourth quarter.

14 Format all cells in the range B30 to F36 in comma format with no decimals.

15 Type **=SUM(B30:E30)** in cell F30.

16 Type **=SUM(B31:E31)** in cell F31.

17 Place a bottom border in cells B31 through F31.

18 Type **=B30+B31** in cell B32 and then fill this formula across from cell C32 to F32.

19 Place a bottom border in cells B32 through F32.

20 Place a bottom border in cells B35 through F35.

21 Type **=SUM(B34:E34)** in cell F34.

22 Type **=SUM(B35:E35)** in cell F35.

23 Type **=B34+B35** in cell B36 and then fill this formula across from cell C36 to F36.

24 Place a bottom border in cells B36 through F36. The investing and financing portion of your cash budget should look like Figure 6.8.

Figure 6.8

Investing and Financing Portion of the Cash Budget

	A	B	C	D	E	F
29	**Investing activities**					
30	Equipment purchases		(300,000)			(300,000)
31	Equipment sales					-
32	Cash from (to) investing activities	-	(300,000)	-		(300,000)
33	**Financing activities**					
34	Loan proceeds		250,000			250,000
35	Loan payments			(20,000)	(20,000)	(40,000)
36	Cash from (to) financing activities	-	250,000	(20,000)	(20,000)	210,000

Cash Budget / Sheet2 / Sheet3

25 Save your work.

You are very close to completing the cash budget.

Finalizing and Formatting the Cash Budget

"To finalize the cash budget we need to compute the net change in cash and compare it to beginning cash to determine our forecasted ending cash balance for the year," comments Kyle. "How much cash will you have at the beginning of the budgeted period?" Kyle asks.

"Right now my best estimate is about $25,000," Nathan responds.

To finalize the cash budget:

1 To add the new assumptions discussed above, type **Beginning cash** in cell A54.

2   Type **25000** in cell B54. Format the cell in comma format with no decimals.

3   Define a name for cell B54 as you've done before.

4   Type **Change in cash** in cell A37.

5   Type **Beginning cash** in cell A38.

6   Type **Ending cash** in cell A39.

7   Type **=B28+B32+B36** in cell B37 to add operating, investing, and financing cash activities for the first quarter.

8   Fill that formula across from cell C37 to F37.

9   Click in cell **B38**, click **Use in Formula** from the Defined Names group on the Formulas tab of the Ribbon, click **Beginning_cash**, and then press [**Enter**]. Format the cell in comma format with no decimals.

10 Type **=B37+B38** in cell B39.

11 Fill that formula across from cell C39 to F39.

12 Type **=B39** in cell C38 to reference ending cash from the first quarter to beginning cash in the second quarter.

13 Fill that formula across from cell D38 to E38.

14 Type **=B38** in cell F38 to reference beginning cash from the first quarter to beginning cash for the year.

15 Place a bottom border in cells B38 through F38.

16 Place a bottom double border in cells B39 through F39.

17 Save your work.

18 Click the **Microsoft Office** button and then click **Print.**

19 Click **OK** to print the cash budget (two pages) shown in Figure 6.9 and Figure 6.10.

20 Press the [**Ctrl**] and [`] (grave accent key) keys simultaneously to switch to Formula view. Part of your window should look like Figure 6.11.

21 Click the **Microsoft Office** button and then click **Print.**

22 Click **Preview** and then click **Page Setup.**

23 Choose the **Landscape** option for orientation and then click the **Fit to:** scaling option.

24 Set scaling to 1 page wide by 1 tall and then click **OK** in the Page Setup window.

25 Click **Print** in the Print Preview window and then click **OK** to print the cash budget in Formula view.

Figure 6.9

Completed Cash Budget

Coast Jewelers	1st	2nd	3rd	4th	
Cash Budget	Quarter	Quarter	Quarter	Quarter	Year
Operating activities					
Operating cash receipts					
Estimated repair hours	1,500	1,600	1,700	1,800	6,600
Professional services revenue	75,000	80,000	85,000	90,000	330,000
Product sales revenue	425,000	400,000	375,000	450,000	1,650,000
Total revenue	500,000	480,000	460,000	540,000	1,980,000
Current quarter collections	400,000	384,000	368,000	432,000	1,584,000
Subsequent quarter collections	81,000	100,000	96,000	92,000	369,000
Operating cash receipts	481,000	484,000	464,000	524,000	1,953,000
Operating cash payments					
Purchases					
Cost of expected sales	255,000	240,000	225,000	270,000	990,000
Required ending inventory	192,000	180,000	216,000	240,000	240,000
Beginning inventory	(125,000)	(192,000)	(180,000)	(216,000)	(125,000)
Purchases	322,000	228,000	261,000	294,000	1,105,000
Current quarter payments	241,500	171,000	195,750	220,500	828,750
Subsequent quarter payments	16,000	80,500	57,000	65,250	218,750
Cash payments for purchases	257,500	251,500	252,750	285,750	1,047,500
Selling and administrative expenses					
Advertising expense	25,000	30,000	35,000	40,000	130,000
Payroll expense	125,000	150,000	150,000	185,000	610,000
Utilities expense	15,000	18,000	17,500	19,000	69,500
Selling and administrative expenses	165,000	198,000	202,500	244,000	809,500
Operating cash payments	422,500	449,500	455,250	529,750	1,857,000
Cash from (to) operating activities	58,500	34,500	8,750	(5,750)	96,000
Investing activities					
Equipment purchases		(300,000)			(300,000)
Equipment sales					-
Cash from (to) investing activities	-	(300,000)	-	-	(300,000)
Financing activities					
Loan proceeds		250,000			250,000
Loan payments			(20,000)	(20,000)	(40,000)
Cash from (to) financing activities	-	250,000	(20,000)	(20,000)	210,000
Change in cash	58,500	(15,500)	(11,250)	(25,750)	6,000
Beginning cash	25,000	83,500	68,000	56,750	25,000
Ending cash	83,500	68,000	56,750	31,000	31,000

Figure 6.10

Cash Budget Assumptions

Assumptions	
Hourly repair rate	50
Pct. collections in current quarter	80%
Pct. collections in subsequent quarter	20%
Beginning accounts receivable	81,000
Cost of expected sales	60%
Required ending inventory	80%
Beginning inventory	125,000
Product sales 1st quarter of next year	500,000
Beginning accounts payable	16,000
Pct. of purchases paid in current quarter	75%
Pct. of purchases paid in subsequent quarter	25%
Beginning cash	25,000

26 Press the [**Ctrl**] and [`] (grave accent key) keys simultaneously to switch back to Value view.

27 Double-click between each column to resize that column to fit its contents.

28 Save your work.

Double-click here to resize column A to fit its contents

Figure 6.11

Partial Formula View of the Cash Budget

	A	B
1	Coast Jewelers	1st
2	Cash Budget	Quarter
3		
4	**Operating activities**	
5	Operating cash receipts	
6	Estimated repair hours	1500
7	Professional services revenue	=B6*Hourly_repair_rate
8	Product sales revenue	425000
9	Total revenue	=B7+B8
10	Current quarter collections	=Pct._collections_in_current_quarter*B9
11	Subsequent quarter collections	=Beginning_accounts_receivable
12	Operating cash receipts	=B10+B11
13	Operating cash payments	
14	Purchases	
15	Cost of expected sales	=Cost_of_expected_sales*B8
16	Required ending inventory	=Required_ending_inventory*C15
17	Beginning inventory	=-Beginning_inventory
18	Purchases	=SUM(B15:B17)
19	Current quarter payments	=Pct._of_purchases_paid_in_current_quarter*B18
20	Subsequent quarter payments	='Cash Budget'!B50
21	Cash payments for purchases	=SUM(B19:B20)
22	Selling and administrative expenses	
23	Advertising expense	25000
24	Payroll expense	125000
25	Utilities expense	15000
26	Selling and administrative expenses	=SUM(B23:B25)
27	Operating cash payments	=B21+B26
28	Cash from (to) operating activities	=B12-B27

Cash Budget / Sheet2 / Sheet3

"I like using names in Excel," says Nathan. "It is much easier to follow the formula logic when I see descriptions of what is going on rather that just cell references."

"I agree," responds Meagan. "It's not much of a hassle to create and use the names, because Excel gives you the 'Create from Selection' option for naming cells and the 'Use in Formula' option for using names."

Excel also has a grouping feature that can dramatically change the way this budget is viewed. Kyle explains that the entire budget can be summarized horizontally (by rows) down to the entries for cash from (to) operating, investing, and financing activities, the net change in cash, beginning cash, and ending cash. The budget can also be grouped vertically to collapse columns and show only the year amounts. Kyle offers to show you Excel's grouping feature by creating five different levels of grouping.

To use Excel's grouping feature on the cash budget:

1 Click and select rows **6, 7,** and **8,** as shown in Figure 6.12, to group total revenues.

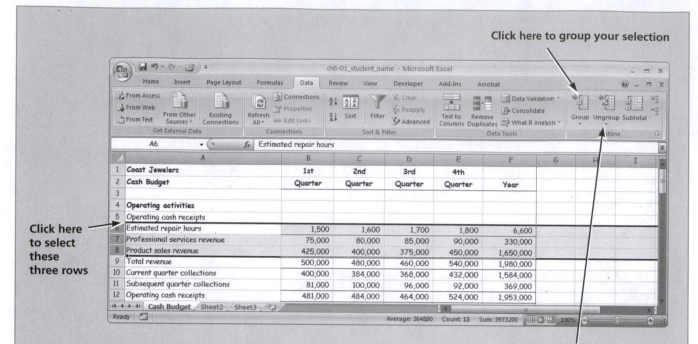

Figure 6.12

Grouping

2 Click **Group** in the Outline group on the Data tab of the Ribbon.

   Trouble? What if you accidently group the wrong rows? No problem, just reselect those rows that you grouped and then click Ungroup from the Outline group on the Data tab of the Ribbon.

3 Click and select rows **5** through **11** to group operating cash receipts.

4 Click **Group** in the Outline group on the Data tab of the Ribbon.

5 Click and select rows **14** through **17** to group purchases.

6 Click **Group** in the Outline group on the Data tab of the Ribbon.

7 Click and select rows **14** through **20** to group cash payments for purchases.

8 Click **Group** in the Outline group on the Data tab of the Ribbon.

9 Click and select rows **22** through **25** to group selling and administrative expenses.

10 Click **Group** in the Outline group on the Data tab of the Ribbon.

11 Click and select rows **13** through **26** to group operating cash payments.

12 Click **Group** in the Outline group on the Data tab of the Ribbon.

13 Click and select rows **4** through **27** to group operating activities.

14 Click **Group** in the Outline group on the Data tab of the Ribbon.

15 Click and select rows **29** through **31** to group investing activities.

16 Click **Group** in the Outline group on the Data tab of the Ribbon.

17 Click and select rows **33** through **35** to group financing activities.

18 Click **Group** in the Outline group on the Data tab of the Ribbon.

19 Click and select columns **B** through **E** to group quarters.

20 Click **Group** in the Outline group on the Data tab of the Ribbon.

21 Click **1** to collapse the column group to the first level.

22 Click **1** to collapse the row group to the first level. Your worksheet should look like Figure 6.13.

Click here to collapse rows to level 1

Click here to collapse columns to level 1

Figure 6.13

Cash Budget Grouped at Level-1 Rows and Level-1 Columns

	A	F
1	Coast Jewelers	
2	Cash Budget	Year
3		
28	Cash from (to) operating activities	96,000
32	Cash from (to) investing activities	(300,000)
36	Cash from (to) financing activities	210,000
37	Change in cash	6,000
38	Beginning cash	25,000
39	Ending cash	31,000

Cash Budget / Sheet2 / Sheet3

23 Click **2** to collapse the column group to the second level.

24 Click **2** to collapse the row group to the second level. Your worksheet should look like Figure 6.14.

Click the plus sign to expand rows or click the minus sign to collapse rows

	A	B	C	D	E	F
1	Coast Jewelers	1st	2nd	3rd	4th	
2	Cash Budget	Quarter	Quarter	Quarter	Quarter	Year
3						
4	Operating activities					
12	Operating cash receipts	481,000	484,000	464,000	524,000	1,953,000
27	Operating cash payments	422,500	449,500	455,250	529,750	1,857,000
28	Cash from (to) operating activities	58,500	34,500	8,750	(5,750)	96,000
29	Investing activities					
30	Equipment purchases		(300,000)			(300,000)
31	Equipment sales					-
32	Cash from (to) investing activities	-	(300,000)	-	-	(300,000)
33	Financing activities					
34	Loan proceeds		250,000			250,000
35	Loan payments			(20,000)	(20,000)	(40,000)
36	Cash from (to) financing activities	-	250,000	(20,000)	(20,000)	210,000
37	Change in cash	58,500	(15,500)	(11,250)	(25,750)	6,000
38	Beginning cash	25,000	83,500	68,000	56,750	25,000
39	Ending cash	83,500	68,000	56,750	31,000	31,000

Cash Budget / Sheet2 / Sheet3

Figure 6.14

Cash Budget Grouped at Level-2 Rows and Level-2 Columns

25 Trying clicking the + and − signs to see the different possible levels you can view.

26 Save your work.

The resulting cash budget leaves the company with only $31,000 at the end of the fourth quarter—which, as Nathan explains, is not acceptable. "We must have done something wrong. I'm sure the bank will reject my application if I present them this budget," he says.

Using What-If Analysis and Goal Seeking with the Cash Budget

"Perhaps we can use Excel's What-If feature to manipulate the budget and give us a better ending balance?" Meagan says. "I propose we increase the hourly rate we charge for repairs from $50 to $75 per hour."

"We can also use the goal seek feature we used before to determine what changes need to be made to achieve a certain target value for ending cash," you suggest. "For instance, if we want an ending cash balance of $50,000, what cost of expected sales percentage could you use?"

Kyle suggests you experiment with your newly created cash budget by using what-if analysis and goal seeking for the two scenarios described.

To use what-if analysis and goal seeking with the cash budget:

1 Change the hourly rate charged for repairs to $75 in cell B42.

2 The result should be ending cash of $187,000, assuming the change in hourly rate had no effect on the projected repair hours.

3 Change the hourly rate charged for repairs back to $50.

4 Use goal seek by setting cell F39 (ending cash) on the cash budget to $50,000 by changing cell B46 (the cost of expected sales). The result should be a percent cost of sales of 59 percent (actually, 59.0142671854734 percent before rounding).

5 Close the workbook without saving changes.

"Now, that is a powerful tool." Nathan says. "I think I can shave off a little on the percentage of cost of sales by increasing my markup slightly."

End Note

You've applied some of what you learned in the first five chapters to better understand how Excel can be used to create a cash budget. In doing so, you created an operating cash receipts budget based on budgeted sales and a predicted pattern of expected cash collections. You also created an operating cash payments budget based on budgeted purchases and a pattern of expected cash payments. To round out the cash budget you created a budget for investing and financing activities and pulled it all together with Excel's grouping feature to create a complete annual cash budget. In addition, you applied the what-if analysis and goal seek features of Excel to answer common questions posed when analyzing budgets. Finally, you used names extensively to better understand formulas and calculations in Excel. In the next chapter you'll explore some more advanced features in Excel.

Chapter 6 Questions

1 Why should you locate budget assumptions in a special section of the worksheet?

2 What information is provided in the operating cash receipts portion of the cash budget?

3 Why does the typical cash budget spread collection of sales revenue over more than one month?

4 What information is provided in the operating cash payments portion of the cash budget?

5 What factors determine monthly purchases in the cash budget?

6 Why does the typical cash budget spread payment of purchases over more than one month?

7 What information is provided in the investing activities portion of the cash budget?

8 What information is provided in the financing activities portion of the cash budget?

9 How is the goal seeking feature used in this chapter?

10 How is grouping used with the cash budget?

Chapter 6 Assignments

1 Create a new Coast Jewelers' Operating Cash Receipts Budget

Using the ch6-02 file to start your work, create a worksheet similar to the one created in this chapter to budget operating cash receipts by month for 3 months. Place assumption information in the cells provided, and define and use names extensively. The company expects to incur repair hours of 600, 700, and 800 in January, February, and March (respectively) at an expected hourly rate of $60. Product sales revenue of $150,000, $165,000, and $175,000 is expected in January, February, and March, together with interest revenue of $14,000, $13,000, and $17,000, respectively. Professional service revenue and interest revenue are all collected in the month earned. It is anticipated that 70 percent of product sales revenue will be collected in the same month as earned, 20 percent collected in the next month, and 10 percent in the following month. Product sales revenue last November was $180,000 and last December was $190,000. (*Hint:* Use these amounts in your budget to determine cash collections in the current 3 months of January, February, and March as a function of prior product sales. Use Excel's grouping feature to group "revenues" rows together and to group the three monthly columns together. Save your file as ch6-02_student_name (replacing student_name with your name).

a. Print the newly completed worksheet in Value view, with your name and date printed in the lower left footer and the file name in the lower right footer.

b. Print the worksheet from part a (above) in Formula view, with your name and date printed in the lower left footer and the file name in the lower right footer. Print only the January cash budget, no assumptions.

c. Collapse all rows and columns and then print the worksheet in Value view, with your name and date printed in the lower left footer and the file name in the lower right footer. Print only the total cash budget, no assumptions.

d. Expand all rows and columns. Use what-if analysis to calculate operating cash receipts if 80 percent of product sales revenue were collected in the same month as earned, 15 percent in then next month, and 5 percent in the following month. Print the resulting worksheet in Value view, with your name and date printed in the lower left footer and the file name in the lower right footer.

e. Reset the collection expectations to their original values (of 70, 20, and 10 percent). Use goal seek to determine what number of repair hours must be worked in January in order to achieve operating cash receipts of $180,000 in January. Print the resulting cash budget, no assumptions in Value view, with your name and date printed in the lower left footer and the file name in the lower right footer.

2 Create a new Coast Jewelers' Operating Cash Payments Budget

Using the ch6-03 file to start your work, create a worksheet similar to the one created in this chapter to budget operating cash payments by month for 3 months. Place assumption information in the cells provided, and define and use names extensively. Product sales revenue of $150,000, $165,000, $175,000, and $180,000 is expected in January February, March, and April respectively. Purchases cost 75 percent of product sales. The company would like to maintain an ending inventory equal to 60 percent of the next month's purchases. At the beginning of January, the company had $75,000 in inventory and $15,000 in accounts payable; 90 percent of a month's purchases are paid in the current month, with the remaining paid in the following month. Selling expenses are expected to be $6,000, $7,000, and $8,000 in January, February, and March (respectively), while general and administrative expenses are expected to remain constant at $40,000 per month. All expenses are paid in the month incurred. Use Excel's grouping feature to group purchases, payments for purchases, and expense rows together and to group the three monthly columns together. Save your file as ch6-03_student_name (replacing student_name with your name).

   a.   Print the newly completed worksheet in Value view, with your name and date printed in the lower left footer and the file name in the lower right footer.

   b.   Print the worksheet from part a (above) in Formula view, with your name and date printed in the lower left footer and the file name in the lower right footer. Print only the January cash budget, no assumptions.

   c.   Collapse all rows and columns and then print the worksheet in Value view, with your name and date printed in the lower left footer and the file name in the lower right footer.

   d.   Expand all rows and columns. Use what-if analysis to calculate operating cash payments if 85 percent of purchases are paid in the current month and 15 percent are paid in the following month. Print the resulting worksheet in Value view, with your name and date printed in the lower left footer and the file name in the lower right footer.

   e.   Reset the payments expectations to the original 90 percent and 10 percent values. Use goal seek to determine what cost of expected sales percentage would cause the operating cash payments to be $500,000 for the quarter. Print the resulting worksheet in Value view, with your name and date printed in the lower left footer and the file name in the lower right footer.

Chapter 6 Case Problem 1:
KELLY'S BOUTIQUE

Kelly's Boutique is contemplating several means of financing their acquisition of $100,000 in special equipment. One alternative is to borrow $100,000 from a local bank for 10 years at 12 percent per annum. The bank has asked them to produce a 1-year cash budget broken down by months (January through December). Sales of $30,000 are expected in the first month, with each month thereafter increasing 2 percent. Purchases are based on an expected cost of sales of 55 percent and a required ending inventory of 70 percent of next month's sales. Beginning inventory was $11,000. Sales for January next year are expected to be $40,000. Sales in the previous November and December were $29,000 and $28,000, respectively. Expenses include advertising expense of $900, depreciation expense of $800, interest expense of $1,000, payroll expense of $8,000, supplies expense of $500, and utilities expense of $600 per month throughout the year. All expenses except depreciation are paid in the month during which they are incurred. Collections in the month of sale are expected to be 50 percent, collections in the first month following a sale 40 percent, and in the second month 10 percent. Payments in the month of purchase are expected to be 75 percent, payments in the first month following a purchase 15 percent, and payments in the second month to be 10 percent. Purchases in the previous November and December were $16,000 and $17,000, respectively. Proceeds from the $100,000 loan are expected in June, and $100,000 of equipment will be purchased in July. Monthly payments of $1,400 on the loan also begin in July. The beginning cash balance in January was $22,000.

Using the ch6-04 file to start your work, create a cash budget (as you did in the chapter) that is based on the assumptions listed in the previous paragraph. Use Excel's grouping feature to group operating cash receipts, operating cash payment, cash from (to) operating activities, cash from (to) investing activities, and cash from (to) financing activities and also to group the twelve monthly columns together. Save your file as ch6-04_student_name (replacing student_name with your name).

a. Print the newly completed worksheet in Value view, with your name and date printed in the lower left footer and the file name in the lower right footer.

b. Print the worksheet from part a (above) in Formula view, with your name and date printed in the lower left footer and the file name in the lower right footer. Print only columns A and B of the cash budget, no assumptions.

c. Collapse rows to level 2 and columns to level 1, and then print the worksheet in Value view with your name and date printed in the lower left footer and the file name in the lower right footer. Print cash budget only, no assumptions.

d. Collapse rows to level 2 and columns to level 1, and then use what-if analysis to calculate end-of-year cash if the sales growth each month were 105 percent and payroll expense were $20,000 per month. Print the resulting worksheet in Value view, with your name and date printed in the lower left footer and the file name in the lower right footer. Print cash budget only, no assumptions.

e. Undo the what-if analysis performed in part d. Collapse rows to level 2 and columns to level 1, and then use goal seek to determine what sales growth would be needed to produce an ending cash balance of $100,000. Print the resulting worksheet in Value view with your name and date printed in the lower left footer and the file name in the lower right footer. Print cash budget only, no assumptions.

Chapter 6 Case Problem 2:
WINE DEPOT

The Wine Depot is contemplating several alternative means of financing their annual acquisition of $75,000 in wine storage facilities. One option is to borrow $300,000 from a local bank for 5 years at 11 percent per annum. The bank has asked them to produce a 4-year cash budget broken down by year (2010 through 2013). Sales of $500,000 are expected in the first year, with sales increasing each year thereafter by 22 percent. Sales in 2009 were $450,000. Purchases are based on an expected cost of sales of 45 percent and a required ending inventory of 10 percent of next year's sales. Purchases in 2009 were $200,000, and beginning inventory was $32,000. Annual expenses include advertising expense of $10,000, marketing expense of $6,000, depreciation expense of $8,000, interest expense of $35,000, salaries expense of $150,000, wages expense of $65,000, supplies expense of $7,500, and utilities expense of $10,000. All expenses except depreciation are paid in the year in which they are incurred and are expected to increase 5 percent each year. Collections in the year of sale are expected to be 94 percent, with the remaining 6 percent collected in the next year. Payments in the year of purchase are expected to be 93 percent, with the remaining 7 percent paid in the next year. Proceeds from the $300,000 loan are expected in 2010, and $75,000 of facilities will be purchased each year. Proceeds from expected equipment sales each year are expected to amount to $10,000. Annual payments of $81,171 on the loan also begin in 2010. The beginning cash balance in 2010 was $20,000.

Using the ch6-05 file to start your work, create a cash budget (as you did in the chapter) based on the assumptions just provided. Use Excel's grouping feature to group operating cash receipts, operating cash payment, cash from (to) operating activities, cash from (to) investing activities, and cash from (to) financing activities. Save your file as ch6-05_student_name (replacing student_name with your name).

a. Print the newly completed worksheet in Value view, with your name and date printed in the lower left footer and the file name in the lower right footer.

b. Print the worksheet from part a (above) in Formula view, with your name and date printed in the lower left footer and the file name in the lower right footer. Print only columns A, B, and C of the cash budget, no assumptions.

c. Collapse rows to level 2; then print the worksheet in Value view, with your name and date printed in the lower left footer and the file name in the lower right footer. Print cash budget only, no assumptions.

d. Collapse rows to level 2, and then use what-if analysis to calculate end-of-year cash if the sales growth each year were 10 percent. Print the resulting worksheet in Value view, with your name and date printed in the lower left footer and the file name in the lower right footer. Print cash budget only, no assumptions.

e. Undo the what-if analysis performed in part d. Collapse rows to level 2, and then use goal seek to determine what annual sales growth would be needed to produce an ending cash balance of $50,000 in 2013. Print the resulting worksheet in Value view, with your name and date printed in the lower left footer and the file name in the lower right footer. Print cash budget only, no assumptions.

Access for Accounting

part

2

Access Tour

In this chapter you will learn:

- Access's capabilities and new features
- How to start, navigate, and work with Access files
- How to use Access help
- How Access is used in accounting

Case: **Coast Jewelers, Inc.**

Nathan and Meagan have expressed an interest in other software that might be able to help them in their jewelry business. Kyle asks them what kinds of records they keep for customer orders and inventory control.

"We keep records by hand now, and it is very tedious and problematic," Meagan responds. "I have a file for customers, suppliers, products, et cetera, but often they get misplaced and are frequently out of date. It's difficult to keep track of it all!"

"Well, perhaps a database management system might help you out," suggests Kyle.

"What's a database management system?" asks Nathan.

Kyle explains that, as their business grows, the information available to them will increase as well. A database management system (DBMS) can help. "Essentially, a DBMS is a tool for storing, retrieving, and interpreting information in an effective and useful way. These days, Microsoft's Access program, a relational database management system, has proven to be a very successful tool in combating information overload."

"Hold on," warns Nathan. "What is a relational database?"

"Ok, let's go slowly," responds Kyle. "Let me walk you and our student assistant through the basics and I'll define relational database then."

"Great," you respond. "I know businesses use databases every day, and this way I can get a better insight on how they are created and used."

Understanding Access's Capabilities and New Features

Access is a DBMS, which organizes a collection of related information used for a specific purpose. For example, information about Coast's customers, its suppliers, and its products could be three different databases in and of themselves. A relational database is one in which information is divided into separate stacks of logically related information, each of which is stored in a separate table in the file. Thus, tables are a critical part of a DBMS, and the relations among the tables are key to its success.

Tables can be related in three different ways: one-to-many, one-to-one, and many-to-many. For instance, the supervisor of an accounting department may have many employees who work under her; however, all the employees who work for her have only one supervisor. This would be a one-to-many relationship: one supervisor to many employees. Another example is the chief financial officer (CFO), who reports to the chief executive officer (CEO). This is a one-to-one relationship because there is only one CEO and one CFO. Still another example is the construction worker who works on many different jobs and each job requires many different workers. This is an example of a many-to-many relationship. The most common of these, and the ones you'll experience here, are the one-to-many relationships.

The DBMS includes more than just tables, of course. Queries, forms, and reports based on the data stored in tables are what make up the management component of DBMS. Before you get too far, Kyle suggests you learn how to start Access.

Access 2007 has been updated with a fresh look so that you can easily create, modify, and work with database solutions. You can also use the Microsoft Office Fluent user interface, tabbed windows view, status bar, scroll bars, and title bar in order to give applications built on Access 2007 a contemporary look. New features such as the Add New Field column and improved selection capabilities make the experience similar to that of Microsoft Office Excel 2007.

The Office Fluent user interface—which replaces the old Access menus, toolbars, and most task panes—is context sensitive and optimized for efficiency and discoverability. With the new Navigation Pane in Access 2007, you get a comprehensive view of tables, forms, queries, and reports. You can even create custom groups to organize and see all the forms and reports that are related to a single table.

Starting, Navigating, and Working with Access Files

Kyle asks you if you are familiar with starting programs in Windows XP. Nathan and Meagan don't know much about computers, so you offer to demonstrate. First you explain that starting Access is the same regardless of whether the computer's operating system is Windows XP or Windows Vista, and then you offer to demonstrate the process for starting Access in Windows XP.

To start Access:

1 Click the **Start** button.

2 Select Microsoft Office Access 2007. Your window may look like Figure 7.1.

3 Click **Microsoft Office Access 2007** to start the application.

Trouble? Your start menu may be completely different from that shown in Figure 7.1. See your instructor or lab personnel for instructions on starting Access.

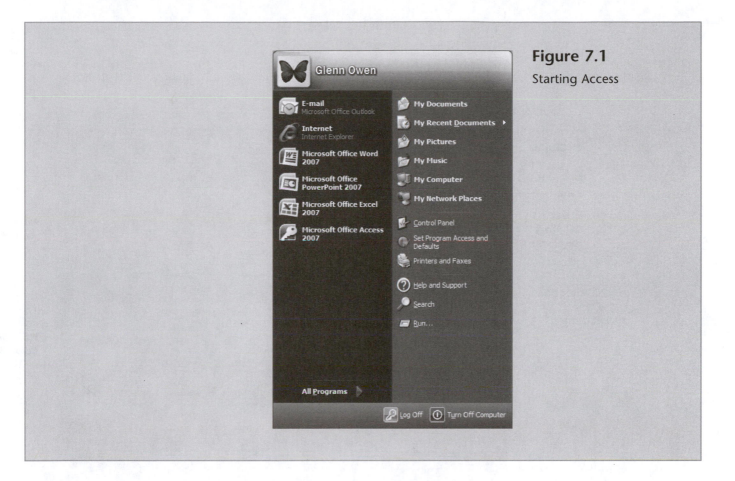

Figure 7.1
Starting Access

Nathan's laptop has Access installed as well, so he has been duplicating Kyle's actions on his own computer, whose screen looks somewhat different than Kyle's —in particular, Kyle's Quick Access Toolbar and Ribbon seem different. Kyle explains that screen size can change the appearance of the Ribbon and that, just like Access itself, both its Ribbon and Quick Access Toolbar can be customized.

To illustrate, Kyle starts Access and creates a new blank database file named Database1. He has captured his Access window (see Figure 7.2) and provided callouts and an explanation of the Access window characteristics. He reminds you that the user interface described here is similar to Excel's interface, so much of this will sound familiar.

Microsoft Office Button – This button, located in the upper left-hand corner of the Access window, is available in all Office 2007 applications. The Microsoft Office Button replaces the File menu and is located in the upper left corner of these Microsoft Office programs. When you click the Microsoft Office Button, you see the same basic commands available in earlier releases of Microsoft Office to open, save, and print your file.

Quick Access Toolbar – At the top of the Access window is the Quick Access Toolbar, which is designed to provied an easy way to execute the commands used most often. The default setting in Access provides access to the Save, Undo, and Redo commands.

Ribbon – There are three basic components of the Ribbon. Tabs: There are seven of them across the top; each represents core tasks you do in Access. Groups: Each

Figure 7.2

The Access Window

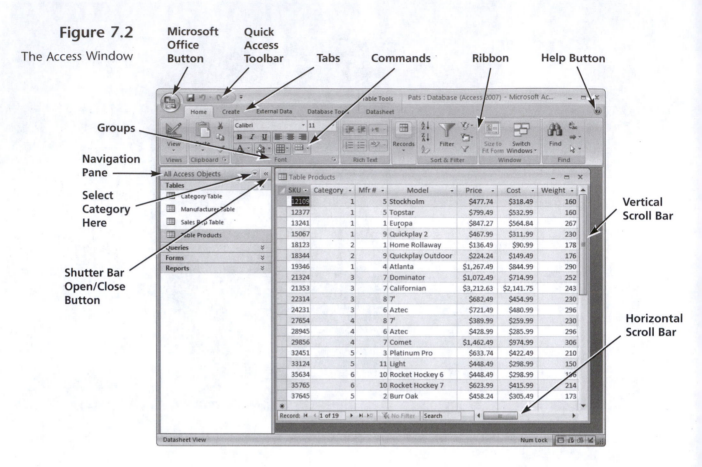

tab has groups that show related items together. Commands: A command is a button, a box to enter information, or a menu. The principal commands in Access are gathered on the first tab, the Home tab. The commands on this tab are those that Microsoft has identified as the most commonly used when people do basic tasks with databases. For example, the Paste, Cut, and Copy commands are arranged first on the Home tab, in the Clipboard group. Font formatting commands are next, in the Font group. Groups pull together all the commands you're likely to need for a particular type of task, and throughout the task they remain on display and readily available, instead of being hidden within menus. These vital commands are visible above your work space.

The commands on the Ribbon are the ones you use the most. Instead of showing every command all the time, Access 2007 shows some commands in response to an action you take. When you see an arrow (called the Dialog Box Launcher) in the lower right corner of a group, there are more options available for the group. Click the arrow, and you'll see a dialog box or a task pane.

Navigation Pane – At the left of the Access window is the Navigation Pane. New in Microsoft Office Access 2007, it is a central location from which you can easily view and access all database objects such as tables, queries, forms, and reports.

The Navigation Pane replaces the Database window, which was used in earlier versions of Access.

Other Access Window Items – Like all Windows screens, scroll bars control your view of the worksheet (horizontal and vertical).

To demonstrate some of Access's features, Kyle suggests you follow along while he opens an Access file:

1 Open Access, if you closed it previously.

2 Click the **Microsoft Office** Button, and then right-click **Open.**

3 Click **Add to Quick Access Toolbar.** Note that your Quick Access Toolbar now shows a folder icon, which gives you a quick way to open new files.

4 Click the new **Open** icon in the Quick Access Toolbar to open a new file. (*Note:* If you are using Access in a computer lab environment, your changes to the Quick Access Toolbar may not reappear the next time you start Access.)

5 Navigate the Open window to the location of this text's student files. (The location would be the CD provided with the text or from your computer lab's server.)

6 Double-click the file **ch7-01**, which should be located in a Ch 07 folder.

7 Click the **Shutter Bar Open/Close** button a few times to see how it opens and closes the Navigation pane.

8 With the Shutter Bar Open, select **All Access Objects** as the category and **Object Type** as the category view.

9 Click the **Table** header a few times to see how you and hide or show its contents. (*Note:* This works for all group headers like tables, queries, forms, and reports. The navigation pane does not display empty groups; if this database did not have any reports, the group header would not display.)

10 Double-click the **Table Products** table. The table shown in Figure 7.3 should appear.

11 Click the **Microsoft Office** Button and place the cursor over the text **Save As**; then click **Access 2007 Database** under the Save the database in another format title. (This is done to keep your original student file available, in case need it again, and also to provide a unique name for your file.)

T r o u b l e ? If you click Save As instead of just putting the cursor over the Save As text, Access will ask if you want to save the object. This is not what you want to do. Click Cancel, and then be sure to just put the cursor over the Save As text and then follow the instructions.

Figure 7.3

Sample Table

12 Click **Yes** when asked if you want Access to close all open objects.

13 Add your name to the file name using the underscore key, as shown in Figure 7.4. In this example the file will be saved as ch7-01_student_name into a folder called My Access Files. You should replace "student_name" with your name.

Figure 7.4

Saving a Database

14 Click **Save.**

Now that you've had a brief view of how to start, navigate, and work with Access files, it's time to become familiar with Access's help features.

Getting Access Help

Access's help features are quite extensive. Whenever you are working with Access and are not certain how to create tables, queries, forms or reports you should press the [F1] function key or click the blue and white question mark on the Tab bar. To illustrate, Kyle decides to show you Access's help feature while trying to create a new table.

To view Access's help to create a new table:

1 Press the [**F1**] function key or click the blue and white question mark to open Access's help window, as shown in Figure 7.5.

Figure 7.5

Access's Help Window

Trouble? You do not have to be connected to the Internet to get Access help. However, the online help is much more extensive. This example assumes you are connected to the Internet. If you are not connected, click the text **Show me offline help from my computer** to view Access help, keeping in mind your window may not match the Figures shown in the text.

2 Click **Tables** from the Access Help window.

3 Click the text **Create a table** to expand the help text. The Create a table help window shown in Figure 7.6 should appear.

Figure 7.6

Access Help for Creating a Table

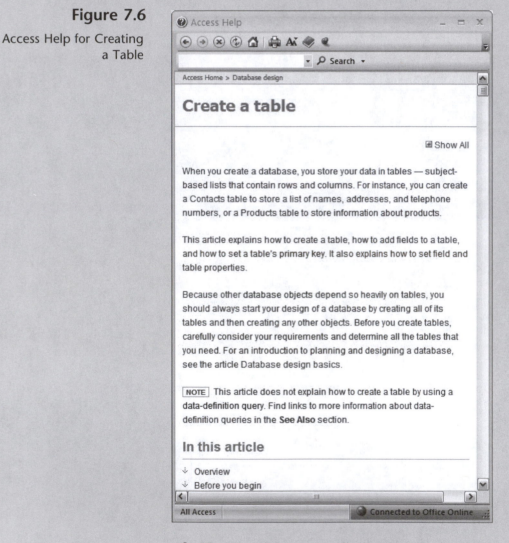

4 Note that the text now displayed gives you more details on how to create a new table. Close the Help window.

Now that you're familiar with Access's help feature, Kyle thinks it would be a good idea to explore how Access is used in the accounting field.

Examples of How Access Is Used in Accounting

There are an unlimited number of ways Access can be used in accounting. This text will focus on how Access can be used to track inventory, but of course that is just one example.

Accounting programs like QuickBooks and Peachtree are nothing more than sophisticated databases. Each organizes information by accounts, such as assets (cash, accounts receivable, inventory, etc.), liabilities (e.g., accounts payable), and equities (common stock and retained earnings). Revenue and expense transactions are also organized by accounts. A user who wants to create an income statement is simply creating a query that says, in essence, "give me the sum of all revenues and all expenses that occurred for a specific period." Thus the transactions are filtered by date and by account types.

All the major asset and liability accounts are supported by a database. For example, the accounts receivable balance sheet account is supported by a detailed subsidiary ledger that can explain how much each customer owes at any point in

Figure 7.7

Assets by Category

time, and a query can be generated that filters the information by date and by customer. Fixed assets accounts (e.g., furniture and fixtures, equipment, buildings) are supported by a detailed subsidiary ledger that can explain the cost of each asset, its economic useful life, its accumulated depreciation, and so forth. The accounts payable balance sheet account is supported by a detailed subsidiary ledger that can explain how much the company owes each vendor at any point in time; a query can be generated that filters the information by date and by vendor. Figure 7.7 shows a report that summarizes a firm's fixed assets by category. This report was created from an Access database designed to capture fixed assets used in a business. Figure 7.8 illustrates a second report generated by the same Access database; this report identifies assets by location.

Payroll is supported by a database as well. Information is collected from employees that includes Social Security number, address, pay rate, exemptions, and deductions. Time-keeping databases collection information about how many

Figure 7.8

Assets by Location

Figure 7.9

Billable Hours by Employee

hours an employee worked on a particular job, day, or area. All of this information is stored in employee tables and payroll time tables and is then used to compute payroll expenses, withholding, paychecks, and cost distributions. Figure 7.9 shows a report used to summarize billable hours by employee. This report was created from an Access database designed to capture time-card information.

The list of database applications for accounting is unlimited, and the illustrations given here are just the tip of the iceberg. However, the goal of this text is to introduce you to the fundamentals of database design and use, so we will focus on how to create tables, queries, forms, and reports that are related to inventory control only.

End Note

The three of you are impressed by your first exposure to Access and pleased with your accomplishments so far. You've learned some of Access's capabilities and new features; how to start, navigate, and work with Access files; how to use Access help; and how Access is used in accounting

In the next chapter you will learn how to create tables, queries, forms, and reports as well as how to print in Access.

Chapter 7 Questions

1 What is a DBMS?

2 What is a relational database?

3 How are tables related?

4 Identify some new features in the 2007 version of Access.

5 What and where is the Microsoft Office Button?

6 What and where is the Quick Access Toolbar?

7 Describe the Ribbon.

8 What and where is the navigation pane?

9 What is the quickest way to access help while in Access?

10 Describe ways in which Access is used in Accounting.

Access Basics

In this chapter you will learn:

- How to create and print tables
- How to create and print queries
- How to create and print forms
- How to create and print reports

Case: **Coast Jewelers, Inc.**

Kyle explains to Nathan, Meagan, and you that the key to understanding how to create and use a database is to understand a database's elements: tables, queries, forms, and reports.

Tables store like information together. Once a table is designed with fields and attributes, information is then collected into tables for later queries, forms, and reports.

Queries allow the database user to ask questions of the information stored in tables. For example, a database user might want to know what inventory balances are for each item as of a particular date or how many units of a particular item were sold to a particular customer.

Forms allow the database user to view, update, add, and delete information stored in tables but organized in traditional forms or source documents like sales invoices, inventory cards, purchase orders, and so forth. Change management experts agree that users of databases prefer information presented in traditional formats even though the raw data might be stored in a different manner (i.e., in tables).

Reports allow the database user to communicate information stored in the database in more usable formats. This might include sorting the information in a certain way—for example, from largest value to smallest value. It might also include grouping the information in a certain way: by customer, salesperson, or product. Finally, reports allow us to "filter" the information and so view only what is needed; examples include sales for a particular month, inventory balances as of a particular date, and accounts receivables for certain specified customers.

Kyle suggests you practice by creating some tables, queries, formats, and reports for Coast's inventory system.

Tables

Step 1 in the creation of any database is developing an understanding of the business and its information needs. Initially, this will take the form of table creation and separation. Rather than placing all information in one table, it's important to separate information into manageable "chunks," or tables. In our inventory example, Coast has information about its products, product suppliers, and product categories that could be combined. However, since every product has one supplier but some suppliers provide more than one product, a one-to-many relation exists between suppliers and products. Likewise, every product falls under one category, but most categories include many products. Thus, we should separate product, supplier, and category information into three separate tables with the common relationship being the supplier identification (ID) number and category ID number.

Step 2 is deciding what information we need for each table, what form (or data type) that information takes, and what properties exist for each field. This means that, for each table (product, supplier, and category), we must identify fields where information is to be stored. A common technique in database creation is to establish a unique ID number field for each record. This field will also be identified as our *Primary Key* field, which by definition holds data that uniquely identifies each record in a table. Thus, our first field, common to all information entered into the table, is a product ID. Next would be a product name, description, and so on. For each field, a corresponding data type (number, text, currency, etc.) must be established and, depending on the data type, properties for each field must be identified (field size, format, caption, etc.).

Step 3 is inputting the information into the tables. This is where we gather information about each product, supplier, and category. "How about running all that by me one more time?" you ask.

"I'll do you one better," responds Kyle. "I'll let you watch me create the product table."

Creating the Product Table

Kyle explains that—in addition to creating fields for a product ID, name, and description—he will create fields that link the product to a specific inventory category supplier and that identify the product's serial number, unit price, reorder level, and required lead time.

To create the product table:

1 Start Access.

2 Click the **Microsoft Office** button and then click **New** to create a new database file.

3 Type **ch8-01_student_name** (replacing "student_name" with your name, as before) into the File Name: text box as shown in Figure 8.1. (In the figure, the file is being saved into an Access Database Files folder located on a USB drive labeled K. You should place your newly created file into a folder and drive you will be able to access later. Do this by clicking the folder icon next to the text box and navigating to your desired location. Once you've specified your location, your file name text box should show Ch8-01_student_name.accdb, which reflects the five-character extension for Access 2007 database files.)

Figure 8.1
Creating a New Blank Database

4   Click **Create.** A new blank database should open with a new table and with the table tools showing in the ribbon, as shown in Figure 8.2.

Figure 8.2
New Database Window

5   Click **View** and then click **Design View.**

6   Type **Product Table** as the name of the new table you are about to create and then click **OK.**

7 Change the first field name from ID to ProductID, leaving the data type as AutoNumber.

8 Enter the additional field information shown in Figure 8.3 exactly as typed. (*Note:* Each data type has different field property characteristics, but all allow you to specify a caption. Be sure to separate the field name for clarification and enter it as each field's caption; see Figure 8.3, Product ID, for an example.) Continue with the rest of the fields, changing ProductName to Product Name, ProductDescription to Product Description, et cetera.

Figure 8.3

Product Table

Trouble? Do not change AutoNumber in the Data Type column. AutoNumber is a data type, not a field name.

9 Once you have entered all the field names, data types, and correct captions, be sure that ProductID is designated as the Primary Key. If it is not, select the field and then click the **Primary Key** tool from the Tools group on the Design ribbon.

10 Close the Product Table window and click **Yes** when asked if you want to save changes to the design of the Product Table.

You have created a placeholder for product information. Now it's time to create a placeholder for supplier information.

Creating the Supplier Table

As with the product table creation, once again several fields will be required to capture information about each supplier. A supplier ID, supplier name, and contact name are just a few of the critical pieces of information necessary. In addition, Kyle suggests you should also include information about the contact's title, address, and phone and fax numbers.

To create the supplier table:

1 Click the **Create** tab on the ribbon.

2 Click **Table Design** from the Tables group on the ribbon.

3 Enter the information shown in Figure 8.4 exactly as typed. (*Note:* Each data type has different field property characteristics, but all allow you to specify a caption. Be sure to separate the field name for clarification and enter it as each field's caption.) Continue with the rest of the fields, changing SupplierName to Supplier Name, ContactName to Contact Name, and so forth. (Observe that changing a field's caption does not change the field's name.)

4 Once you have entered all the field names, data types, and correct captions, click the **SupplierID** field name and then click the **Primary Key** tool on the ribbon.

5 Close the table window and click **Yes** when asked if you want to save changes to the design of the table Table1.

6 Type **Supplier Table** as the table name in the Save As text box and then click **OK.**

7 In the Navigation pane, select **All Access Objects** from the drop-down list of categories.

Figure 8.4

Supplier Table

You have now created a placeholder for supplier information. All that is left is to create a table with category information so that you can separate products into identifiable categories.

Creating a Category Table

The final table necessary to complete the inventory database is a category table, which will consist of only two fields: a category ID and a category name. "Why not just add the category to each product in the product table?" you ask.

"Because," Kyle responds, "in a relational database we try to conserve space and eliminate redundancy."

To create a category table:

1 Click the **Create** tab on the ribbon.

2 Click **Table Design** from the Tables group on the ribbon.

3 Create two fields: CategoryID as an AutoNumber data type and CategoryName as a Text data type.

4 Change the caption names as in previous tables.

5 Set the CategoryID field as the primary field, as in previous tables.

6 Close the table window and save the table as Category Table.

Your table structure is complete. All you need now is information.

Entering Data into Tables

With the table structure complete, you volunteer to enter information about the company's products, suppliers, and categories. Nathan provides the information for each category, product, and supplier.

To enter data into the three tables:

1 Double-click the **Category Table.**

2 Type **Watches** as the first Category Name. (*Note:* The Category ID field will be automatically assigned as you tab to the Category Name field and enter information.) After you type each record, press the [**Enter**] key to begin a new category.

3 Type **Rings**, **Necklaces**, and **Earrings** as the next three Category Names. Your screen should look like Figure 8.5.

4 Close the Category Table window after you have typed all the information.

5 Click **Yes** to save changes.

6 Double-click the **Supplier Table.**

7 Enter the information as specified in Table 8.1. (The Supplier ID field will be automatically assigned as you tab to the Supplier Name field and enter information.) After you type each record, press the [**Enter**] key to begin a new supplier.

8 Close and save the Supplier Table after you have typed all the information.

9 Double-click the **Product Table.**

Figure 8.5

Completed Category Table

10 Enter the information as specified in Table 8.2. (Again, the Product ID field will be automatically assigned as you tab to the Product Name field and enter information.) After you type each record, press the [**Enter**] key to begin a new product.

11 Close and save the Product Table window after you have typed all the information.

"Remember," Kyle says, "in this case every product has one category, but every category may have multiple products. Thus we have a one-to-many relationship." Next up: establishing relationships among the three tables.

Table 8.1   Supplier Table Information

Supplier ID	1	2	3	4	5
Supplier Name	Johnson Wholesale Jewelry Supply	Jewelry Inc.	Seiko USA	Robert Rose	Casio USA
Contact Name	Ben Nimitz	Sara Munoz	Nancy Bearfoot	Paul Moo	Kelly O'Leary
Contact Title	VP Sales	Sales	Western Sales	Salesman	Regional Sales
Address	100 8th Ave.	909 S. Washington	111 Macarthur Blvd.	385 5th Ave.	571 Mount Pleasant
City	New York	Pilot Pt.	Mahwah	New York	Dover
Postal Code	10035	76258	07430	10001	07801
State Or Province	NY	TX	NJ	NY	NJ
Country	USA	USA	USA	USA	USA
Phone Number	212-555-1354	940-555-0817	201-555-5730	212-555-4166	201-555-3215
Fax Number	212-555-6874	940-555-1187	201-555-3872	212-555-9718	201-555-8741

Table 8.2 Product Table Information

Product ID	1	2	3	4	5	6	7
Product Name	Flower Drop Earrings	Kinetic Auto Relay	LeGrand Sport	G-Shock	Engagement Ring	Diamond Earrings	Diamond Heart Slide
Product Description	These elegant earrings have a classy, refined look. The crystal stone top is attention-getting marcasite look, followed by a dainty drop that is a faceted black bead.	Energy storage for up to four years of time memory.	Step-motion second hand will move at 2-second intervals.	Shock resistant daily and schedule alarm.	This engagement ring is set in 14K white and yellow gold.	A dazzling pair of dangle diamond earrings.	A gorgeous diamond heart slide is designed in 14K white and yellow gold.
Supplier ID	4	3	3	5	1	2	1
Category ID	4	1	1	1	2	4	3
Product#	136305	SMA113	SKA040	DW004B-4V	LGR29	ER-764	PD-241
Unit Price	$6.00	$425.00	$275.00	$49.00	$400.00	$510.00	$525.00
Reorder Level	5	2	2	2	1	1	2
Lead Time	10	11	14	10	15	30	30

Establishing Table Relationships

One final step is necessary when you create multiple tables: creating relationships between the tables. Recall our previous discussion (see Chapter 7) about one-to-one, one-to-many, and many-to-many relationships. In the Coast Jewelers' database you created three tables, and now you must define each relationship. For example, every product belongs in a particular category and has a supplier. Thus, there is a one-to-many relationship between the supplier table and the product table and a one-to-many relationship between the category table and the product table.

Kyle suggests you establish those relationships using Access's relationship tool.

To establish relationships between tables:

1 Select the **Relationships** tool from the Database Tools tab on the ribbon.

2 Click each table in the Show Table window and click the **Add** button so that all three tables appear in the Relationships window.

3 Click **Close** in the Show Table window.

4 Resize the Product table and the Supplier Table so that all fields are visible and the vertical scroll bars disappear, as shown in Figure 8.6.

Figure 8.6

Relationships Window

5 Click on the **Category ID** field in the Category Table. Hold the mouse button down and drag to the **Category ID** field in the Product Table, and then release the mouse button.

6 When the Edit Relationships window appears, click **Create.**

7 Click on the **Supplier ID** field in the Supplier Table. Hold the mouse button down and drag to the **Supplier ID** field in the Product Table; then release the mouse button.

8 When the Edit Relationships window appears, click **Create.** The Relationships window should now show lines connecting the common fields between each table, as shown in Figure 8.7.

9 Click the **Relationship Report** tool in the Tools group of the Design tab on the Ribbon.

10 Click **Print** and then click **OK** to print the relationships report.

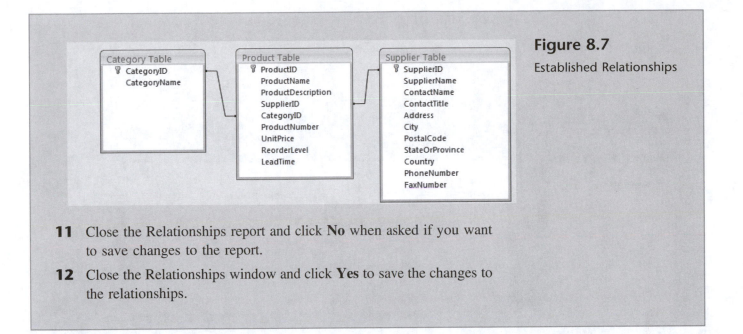

Figure 8.7
Established Relationships

11 Close the Relationships report and click **No** when asked if you want to save changes to the report.

12 Close the Relationships window and click **Yes** to save the changes to the relationships.

Now that relations have been established, you can create queries, reports, and forms that use information from one or more tables. However, it is always important to have a physical copy of your tables for backup and reference.

Printing Tables

Occasionally you may want to print the tables to make sure information has been entered correctly. Later you will use the report feature of Access to print specific information available in the tables in a format that more effectively provides the needed information.

To print all three tables:

1 Double-click the **Category Table.**

2 Place your mouse over the text **Print** in the Microsoft Office button and then click **Print Preview** to view a reduced-size version of the table to be printed.

3 Click once in the table to zoom to a larger size. (*Note:* You may have to move the scroll bars around to find the table to be printed.) Your screen should look like Figure 8.8.

4 Click the **Print** button on the Print Preview tab to print a copy of the table, and then click **OK** to print.

5 Click the **Close Print Preview** button and then close the Category Table window.

Figure 8.8

Print Preview of the Category Table

6 Double-click the **Product Table.**

7 Place your mouse over the text **Print** in the Microsoft Office button and then click **Print Preview** to view a reduced-size version of the table to be printed.

8 Click the **Print** button on the Print Preview tab to print a copy of the table, and then click **OK** to print.

9 Click the **Close Print Preview** button and then close the Product Table window.

10 Double-click the **Supplier Table.**

11 Place your mouse over the text **Print** in the Microsoft Office button and then click **Print Preview** to view a reduced-size version of the table to be printed.

12 Click the **Print** button on the Print Preview tab to print a copy of the table, and then click **OK** to print.

13 Click the **Close Print Preview** button and then close the Category Table window.

Queries

Queries are essentially questions about the information stored in the database, such as: What products do we sell? From whom do we buy products? For any query, it is important to identify where the information can be found, what information is required, what criteria have been established, and how the information is reported.

Creating a Query

Kyle explains that, for each query, tables are identified that contain the information to be requested. He suggests you create a query to list all products. Specifically, he wants you to provide the category name, product name, unit price, supplier name, and supplier phone number.

To create a query:

1 Click the **Create** tab on the Ribbon.

2 Click **Query Wizard** from the Other group on the Create tab.

3 Select **Simple Query Wizard** from the New Query window and then click **OK.**

4 Select **Table: Category Table** from the Table/Queries drop-down list.

5 Click the field **Category Name** from the list of available fields, then click the **>** button. This action will place the field CategoryName into the list of selected fields; see Figure 8.9.

Figure 8.9

Simple Query Wizard

Trouble? If you select the wrong field or click the wrong buttons, you can use the **>** or **<** buttons to move fields back and forth between the list of available fields and the list of selected fields.

6 Select **Table: Product Table** from the Table/Queries drop-down list.

7 Click the field **Product Name** from the list of available fields, then click the > button. This action will place the field ProductName into the list of selected fields.

8 Click the field **Unit Price** from the list of available fields, then click the > button. This action will place the field UnitPrice into the list of selected fields.

9 Select **Table: Supplier Table** from the Table/Queries drop-down list.

10 Click the field **Supplier Name** from the list of available fields, then click the > button. This action will place the field SupplierName into the list of selected fields.

11 Click **Next** in the Simple Query Wizard window.

12 Make sure the Detail button is selected in the window presented, and then click **Next.**

13 Type **Products Query** as the title, click the **Open the query to view information** button, and then click **Finish.**

14 The resulting query lists all seven products, as shown in Figure 8.10.

Figure 8.10

Products Query

Products Query			
Category Name	Product Name	Unit Price	Supplier Name
Earrings	Flower Drop Earrings	$6.00	Robert Rose
Watches	Kinetic Auto Relay	$425.00	Seiko USA
Watches	Le Grand Sport	$275.00	Seiko USA
Watches	G-Shock	$49.00	Casio USA
Rings	Engagement Ring	$400.00	Johnson Wholesale Jewelry Supply
Earrings	Diamond Earrings	$510.00	Jewelry Inc.
Necklaces	Diamond Heart Slide	$525.00	Johnson Wholesale Jewelry Supply

Record: 1 of 7   No Filter   Search

Printing a Query

Occasionally you may want to print the query to make sure information has been properly selected. Later you will use the report feature of Access to print specific information available from a query in a format that more effectively provides the needed information.

To print a query:

1 Double-click **Products Query.**

2 Click the **Microsoft Office** button.

> **3** Place your mouse over the text **Print** in the Microsoft Office button and then click **Print Preview** to view a reduced-size version of the query to be printed.
>
> **4** Click the **Print** button on the Print Preview tab to print a copy of the table, and then click **OK** to print.
>
> **5** Click the **Close Print Preview** button, and then close the Products Query window.

Access has another helpful feature, called *forms*, for capturing or viewing information in a database.

Forms

Forms have a variety of purposes. One purpose is to provide a dialog box for access to predesigned queries, other forms, or reports. Another purpose is to provide a dialog box to capture new information and use it to carry out an action.

Creating a Form

Kyle suggests that you use a form to capture information about additional Coast Jewelers' products. He reminds you that entering information into a form automatically updates the table containing such information. The form itself is just a means to update the table either by editing existing information or by adding new information like a new record.

To create a form to capture additional products:

1 Click the **Create** tab on the Ribbon.

2 Click **More Forms** in the Forms group and then click **Forms Wizard**

3 Select **Table: Product Table** from the Table/Queries drop-down list.

4 Click the **>>** button to select all the fields available then click **Next.**

5 Select the **Columnar** layout, and then click **Next.**

6 Select the **Access 2007** style, and then click **Next.**

7 Type **Products Form** as the new form title, and then click **Finish.** The resulting form should look like Figure 8.11.

8 Do not close this form.

Figure 8.11

Products Form

Next record button   New record button

Using a Form to View, Edit, or Add Information

This newly created form can be used to enter new information, edit existing information, and view existing information for each product. Nathan offers to try out the new form by viewing each record. He also volunteers to enter a new product and edit a reorder level for one product.

To use a form to view and edit existing products and add an additional product:

1 Click the **Next record** button (the right arrow) at the bottom of the Products form and view each product. Continue to view each record until you reach record 5, Engagement Ring.

2 Click in the **Reorder Level** edit box and change the reorder level from 1 to 2.

3 Click the **New record** button (the right arrow with the asterisk).

4 Press the **[Tab]** key to move the cursor to the Product Name field.

5 Type **Diamond Wedding Ring** as the new product name. Note that, once you start typing the new product name, the Product ID field changes to 8 as the AutoNumber process executes.

6 Complete the form as shown in Figure 8.12.

Figure 8.12

Product Form with New Record

Products Form

Product ID	8
Product Name	Diamond Wedding Ring
Product Description	A dazzling engagement set that consists of a .25ct. round brilliant cut diamond accented by twelve round brilliant cut diamonds all near colorless and SI1 clarity.
Supplier ID	1
Category ID	2
Product Number	CJ-2275-7
Unit Price	$650.00
Reorder Level	2
Lead Time	25

Record: ◄ ◄ 8 of 8 ► ►l ►⊞ No Filter Search

Previous record button

7 Do not close this form.

Nathan has completed the form and, in so doing, has edited an existing record and added a new one. This new product is now a part of the product table and will be present for future queries or reports. Most of the information in a form comes from an underlying record source. For Coast Jewelers this includes some of the product information derived from the product table. Using graphical objects called *controls*, Nathan created a link between the form and its record source, the product table. He used the most common type of control used to display and enter data: a text box.

Other information in the form is stored in the form's design. In the Coast Jewelers form just created, this includes the descriptive text (such as headers and footers) as well as graphic elements (such as the horizontal rule). In other forms this might include a calculation that comes from an expression stored in the form's design.

Printing a Form

Occasionally you may want to print a single form.

To print a single form:

1 Click the **Previous record** button until you reach Record 2.

2 Click the **Microsoft Office** button and then click **Print.**

3 Click **Selected Record(s)** to print the form of record 2. Note that only record 2 will be printed, because you were in record 2 when you activated the Print window.

4 Click **OK** to print the selected record.

5 Close the Products form.

"How do I get a report of the information in my new database?" asks Nathan. "Good question," Kyle answers. "Let's generate a report for you now."

Reports

Reports are a way for a user to get information out of a database in a format that helps the analytical process. To be useful, reported information needs to be properly formatted, sorted, and/or grouped. Reports are more than listings of information. For instance, a user may want to create mailing labels, which would require a different level of formatting than a report of items grouped in particular categories. Your report may need a chart, a logo, subtotals, or grand totals. It may need a date, a special title, headers and footers by item or category, et cetera. Finally, your requirements may necessitate the reporting of only certain items in your database that meet specific criteria, such as those items that cost more than a certain dollar amount or those items from a particular category only.

Creating a Report

Kyle suggests that your first report utilize Access's Reports Wizard and simply list, by product number, all the products together with their product ID, product name, and unit price. There are five steps to creating a report:

- Identify which fields you want in your report and in what tables those fields are present.
- Specify grouping levels, if any.
- Specify sort order, if any.
- Specify a report layout.
- Specify a report style.

To create a report of all products listed by product number:

1 Click the **Create** tab on the Ribbon.

2 Click **Reports Wizard** from the Reports group.

3 Click **Product Table** from the list of Tables/Queries.

4 Click **Product ID** from the list of Available Fields; then click the **>** button to move ProductID from the list of Available Fields to the list of Selected Fields. Your screen should look like Figure 8.13.

Figure 8.13

Report Wizard

5 Click **Product Name** from the list of Available Fields, then click the
> button to move ProductName from the list of Available Fields to
the list of Selected Fields.

6 Click **Unit Price** from the list of Available Fields, then click the >
button to move UnitPrice from the list of Available Fields to the list
of Selected Fields.

7 Click the **Next** button.

8 Click the **Next** button again, since no grouping is required for this
report.

9 Select **Product ID** in the first sort order list box. Make sure the sort
order is Ascending, as shown in Figure 8.14, and then click **Next.**

10 Click **Tabular** Layout, **Portrait** Orientation, and make sure the
Adjust the field width so that all fields fit on a page check box is
checked; then click **Next.**

11 Click **Aspect** from this list of available report styles, and then click
Next.

12 Type **Products by Product ID** as the name of the report. Select the
Preview the Report option button, and then click **Finish.** Your
window should look like the one shown in Figure 8.15.

13 Click **Close Print Preview** to reveal the report's design view, as
shown in Figure 8.16.

14 Leave the resulting report design view window open.

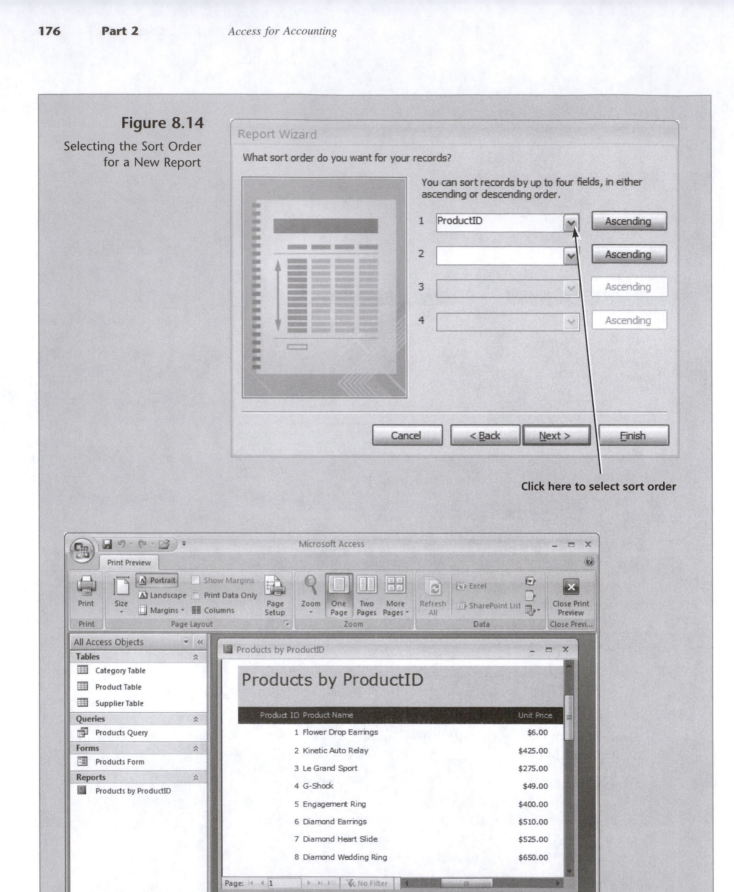

Figure 8.14

Selecting the Sort Order for a New Report

Click here to select sort order

Figure 8.15

Product Report

Figure 8.16

Design View

Editing a Report

You can edit this report at any point and change its characteristics. When you closed the Report window, a Design View window appeared. You can switch between Report, Layout, and Design view by clicking on the View tool.

The *Design view* gives you a more detailed view of the structure of your report. You can see the header and footer bands for the report, page, and groups. The report is not actually running in Design view, so you cannot see the underlying data while working; however, there are certain tasks you can perform more easily in Design view than in Layout view. You can add a wider variety of controls to your report, such as labels, images, lines, and rectangles. You can also edit text-box control sources in the text boxes themselves (without using the property sheet) and change certain properties that are not available in Layout view.

The *Layout view* is the most intuitive view to use for report modification, and it can be used for nearly all the changes you would want to make to a report in Office Access 2007. In Layout view the report is actually running, so you can see your data much as it will appear when printed. Nonetheless, you can still make changes to the report design in this view. Because you can see the data while you are modifying the report, it's a useful view for setting column widths, adding grouping levels, or performing almost any other task that affects the appearance and readability of the report.

Meagan suggests that the report just generated could be improved be centering the product ID title and data, narrowing the width of the unit price field, and narrowing the horizontal rule. You offer to make the changes she has suggested by using the Design view.

To edit the "Products by Product ID" report:

1 Change to the Layout view by clicking the **View** button tool and clicking **Layout View.** Note the differences between the Layout view shown here in Figure 8.17 below and the Design view shown previously in Figure 8.16. (More on this later.)

Figure 8.17

Layout View

2 Change back to the Design view by clicking the **View** button tool and clicking **Design View.**

3 Click **Product ID** (located in the Page Header section), then click the **Center** tool in the Font group in the Home tab of the Ribbon.

4 Click **Product ID** (in the Detail section) and then click the **Center** tool.

5 Click **Unit Price** (in the Page Header section). Hold the Shift key down and click **Unit Price** in the Detail section as well. (*Note:* Holding the Shift key down allows you to select both the header and the detail field at the same time.)

6 Click the right side on the **Unit Price** field and drag to the left until the rightmost edge of both the UnitPrice field and the Unit Price header are lined up with the 4-inch marker on the ruler. (*Note:* You may have to do the same for the ProductName field and header to line controls up.) See Figure 8.18.

7 Click anywhere in the Report window to unselect the Unit Price fields.

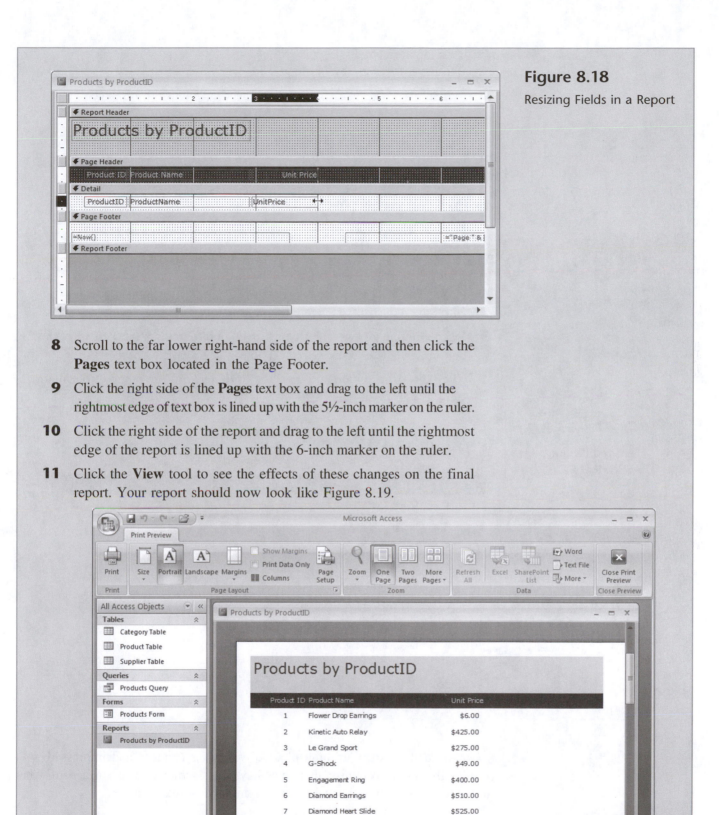

Figure 8.18
Resizing Fields in a Report

8   Scroll to the far lower right-hand side of the report and then click the **Pages** text box located in the Page Footer.

9   Click the right side of the **Pages** text box and drag to the left until the rightmost edge of text box is lined up with the 5½-inch marker on the ruler.

10   Click the right side of the report and drag to the left until the rightmost edge of the report is lined up with the 6-inch marker on the ruler.

11   Click the **View** tool to see the effects of these changes on the final report. Your report should now look like Figure 8.19.

Figure 8.19
Resized Report in Print Preview

12 Close the Products by ProductID report.

13 When prompted, click **Yes** to save the changes in the Products by ProductID report.

Printing a Report

Often you will want to print the reports created.

To print the "Products by Product ID" report:

1 Double-click the **Products by Product ID** report.

2 Click the **Microsoft Office** button.

3 Place your cursor over the **Print button** and then click the **Print Preview** button to view a reduced-size version of the report to be printed

4 Click the **Print** button and then click **OK** to print the report. Your report should look like Figure 8.20.

Figure 8.20

Printed Products by Product ID Report

Products by ProductID

Product ID	Product Name	Unit Price
1	Flower Drop Earrings	$6.00
2	Kinetic Auto Relay	$425.00
3	Le Grand Sport	$275.00
4	G-Shock	$49.00
5	Engagement Ring	$400.00
6	Diamond Earrings	$510.00
7	Diamond Heart Slide	$525.00
8	Diamond Wedding Ring	$650.00

5 Close the Products by ProductID report window.

Nathan and Meagan are both pleased with your changes and impressed with your skills. They recognize that they have just scratched the surface of what Access can do for their business and are anxious to learn more.

End Note

In this chapter you have learned about some basics of the Access program, some features of the help system, and how to work with tables, queries, forms, and reports. There is much more to the Access program and much more to know about tables, queries, forms, and reports. The following four chapters will elaborate on each of these, bringing you a keener understanding of how Access is used in accounting.

Chapter 8 Questions

1 Why isn't all information entered into a single table?

2 Identify and describe the first three steps followed in the creation of a database.

3 Which tool is used to establish relationships between tables?

4 What are queries?

5 What facts must be identified for each query?

6 What questions are asked by the Simple Query Wizard?

7 What are the purposes of forms?

8 From where does most of the information in a form come?

9 How are controls used to create forms?

10 Are headers and footers also a part of the record source?

11 What questions does the Simple Form Wizard ask?

12 What are reports?

13 To be useful, how should reports be organized?

14 What questions does the Report Wizard ask?

15 What are the five steps necessary to create a report?

16 How do you switch between the Design view and the Layout view when creating reports?

Chapter 8 Assignments

1 Create new queries for Coast Jewelers (use the Ch8-02 file)

   a. Create and print a query for Coast Jewelers that lists the supplier name, contact name, and phone number of every supplier. (*Note:* Be sure to use the supplier table to locate field names.) Save the query as Supplier Query 1.

   b. Create and print another query for Coast Jewelers that lists the supplier name, address, city, and state of every supplier. (*Note:* Be sure to use the supplier table to locate field names.) Save the query as Supplier Query 2.

2 Create new forms for Coast Jewelers (use the Ch8-02 file)

    a. Create and print a form for Coast Jewelers that lists all fields from the supplier table in a columnar format, Apex style. (*Note:* Once again, use the supplier table to locate field names.) Save the form as Supplier Form, and print the first record only.

    b. Create and print a form for Coast Jewelers that lists all fields from the category table in a columnar format, Apex style. (*Note:* Use the category table to locate field names.) Save the form as Category Form, and print the first record only.

3 Create new reports for Coast Jewelers (use the Ch8-02 file)

    a. Create and print a report for Coast Jewelers that lists the supplier ID, supplier name, and city from the supplier table. (Use the supplier table to locate field names.) The report should have no grouping, be sorted by supplier ID in ascending order, and be formatted in a tabular layout with portrait orientation and Apex style. Save the report as Suppliers by Supplier ID. Make sure all field information is visible.

    b. Create and print a report for Coast Jewelers that lists the supplier name, contact name, contact title, and phone number from the supplier table. (Use the supplier table to locate field names.) The report should have no grouping, be sorted by supplier name in ascending order, and be formatted in a tabular layout with portrait orientation and Apex style. Save the report as Suppliers by Supplier Name. Make sure all field information is visible.

4 Create and edit tables for Coast Jewelers (use the Ch8-02 file)

    a. Create a new table for Coast Jewelers that includes fields labeled Buyer ID, Buyer Name, and Buyer Phone. The first field (Buyer ID) is an AutoNumber data type; the rest are Text data types. All should have captions that separate each word (e.g., Buyer ID). Set the Buyer ID field as the Primary Key and save the new table as Buyers Table. Enter the following buyer information into the Buyers table, and then print the new table.

Buyer ID	Buyer Name	Buyer Phone
1	Lopez	555-7894
2	Ng	555-1324
3	Fortier	555-9137

    b. Add a field to the Product table called BuyerID, a Number data type. Add the specific BuyerID information to the following products in the Products table and then print the new table.

Product ID	Buyer ID
1	3
2	3
3	2
4	1
5	2
6	3
7	1
8	2

c. Establish a one-to-many relationship between the Buyers table and the Product table using BuyerID as the related field. Print the relationships report.

d. Create and print a query for Coast Jewelers that lists the product name, buyer name, and buyer phone number for every product. (*Note:* Be sure to use both the product and buyer tables to locate field names.) Save the query as Product Buyer Query.

Chapter 8 Case Problem 1:
KELLY'S BOUTIQUE

Recall from Chapter 2 that Kelly's Boutique sells books as well as women's shoes. Kelly's son Casey, a college accounting student who is home for the holidays, is eager to help his mom incorporate computers in her business. In this chapter (and in those that follow), Casey will try teaching Kelly the use of Access as it applies to her accounting and business needs.

Casey suggests that Kelly use a database to keep a record of her book inventory. Kelly has a partial list of books she has purchased that she thinks should be part of the database. This list includes each book's ISBN, department name, related supervisor and phone number of the supervisor, book title, publisher, publisher contact, publisher phone number, author, and list price.

Create a new database file using the following information and name the file ch8-03_student_name (replacing student_name with your name).

a. Use the information below to create a book table, department table, and publisher table in Access. Then print each table.

Book Table

ISBN	Dept	Book Title	Pub Num	Author	List Price
684872153	Adult	Angela's Ashes	7	McCourt	$ 7.99
60244151	Children	Betsy–Tacy	2	Lovelace	$12.95
670175919	Children	Blueberries for Sal	5	McCloskey	$16.99
27136701	Children	Caddie Woodlawn	4	Brink	$17.00
140286276	Adult	Deep End of the Ocean	3	Mitchard	$12.95

ISBN	Dept	Book Title	Pub Num	Author	List Price
60173289	Adult	Divine Secrets of the YaYa Sisterhood	2	Wells	$24.00
394800168	Children	Green Eggs and Ham	6	Seuss	$ 7.99
439064864	Children	Harry Potter and the Chamber of Secrets	9	Rowling	$17.95
439136350	Children	Harry Potter and the Prisoner of Azkaban	9	Rowling	$17.95
590353403	Children	Harry Potter and the Sorcerer's Stone	9	Rowling	$17.95

Dept Table

Dept	Supervisor	Phone
Adult	Nancy Wine	555-9754
Children	Barbara Manchester	555-1974

Publisher Table

Pub Num	Publisher	Contact	Phone
1	Mass Market Paperback	Smith	555-9745
2	Harper Collins	Potter	555-7481
3	Penguin	Frued	555-8974
4	Simon & Schuster	Gonzalez	555-9874
5	Viking Press	Hu	555-1654
6	Random House	Ouimet	555-9144
7	Scholastic Press	Salazar	555-9888
8	Touchstone Books	Chi	555-1112
9	Arthur A. Levine Books	Robinson	555-5118

b. Establish the appropriate relationship between each table. Print the relationships report.

c. Create and print a query that lists department, book title, author, supervisor, publisher, and contact. Save this query as Books by Department.

d. Create a form that shows all fields from the book table in a columnar format with Apex style. Save it as Book Form, and print the first record.

e. Create and print a report that contains the book title, ISBN, publisher, and phone number. The report should have no grouping, be sorted by book title in ascending order, and be formatted in a tabular portrait layout with Apex style and the title Book Report. All field information should be visible.

f. Make sure you keep a copy of this file for use in the next chapter.

Chapter 8 Case Problem 2:
WINE DEPOT

The Wine Depot is interested in more effectively managing their inventory. Barbara would like you to put together a database of their current wine inventory. Create a new database file using the following information and name the file ch8-04_student_name (replacing student_name with your name).

a. Use the following information to create and print a wine products table, a buyer table, and a winery table.

SKU	Type	Winery	Price	Cost	Size	Vintage	Quantity
13883	Chardonnay	7	41.00	24.60	750	1998	12
14539	Merlot	8	36.00	21.60	750	1999	5
15347	Cabernet Sauvignon	3	120.00	72.00	750	1989	7
15966	Pinot Noir	2	65.00	39.00	750	1999	24
16528	Chardonnay	15	30.00	18.00	750	2001	12
16554	Sauvignon Blanc	18	21.00	12.60	750	2001	8
16716	Chardonnay	11	20.00	12.00	750	2001	10
16739	Chardonnay	17	61.00	36.60	750	1999	5
16769	Syrah	6	34.00	20.40	750	2000	10
16874	Syrah	5	35.00	21.00	750	2000	15
17024	Sauvignon Blanc	4	22.00	13.20	750	2001	10
17275	Sauvignon Blanc	14	16.00	9.60	750	2002	1
17425	Zinfandel	10	28.00	16.80	750	2001	7
17454	Sauvignon Blanc	13	15.00	9.00	750	2002	24
17521	Chardonnay	1	24.00	14.40	750	2001	4
17539	Cabernet Sauvignon	19	75.00	45.00	750	2000	3
17549	Zinfandel	9	22.00	13.20	750	2000	3
17578	Cabernet Sauvignon	12	11.00	6.60	750	2001	2
17840	Red Chianti	16	32.00	19.20	750	1999	12

Buyer	Name	Phone
101	James Taylor	555-1245
102	Johnny Rivers	555-8794
103	Michael Jackson	555-9743
104	Aden Mikowicz	555-2914

Winery	Name	Location	Buyer
1	Babcock	American	101
2	Bass Phillip	Australia	104
3	Beringer	American	101
4	Brander	American	101
5	Cafaro	American	101
6	Carhartt	American	101
7	Clarendon	Australia	104
8	Gainey	American	102

Winery	Name	Location	Buyer
9	Gary Farrell	American	102
10	Joel Gott	American	102
11	Melville	American	102
12	Miguel Torres	Chile	104
13	MudHouse	New Zealand	104
14	Neil Ellis	South Africa	103
15	Neyers	American	103
16	San Vincenti	Italy	104
17	Talbot	American	103
18	Voss	American	103
19	Woodward	American	103

b. Establish the appropriate relationship between each table and then print the relationships report.

c. Create and print a query that lists SKU, Type, Winery, Buyer, and Buyer Phone for all products. (Save as Wine Products Query 1.)

d. Create and print a form for entering new products; use whatever style you'd like. (Save the form as Wine Products Form 1, and print the first record only.)

e. Create and print a report with the fields Type, Name (Name of Winery), Vintage, and Price for all products. The report should be sorted by Type in ascending order and be formatted in a Tabular layout with Portrait orientation and Aspect style. (Save the report as Wine Products Report 1.) All field information should be visible.

f. Make sure you keep a copy of this file for use in the next chapter.

Tables

In this chapter you will learn:

- Add, change, and delete records
- Add a picture with an OLE field
- Change the structure of a database
- Change field data types, row heights, and column widths
- Create field validation rules
- Create field default values
- Create field formats
- Specify referential integrity
- Document a database

Case: **Coast Jewelers, Inc.**

Nathan and Meagan are impressed with the features of Access as a database program. Kyle cautions them that there is a lot more to Access than what they have seen so far. He explains that the tables they have created can be structured in different ways and that each field can be set up with specific formats, default values, validation rules, and so on.

"Wait just a minute," exclaims Nathan. "This sounds more complicated than what we might need!"

"On the contrary," responds Kyle. "These table features—and ones I'll explain later for queries, forms, and reports—are important to the validity of the data included in your database and helpful in making your database useful."

"Let's just take it one step at a time," says Meagan.

Kyle then enlightens them both on the importance of data validity and integrity. He explains that information in your database is of little use if it is incorrect, incomplete, or in an inconsistent format. Over the next few days he plans on explaining tables in more detail. Let's begin by reviewing the basic procedures for adding, changing, or deleting records from a table.

Add, Change, and Delete Records

In this section, you will learn how to add, change, and delete records from tables. This process can also be done via forms, which will be discussed in Chapter 11.

Add Records

You have already added records to the inventory database in Chapter 7 but decide to practice it again. Kyle observes your input of adding one more record to the Product table.

To add a new record to a table:

1 Start Access.

2 Click the **Microsoft Office** button and then click **Open.**

3 Navigate the Open window to the location of this text's student files. (The location would be the CD provided with the text or from your computer lab's server.)

4 Double-click **ch09-01**, which should be located in a Ch 09 folder. (This is the completed Coast Jewelers Inventory file from Chapter 8.)

5 Click the **Microsoft Office** button and then place the mouse over the words **Save As.**

6 Click **Access 2007 Database** under the section Save the database in another format.

7 Navigate the Save As window to the location you wish to save this file and type **Ch09-01_student_name** in the File Name: text box (replacing "student_name" with your name).

8 Click **Save.**

9 Double-click **Product Table.**

10 Click in the **Product Name** field of a new record next to the (AutoNumber) reference in the Product ID field. Type **Diamond Pendant** in the Product Name field.

11 Press the **[Tab]** key and type **A one caret top of the line diamond in a gold leaf setting.** in the Product Description field.

12 Press the **[Tab]** key and type **3** as the Supplier ID.

13 Press the **[Tab]** key and type **3** as the Category ID.

14 Press the **[Tab]** key and type **1235** as the Product Number.

15 Press the **[Tab]** key and type **375** as the Unit Price.

16 Press the **[Tab]** key and type **2** as the Reorder Level.

17 Press the **[Tab]** key and type **10** as the Lead Time.

18 Press the **[Tab]** key and type **1** as the Buyer ID.

19 Press the **[Tab]** key again and note that a new record (product) has been added to the table, as shown in Figure 9.1.

20 Do not close this file.

Figure 9.1

Partial View of Updated Product Table

Change Records

Changing records in the table is equally as easy. Kyle suggests you change the supplier for the diamond pendant you just entered from **3** to **2** and change the buyer from **1** to **3**.

To change a record in a table:

1 Double-click the **Supplier ID** field for the Diamond Pendant you just entered. Type **2** to replace the 3 currently listed in this field.

2 Double-click the **Buyer ID** field for the Diamond Pendant you just entered. Type **3** to replace the 1 currently listed in this field. You may have to use the horizontal scroll bars at the bottom of the table to view this field.

3 Press the [**Tab**] key to move to a new record.

Changing fields for a particular record in a table is easy. So is the procedure for deleting a record.

Delete Records

Kyle warns you that deleting records in a table is a permanent act. It is important to be sure you want to delete a record before proceeding. Access will warn you of this and give you an opportunity to undo your deletion.

To delete a record from a table:

1 Click on the far left side of the table next to the row containing information on Product ID 7.

2 With the Product ID 7 record selected, right-click anywhere in that record to bring up a shortcut menu.

3 Point your mouse to the text Delete Record as shown in Figure 9.2.

Product ID	Product Name	Product Descri	Supplier ID	Category ID	Product Number
1	Flower Drop Earrings	These elegant ea	4	4	136305
2	Kinetic Auto Relay	Energy storage fc	3	1	SMA113
3	Le Grand Sport	Step-motion secc	3	1	SKA040
4	G-Shock	Shock resistant, c	5	1	DW004B-4V
5	Engagement Ring	This is a very unic	1	2	LGR29
6	Diamond Earrings	A dazzling pair of	2	4	ER-764
7	Diamond Heart Slide	A gorgeous diam	1		
8	Diamond Wedding Ring	A dazzling engag	1		
9	Diamond Pendant	A one caret top o	2		

Product Table

Record: 7 of 9   No Filter   Search

Shortcut menu: New Record / Delete Record / Cut / Copy / Paste / Row Height...

Figure 9.2

Deleting a Record from a Table

4 Click **Delete Record.**

5 An Access dialog warning box appears asking if you are sure you want to delete this record. See Figure 9.3.

Figure 9.3

Delete Warning

Microsoft Office Access

You are about to delete 1 record(s).

If you click Yes, you won't be able to undo this Delete operation. Are you sure you want to delete these records?

[Yes]   [No]

6 Click **Yes,** and the record is deleted.

"That was easy," you comment. "Let's continue."

Add a Picture with an OLE Field

In this section, you will add a special field to the table and insert pictures to enhance the database. The process requires two steps. Step one is adding a new field to the table; step two is adding a picture to each record.

Add an OLE Field to a Table

Kyle decides to add a picture field to the Product table. The picture—in this case, pictures of the jewelry Coast Jewelers sells—is created either by taking a digital picture of each product or by scanning a picture of each product. Nathan has taken digital pictures of each product and saved them as bitmaps (.bmp) files. Because these objects were not created by Access but instead by with another application, they need to be inserted as objects into the database. OLE (Object Linking/ Embedding) is the integration of objects from other applications.

To add an OLE field to the Product table:

1 Click **View** and then click **Design View.**

2 Scroll down the Design view and click in the **blank field name** under Buyer ID.

3 Type **Picture** as the new field name.

4 Press [**Tab**] to move the cursor to the Data Type column.

5 Select **OLE Object** from the drop-down list of data types as shown in Figure 9.4.

Figure 9.4

Adding a New OLE Field

6 Save the modified table by clicking the **Save** tool on the Quick Access toolbar.

The table is now ready for additional data. You will need to switch from the design view of the table back to the datasheet view in order to add pictures of each product.

Add Pictures to the Table

To add pictures to the table you will need your student disk, which contains all the bitmap files that you'll need to insert into the Product table.

To add a picture to the Product table:

1 Click **View** and then click **Datasheet View.**

2 Scroll to the right of the table to view the Picture field.

3 Right-click the **Picture** field on the first record to reveal the Shortcut menu; then click **Insert Object**, as shown in Figure 9.5.

Figure 9.5

Inserting an Object

Product Number	Unit Price	Reorder	Lead Time	BuyerID	Picture	Add New Field
136305	$6.00	5	10	3		
SMA113	$425.00	2	11	3		Cut
SKA040	$275.00	2	14	2		Copy
DW004B-4V	$49.00	2	10	1		Paste
LGR29	$400.00	2	15	2		Sort Ascending
ER-764	$510.00	1	30	3		Sort Descending
CJ-2275-7	$650.00	2	25	2		Clear filter from Picture
1235	$375.00	2	10	3		Is Not Blank
*						Insert Object...

Record: 1 of 8 — No Filter — Search

4 Click the **Create from File** option.

5 Click **Browse.**

6 Navigate the Browse window to the location of this text's Images folder. (The location would be the CD provided with the text or from your computer lab's server.)

7 Several images should be available, as shown in Figure 9.6.

8 Double-click on **1** to insert that picture into the Product ID 1 record.

9 Click **OK** in the Insert Object window. This window should then close, and the table should now contain the words Bitmap Image in the Picture field of the Product ID 1 record. (*Note:* The name of the image corresponds to the product number for each product.)

10 Follow the same procedures to add pictures to the next *three* products.

11 Close the Product table.

Figure 9.6

Images Available

You have now added both a placeholder and some data for the picture field. You will enter more pictures later.

"Why don't I see the pictures in the table?" Meagan asks.

"The pictures are there, they are just not shown." Kyle responds.

"You'll need to add the picture field to your previously created Product Form to view each picture. We can do that next week when we spend time modifying and creating new forms."

Change the Structure of a Database

When you initially created the Inventory database, you defined its structure by specifying the names, data type, and sizes of all the fields in each table. Often, as when you added a picture field, you will need to change the structure of the database. In addition to adding fields, you may also need to change the field size, resize the field rows or columns, or change the data type. Additional changes that affect the validity of the data entered include the creation or modification of field validation rules, default values, and field formats.

"That is an important issue for us," says Nathan. "We can't use this database if the information isn't accurate and reliable. We also need to make it easier for our employees to enter data into the database."

"Exactly the reason for validation rules, default value, and field formats!" Kyle replies.

Change a Field Size, Row Height, Column Width, and Data Type

Recall that, when you first created the Inventory tables, every field you created with a Data Type = Text set the initial field size to 50. That means that a maximum of 50 characters could be entered into that field. In some cases, limiting the field size helps prevent errors. For instance, the supplier table has a field for State or Province. If you wanted only a two-character designation for each State or Province, you could set the field size to 2.

To change a field size:

1 Double-click the **Supplier Table.**

2 Click **View** and then click **Design View.**

3 Click the **State Or Province** field name.

4 Under Field Size for the StateOrProvince field, type **2** (replacing 50). See Figure 9.7.

Figure 9.7

Changing a Fields Field Size Property

Field Name	Data Type	Description
SupplierID	AutoNumber	
SupplierName	Text	
ContactName	Text	
ContactTitle	Text	
Address	Text	
City	Text	
PostalCode	Text	
StateOrProvince	Text	
Country	Text	
PhoneNumber	Text	
FaxNumber	Text	

Field Properties

General | Lookup

Field Size	2
Format	
Input Mask	
Caption	State or Province
Default Value	
Validation Rule	
Validation Text	
Required	No
Allow Zero Length	No
Indexed	No
Unicode Compression	Yes
IME Mode	No Control
IME Sentence Mode	None
Smart Tags	

The maximum number of characters you can enter in the field. The largest maximum you can set is 255. Press F1 for help on field size.

5 Click the **Save**.

6 A warning should appear. Click **Yes** to continue.

7 Click **View** and then click **Datasheet View**.

8 Scroll across Supplier ID 5 under the StateOrProvince field. Try to type **New Jersey**. Note that you are restricted to two characters.

9 Type **NJ** into the StateOrProvince field for Supplier ID 5.

10 Close the Supplier table.

Viewing data in table format is a quick way to look at all the information available in the table without generating a query or report. Sometimes, however, the information in a table is not very readable. Take, for instance, the Product table and the related product description. Only part of the description is viewable. That is easily fixed by modifying the row height of each record.

"There is also a lot of wasted space in those tables where the columns are too wide as well," remarks Meagan.

"Let's fix them both," says Kyle.

To modify the Product table's row height and column width:

1 Double-click **Product table.**

2 Place the cursor between Product ID 1 and 2.

3 Click and drag down until the entire product description is revealed, as shown in Figure 9.8. Notice how the cursor changed its appearance once it was over the line separating each record.

Figure 9.8

Partial View of Product Table after Resizing a Field's Row Height

4 Place the cursor between the Product Name and Product Description fields at the top of the table. Note how the cursor has once again changed its appearance.

5 Double-click the cursor to automatically resize the column width of the Product Name field, as shown in Figure 9.9. (This saves you the time of manually resizing a field's column width.)

Figure 9.9

Partial View of Product Table after Resizing a Field's Column Width

"I have a question," says Meagan. "When I was watching you create the Product table, I noticed you set up the LeadTime field as a data-type text. Why isn't it considered a number?"

"Good question," Kyle responds. "If we plan to use the lead time information as just information for each product, then it doesn't matter whether we set it up as a Number data type or as a Text data type. However, if we later on want to use this field in a calculation, the Text data type wouldn't work. I'll show you how easy it is to change a field's data type."

To change a field's data type:

1 Click **View** and then click **Design View.**

2 Scroll down the fields listed and click in the Data Type column next to the field name LeadTime.

3 Select **Number** from the drop-down arrow as the new data type for this field, as shown in Figure 9.10.

4 Close and save the changed Product table. Click **Yes** in the warning window presented.

Figure 9.10

Changing a Field's Data Type

By changing a table's row height and column width or by editing a field's data type and field size, you change the basic structure of a database. We next address additional changes that can be made to a table: establishing validation rules, default values, and formats.

Create Validation Rules

Kyle explains that validation rules improve data integrity and validity. Validation rules check information entered into the database (e.g., into a field) and test the entry to see if it meets certain criteria. If the information entered passes the test, the entry is allowed. If the entry fails the test, a warning appears and the entry is rejected.

"For example, in the Product table, every product should have a unit price entered and every price should be reasonable. You wouldn't want to have a unit price of $0.00 or something greater than $1,000.00," says Kyle.

"This would then prevent someone from entering an unreasonable price but it wouldn't prevent entering an incorrect price, right?" asks Nathan.

"Right," Kyle responds. "Validation rules can test for limits like greater than 0 and less than 1,000, or just greater than 100." Kyle explains that, in addition to validating a user's entry into a database, the validation rule can also provide specific feedback to a user concerning why the validation test failed. He suggests that you help Meagan and Nathan establish the unit price restriction for the Product table and ensure that a price is entered for every product.

To create a validation rule:

1 Double-click **Product table.**

2 Click **View** and then click **Design View.**

3 Select the **Unit Price** field.

4 With the UnitPrice field selected, click in the Validation Rule text box and type **>0 And <1000.**

5 With the UnitPrice field still selected, click in the Validation Text text box and type **Unit Price must be > $0 and < $1,000**, as shown in Figure 9.11.

Figure 9.11

Validation Rules and Text

Product Table			
Field Name	**Data Type**	**Description**	
ProductID	AutoNumber		
ProductName	Text		
ProductDescription	Memo		
SupplierID	Number		
CategoryID	Number		
ProductNumber	Text		
UnitPrice	Currency		
ReorderLevel	Number		
LeadTime	Number		
BuyerID	Number		
Picture	OLE Object		

Field Properties

General Lookup

Format	Currency
Decimal Places	Auto
Input Mask	
Caption	Unit Price
Default Value	
Validation Rule	>0 And <1000
Validation Text	Unit Price must be > $0 and < $1,000
Required	No
Indexed	No
Smart Tags	
Text Align	General

The error message that appears when you enter a value prohibited by the validation rule. Press F1 for help on validation text.

6 Save your changes to the table by clicking on the **Save** tool on the Quick Access toolbar.

7 Before Access will allow you to save the changes in validation rules, it will first ask if you want to test the existing data in the table (specifically, the UnitPrice field) to see if it meets the new rule. See Figure 9.12.

Figure 9.12
Warning Window

8 Click **Yes** to check the validity of existing information.

9 With the UnitPrice field still selected, select **Yes** the Required text box. (This will require that all new records in the Product table have a unit price entered.)

10 Click **View** and then click **Datasheet View.**

11 Click **Yes** in the dialog box provided to save the revised table design.

12 Click **Yes** in the next dialog box provided to once again test whether existing data meets the new rules.

13 Type **1500** as the new unit price of product ID 1 and then press **[Tab].**

14 The dialog box shown in Figure 9.13 should appear.

Figure 9.13
Validation Rule Dialog Box

15 Click **OK.**

16 Type **6** as the unit price of product ID 1 and then press **[Tab].**

17 Select the unit price of Product ID 2; then press **[Backspace]** and then **[Tab].** The dialog box shown in Figure 9.14 should appear, stating that an entry is required in this field.

Figure 9.14
Required Value Dialog Box

18 Click **OK.**

19 Type **425** as the unit price of product ID 2 and then press **[Tab].**

20 Close the Product table.

You've now established validation rules, text, and field requirement rules, which will help you maintain data integrity. Another way to ensure that valid information is entered into the database is to create default values.

Create Default Values

Default values, as the name implies, provides the person entering data into a database with pre-existing information for certain fields. This helps ensure the validity of entered data and also speeds up the process of entering information into a database.

"Repetitive information or information that is present in many or most records is ideal for Access's Default Value option," Kyle explains.

"For example, if most of your suppliers are located in New York, then you could set the default value for the state field of the supplier table to 'NY'."

"But what if a supplier is not actually located in New York?" you ask.

"Then you simply type over the default value," Kyle answers. "However, since most of your suppliers are in the state of New York, that won't happen very often."

"Could we also set the default value for country, given that most of our suppliers are also located in the United States"?

"Now you're catching on!" Kyle responds.

Kyle instructs you to add a new supplier after you establish NY as the default value for the state field and USA as the default value for the country field of the Supplier table.

To create default values:

1   Double-click **Supplier table.**

2   Click **View** and then click **Design View.**

3   Click the **State Or Province** field.

4   Click in the **Default Value** text box, type **NY**, and then press **[Tab].** Note that Access automatically adds the quotes around NY. The Field Properties section of your screen should look like Figure 9.15.

Figure 9.15

Entering a Default Value for a Field

Field Size	2
Format	
Input Mask	
Caption	State or Province
Default Value	"NY"
Validation Rule	[...]
Validation Text	
Required	No
Allow Zero Length	No
Indexed	No
Unicode Compression	Yes
IME Mode	No Control
IME Sentence Mode	None
Smart Tags	

5   Select the **Country** field.

6   With the Country field selected, click the **Default Value** text box and type **USA.**

7   Close the Supplier table and click **Yes** to save your changes.

"Now that should save us some time as we enter more suppliers," you comment.

Kyle remarks that formats and input masks also help ensure valid data entry while making information more meaningful.

Create Formats and Input Masks

Kyle explains that format properties in tables vary depending on the data type assigned to each field. For example, a Number data type can be pre-formatted as currency ($1,234.56), fixed decimal (1234.56), standard decimal (1,234.56), percent (123%), or other formats. A Date/Time data type can be pre-formatted as a short date (1/23/09), a long date (Sunday, January 23, 2009), et cetera. On the other hand, a Text data type is not usually subject to a particular format.

"I'd like to add a date to our supplier table so that I know how long I've been doing business with each supplier," Nathan comments. "Can that date be formatted like you mentioned?"

"Certainly," Kyle responds.

"How about formatting phone numbers?" Meagan asks. "Can we format phone numbers so that the area code, prefix, and number are always displayed the same?"

"The best way to solve that issue is by using another Access feature called *input masks*," Kyle answers.

He explains that input masks are used to control how data is entered. This is quite different from the format property referred to previously, which affects only how a value is displayed, not how it is stored in the table. A display format is not applied until the data entered is saved—nothing is displayed in the field to suggest or control the format in which data is entered. If you need to control how data is entered, Kyle suggests you use an input mask in addition to (or instead of) a data display format in those cases.

An input mask ensures that the data will fit in the format you define, and only the kind of values specified can be entered in each blank. In Meagan's example, an input mask would require that all entries contain exactly enough digits to make up a U.S. area code and telephone number and also that only digits (not alphabetic characters) be entered in each blank.

Kyle instructs you to work with Nathan and Meagan by adding a "first purchase date" field to the Supplier table and have it displayed in a short date format. In addition, he suggests you modify the Supplier table: phone number field using a phone number mask.

To utilize the format and input mask capabilities of Access:

1　Double-click **Supplier table.**

2　Click **View** and then click **Design View.**

3　Create a new field by clicking in the field name text box located under the last field titled FaxNumber.

4　Type **First purchase date** as the new field name and then press **[Tab].**

5 Select **Date/Time** as the data type for the new field.

6 Select **Short Date** as the format for the new field.

7 Type **First Purchase** as the caption for the new field. Your screen should look like Figure 9.16.

Figure 9.16

Modified Supplier Table

Supplier Table			
Field Name	**Data Type**	**Description**	
SupplierID	AutoNumber		
SupplierName	Text		
ContactName	Text		
ContactTitle	Text		
Address	Text		
City	Text		
PostalCode	Text		
StateOrProvince	Text		
Country	Text		
PhoneNumber	Text		
FaxNumber	Text		
Firstpurchasedate	Date/Time		

Field Properties

General | Lookup

Format	Short Date
Input Mask	
Caption	First Purchase
Default Value	
Validation Rule	
Validation Text	
Required	No
Indexed	No
IME Mode	No Control
IME Sentence Mode	None
Smart Tags	
Text Align	General
Show Date Picker	For dates

The label for the field when used on a form. If you don't enter a caption, the field name is used as the label. Press F1 for help on captions.

Click here and then select the button on the far right to activate the Input Mask Wizard

8 Click **Save** from the Quick Access toolbar.

9 Click the **Phone Number** field.

10 With the PhoneNumber field selected, click in the Input Mask text box and select the button on the far right to activate the Input Mask Wizard.

Trouble? The input mask feature may not be installed on your version of Access. If not installed, a message may pop up asking if you want to install it now. If you are in a lab environment, please check with your lab administrator before proceeding. If you are at your own computer, have your installation disk handy and follow the instructions to install this feature.

11 Click **Phone Number** input mask, as shown in Figure 9.17, and then click **Next.**

Figure 9.17

Input Mask Wizard

12 Click **Next** two times to accept the default input mask for a phone number; then click **Finish.**

13 The Field Properties section of the PhoneNumber field should look like Figure 9.18.

Field Size	50
Format	
Input Mask	!\(999") "000\-0000;;_
Caption	Phone Number
Default Value	
Validation Rule	
Validation Text	
Required	No
Allow Zero Length	No
Indexed	No
Unicode Compression	Yes
IME Mode	No Control
IME Sentence Mode	None
Smart Tags	

Figure 9.18

Input Mask for the Phone-Number Field

14 Click **Save** from the Quick Access toolbar.

15 Click **View** and then click **Datasheet View.**

16 Type **1/1/09** in the First Purchase field of Supplier ID 1.

17 Click in the **First Purchase** field of Supplier ID 2. Note that the date displayed for Supplier ID 1 has changed to 1/1/2009.

18 Type **February 12, 2009** in the First Purchase field of Supplier ID 2.

19 Click in the **First Purchase** field of Supplier ID 3. Note that the date displayed for Supplier ID 2 has changed to 2/12/2009.

20 Type **Mar 20, 2009** in the First Purchase field of Supplier ID 3.

21 Click in the **First Purchase** field of Supplier ID 4. Note that the date displayed for Supplier ID 3 has changed to 3/20/2009.

22 Type **4/30/09** in the First Purchase field of Supplier ID 4 and 5. Part of your screen should look like Figure 9.19.

Figure 9.19

Partial View of Modified
Supplier Table

	Country	Phone Number	Fax Number	First Purchase
⊞	USA	212-555-1354	212-555-6874	1/1/2009
⊞	USA	940-555-0817	940-555-1187	2/12/2009
⊞	USA	201-555-5730	201-555-3872	3/20/2009
⊞	USA	212-555-4166	212-555-9718	4/30/2009
⊞	USA	201-555-3215	201-555-8741	4/30/2009
*	USA			

Supplier Table

Record: I◄ ◄ 6 of 6 ► ►I ►☀ ☒ No Filter Search

23 Add a new supplier to the Supplier table by typing **Rolex** as the Supplier Name and then pressing [**Tab**].

24 Type **Paula Lyon** as the Contact Name, then press [**Tab**].

25 Type **Sales associate** as the Contact Title, then press [**Tab**].

26 Type **10332 5th Avenue** as the Address, then press [**Tab**].

27 Type **New York** as the City, then press [**Tab**].

28 Type **10003** as the Postal Code, then press [**Tab**].

29 Press [**Tab**] twice to accept the default State and Country values of NY and USA.

30 Type **2125551345** as the Phone Number, then press [**Tab**]. Note the input mask will place the parentheses and dashes accordingly. (Although the input mask will affect future entries into this field, it will not affect the form of *existing* entries—e.g., by placing the area code in parentheses.)

31 Type **2125551346** as the Fax Number, then press [**Tab**]. Observe that, in the absence of an input mask, the data is accepted as is.

32 Go back to the Fax Number field and reenter the fax number as **212-555-1346** (to be consistent with previous entries); then press [**Tab**].

33 Type **6/1/09** as the First Purchase field.

34 Click **Save** from the Quick Access toolbar.

35 Close the Supplier table.

You have witnessed the affects and benefits of default values, display formatting, and input masks. Perhaps now is a good time to see how Access can enforce additional constraints on data entry to ensure that only valid data from database tables are entered as a part of a record.

Referential Integrity

In the previous chapter you established relationships between the product, supplier, category, and buyer tables. This action identified the common fields between each table. You can further define that relationship by using referential integrity.

Kyle explains that referential integrity is a system of rules that Microsoft Access uses to ensure not only that relationships between records in related tables are valid but also that you don't accidentally delete or change related data. When referential integrity is enforced, you must observe the following rules.

- You cannot enter a value in the Foreign Key field of the related table that does not exist in the Primary Key of the primary table. A *Foreign Key* is a field that refers to the Primary Key field in another table and indicates how the tables are related: the data in the Foreign Key and Primary Key fields must match, although the field names need not be the same.

- You cannot delete a record from a primary table if matching records exist in a related table.

- You cannot change a Primary Key value in the primary table if that record has related records. If you want Microsoft Access to enforce these rules for a relationship, you should select the Enforce Referential Integrity check box when you create or edit the relationship. If referential integrity is in force and you break one of the rules while changing related tables, Microsoft Access displays an error message and does not allow the change.

"Wait just a minute!" Nathan exclaims. "Primary key, foreign key, referential integrity, I'm confused!"

"I know," responds Kyle. "Let me give you an example. Once I show you how this affects our product, supplier, category, and buyer tables, I think you will have a better understanding."

Kyle explains that one of the foreign keys he was referring to included the SupplierID field located in the Product table. It is considered a Foreign Key field because it refers to a Primary Key field in another table. In this case, the Primary Key to which it refers is the SupplierID field located in the Supplier table. Kyle also notes that this field, SupplierID, is the Primary Key field in the Supplier table as can be seen in Figure 9.20.

Further, Kyle explains, to ensure validity in the Product table we should enforce referential integrity. In doing so, every entry in the SupplierID field of the Product table will have to match one of the records in the SupplierID field of the Supplier table.

"This is still a bit baffling," says Meagan.

"Just watch as I establish referential integrity for the SupplierID field and test it by adding another record," responds Kyle.

To establish referential integrity:

1 Click the **Database Tools** tab on the Ribbon.

2 Click the **Relationships** tool in the Show/Hide group.

3 Move the tables around the screen, so they match Figure 9.20, by clicking the title bar of each window and then dragging it to a new location.

Figure 9.20

Relationships Window

4 Double-click the line that connects the SupplierID field of the Product table with the SupplierID field of the Supplier table.

5 Click the **Enforce Referential Integrity** check box in the Edit Relationships window as shown in Figure 9.21; then click **OK.**

Figure 9.21

Edit Relationships Window

6 Note the changed line connecting the two tables. In particular, note the one-to-many reference shown by the dark line, the 1, and the infinity symbol.

7 Click **Relationship Report** from the Tools group of the Design tab on the Ribbon.

8 Click **Print** and then click **OK** to print the Relationships Report as shown in Figure 9.22.

Figure 9.22

Printed Relationships Report

9 Close the Relationships Report window and click **No** when asked if you want to save changes to the design of Report1.

10 Close the Relationships window and then click **Yes** to save changes to relationships.

11 Double-click the **Product Table.**

12 Type **Diamond Studs** in the Product Name field, then press [**Tab**].

13 Type **A brilliant pair of .5 ct round cut diamonds.** in the Product Description field; then press [**Tab**].

14 Type **10** in the Supplier ID field, then press [**Tab**].

15 Type **4** in the Category ID field, then press [**Tab**].

16 Type **ER 800** in the Product Number field, then press [**Tab**].

17 Type **750** in the Unit Price field, then press [**Tab**].

18 Type **1** in the Reorder Level field, then press [**Tab**].

19 Type **14** in the Lead Time field, then press [**Tab**].

20 Type **1** in the Buyer ID field, then press [**Tab**].

21 Press [**Tab**] again because we do not yet have a picture for this product.

22 Note that the last Tab completes the entry for this new product. However, since you established referential integrity, an error message (see Figure 9.23) appears. This occurred because there is no Supplier ID 10 in the Supplier table and so Access rejected your entry. Click **OK** in the error message to return to the Product table.

Figure 9.23

Error Message

23 Type **2** in the Supplier ID field, and then close the Product table. This time Access accepts the entry in the Supplier ID field because it matches a record found in the Supplier ID field of the Supplier table.

"That makes more sense now," Meagan and Nathan agree.

Documenting a Database

"Now that we've made all these changes to our database, how do we document them?" Nathan asks.

"Good question" responds Kyle. "Access has a feature called the Database Documenter that will provide a list of table, query, form, and report attributes."

Kyle suggests you document some of the changes you made to the product and supplier tables. In particular, he would like to see documentation of the unit price field in the Product table (where you added a validation rule) and documentation of the phone number field in the Supplier table (where you added an input mask).

To document the information requested:

1 Click **Database Documenter** from the Analyze group of the Database Tools tab on the Ribbon.

2 Click the **Tables** tab in the Documenter window.

3 Click the **Supplier Table** check box as shown in Figure 9.24.

Figure 9.24

Documenter Window

4 Click the **Options** button.

5 Check or uncheck boxes and select option buttons as per Figure 9.25.

Figure 9.25
Print Table Definition

6 Click **OK** in the Print Table Definitions window, and then click **OK** in the Documenter window.

7 Click in the lower portion of the **Zoom** button in the Zoom group of the Print Preview tab of the Ribbon.

8 Click **150%.**

9 Navigate to page 4 of the report by clicking the arrows located in the lower left-hand corner of the Print Preview window, and locate information on the PhoneNumber field.

T r o u b l e ? Page 4 on your screen may not contain information on the PhoneNumber field. If not, look on pages 3 or 5 to find it and then change the page you print in step 10 accordingly.

10 Click **Print**, click **Pages** in the Print window, and then type **4** in the From and To: text boxes. Your resulting printout should contain the information shown in Figure 9.26.

11 Click **Close Print Preview.**

12 Click **Database Documenter** from the Analyze group of the Database Tools tab on the Ribbon.

13 Click the **Tables** tab in the Documenter window.

14 Click the **Product Table** check box and then click **OK.**

15 Click in the lower portion of the **Zoom** button in the Zoom group of the Print Preview tab of the Ribbon.

16 Click **150%.**

Figure 9.26

Database Documenter
Information on the Phone
Number Field of the
Supplier Table

PhoneNumber		Text	50
AggregateType:	-1		
AllowZeroLength:	False		
AppendOnly:	False		
Attributes:	Variable Length		
Caption:	Phone Number		
CollatingOrder:	General		
ColumnHidden:	False		
ColumnOrder:	Default		
ColumnWidth:	1830		
DataUpdatable:	False		
DisplayControl:	Text Box		
GUID:	{guid {D396690E-F676-11D3-B511-939E8A1E7E2A}}		
IMEMode:	0		
IMESentenceMode:	3		
InputMask:	!\(999") "000\-0000;;_		
OrdinalPosition:	9		
Required:	False		
SourceField:	PhoneNumber		
SourceTable:	Supplier Table		
TextAlign:	General		
UnicodeCompression:	True		

17   Navigate to page 3 of the report by clicking the arrows located in the lower left-hand corner of the Print Preview window, and locate information on the UnitPrice field.

Trouble? Page 3 on your screen may not contain information on the UnitPrice field. If not, look on pages 2 or 4 to find it and then change the page you print in step 18 accordingly.

18   Click **Print.** click **Pages** in the Print window, and then type **3** in the From and To: text boxes. Your resulting printout should contain the information shown in Figure 9.27.

Figure 9.27

Database Documenter
Information on the Unit
Price Field of the Product
Table

UnitPrice		Currency	8
AggregateType:	-1		
AllowZeroLength:	False		
AppendOnly:	False		
Attributes:	Fixed Size		
Caption:	Unit Price		
CollatingOrder:	General		
ColumnHidden:	False		
ColumnOrder:	Default		
ColumnWidth:	1320		
DataUpdatable:	False		
DecimalPlaces:	Auto		
Format:	$#,##0.00;($#,##0.00)		
GUID:	{guid {FA1F2364-E5F1-11D3-B511-FAF49AA7C228}}		
OrdinalPosition:	6		
Required:	True		
SourceField:	UnitPrice		
SourceTable:	Product Table		
TextAlign:	General		
ValidationRule:	>0 And <1000		
ValidationText:	Unit Price must be > $0 and < $1,000		

19   Click **Close Print Preview.**

Meagan notes that in the Supplier table documentation she can see the input mask created for the PhoneNumber field and that in the Product table documentation she can see the validation rule and validation text created for the UnitPrice field.

"What about all the other information provided for the fields in question?" Meagan asks.

"Helpful," comments Kyle, "but not that important for us right now. It's time to practice!"

End Note

In this chapter, you have learned more about the use of tables in the Access program. You have learned how to add, change, and delete records; how to add a picture with an OLE field; and how to change the structure of a database, which included changing field data types and column widths and changing record row heights. You have also learned how to create field validation rules, default values, and formats. Finally, you learned about the advantages and functionality of specifying referential integrity. In the next chapter you will experience more of the query process.

Chapter 9 Questions

1 Describe the process for deleting a record from a table.

2 Define OLE.

3 What can you do in Access to change the structure of a database?

4 Why would you want to change the column width and/or row height of a table?

5 What do validation rules do?

6 What is the process for adding a validation rule to a field?

7 Why would you establish default values for a field?

8 What are input masks?

9 What is referential integrity?

10 What rules must be followed if referential integrity is enforced?

Chapter 9 Assignments

1 Add, change, and delete records to the Coast Jewelers database (use the Ch9-02 file)

  a. Add the following record to the Buyers table: ID 4, Farley, 555-7187.

  b. Add Bracelets as a category to the Category table.

  c. Delete the following record from the Buyers table: ID 2, Ng.

  d. Change the buyer for the following Product IDs from buyer 2 to buyer 4: Product ID 3, 5, and 8.

  e. Print the first page of the product, buyers, and category tables as modified.

  f. Save your file as Ch9-02_student_name (replacing student_name with your name).

2 Add pictures with an OLE field to the Coast Jewelers database (use the Ch9-02 file)

  a. Add pictures for the remaining products in the Product table using the picture files provided. Each product has a picture associated with it and is labeled with the product ID number.

  b. Print page 2 of the Product table as modified.

   c.   Save your file as Ch9-02_student_name (replacing student_name with your name).

3   Change the structure of the Coast Jewelers database

   a.   Add the following product to the Product table. Product ID: 11; Name: Pearl Necklace; Description: "A 14K gold 18 inch cable chain holds a genuine 6mm round cultured pearl."; Supplier ID: 1; Category ID: 3; Product Number: PRLN652; UnitPrice: 95; Reorder Level: 3; Lead Time: 7; Buyer ID: 1; Image: 11.

   b.   Add the following product to the Product table. Product ID: 12; Name: Swiss Army Watch; Description: "Officer's watch in rugged stainless steel."; Supplier ID: 6; Category ID: 1; Product Number: 24277; UnitPrice: 175; Reorder Level: 3; Lead Time: 10; Buyer ID: 4; Image: 12.

   c.   Resize the column width of each field and the record's row height of the Product table so that they fit on one page when printed. (Don't worry if not all the information is shown or if the field name isn't fully visible when the table is printed.)

   d.   Print the Product table in landscape orientation.

   e.   Resize the column width of each field and the record's row height of the Supplier table so that they fit on one page when printed. (Don't worry if not all the information is shown or if the field name isn't fully visible when the table is printed.)

   f.   Print the Supplier table in landscape orientation.

   g.   Create a validation rule for the Reorder Level field of the Product table, making the field a required one and making sure the reorder level is greater than 0 but less than 100 units. Create your own feedback statement and insert it as the validation text.

   h.   Establish 7 as the default value for the Lead Time field of the Product table.

   i.   Establish a phone number input mask for the BuyerPhone field of the Buyers table.

   j.   Enforce referential integrity between the Product table and the Buyer and Category tables.

   k.   Print the Relationships window.

   l.   Print documentation on the properties of the Reorder Level field of the Product table and the BuyerPhone field of the Buyers table.

   m.   Save your file as Ch9-02_student_name (replacing student_name with your name).

Chapter 9 Case Problem 1:
KELLY'S BOUTIQUE

Note: You must have completed Case 1 in the previous chapter in order to continue working on this case.

In Chapter 8 you created a database for Kelly's Boutique consisting of a Book table, a Department table, and a Publisher table. You also created an initial form, query, and report. Kelly would now like you to make some adjustments to the tables previously created by adding and deleting some records, adding some OLE fields and pictures, and changing the structure of the database. Make the following changes for Kelly using the ch8-03_student_name file you created in Chapter 8. (*Note:* Open your ch8-03_student_name file first, save it as ch9-03_student_name, and then make the listed changes.)

a. Add Warner as the tenth publisher to the Publisher table with a contact Yee and phone 555-7894.

b. Add the following records to the Book table:

ISBN	Dept	Book Title	Num	Author	Price
039480029	Children	Hop on Pop	6	Seuss	7.99
039480001	Children	The Cat in the Hat	6	Seuss	7.99
446676098	Adult	The Notebook	10	Sparks	16.95

c. Add a Picture field for OLE objects to the Book table.

d. Add pictures to the Book table for *Green Eggs and Ham*, *Hop on Pop*, *Harry Potter and the Prisoner of Azkaban*, *Divine Secrets*, and *Deep End of the Ocean*. Picture files are labeled by book name and are located on your student disk.

e. Resize the column width of each field and the record's row height of each table so that they fit on one page when printed.

f. Establish a phone number input mask for the Phone field of the Publisher and Department tables.

g. Enforce referential integrity between the Book table and the Department and Publisher tables.

h. Create a validation rule for the List price field of the Book table, making the field a required one and making sure the price is no less than $1 but no more than $100. Create your own feedback statement and insert it as the validation text.

i. Establish Children as the default value for the Department field of the Book table.

j. Print the Book, Department, and Publisher tables.

k. Print the Relationships report.

l. Print documentation on the properties of the List Price field of the Book table and the Phone field of the Publisher table.

Chapter 9 Case Problem 2:
WINE DEPOT

Note: You must have completed Case 2 in the previous chapter in order to continue working on this case.

In Chapter 8 you created a database for the Wine Depot consisting of a Wine Products table, a Winery table, and a Buyer table. You also created an initial query, form, and report. Barbara has now asked you to make some changes to those files. Make the following changes for Barbara using the ch8-04_student_name file you created in Chapter 8. (*Note:* Open your ch8-04_student_name file first, save it as ch9-04_student_name, and then make the listed changes.)

a. Add buyer 105, Carly Simon, 555-6874 to the Buyer table.

b. Add winery 20 (Robert Mondovi, American, 105) and winery 21 (Wente, American, 104) to the Winery table.

c. Delete wines with SKU 15966 and 16769.

d. Delete winery 2.

e. Add the following records to the Wine Products table:

SKU	Type	Winery	Price	Cost	Size	Vintage	Quantity
12564	Merlot	21	12.99	8.00	750	2000	24
12895	Sauvignon Blanc	4	15.49	9.00	750	2002	12
16900	Syrah	11	24.00	18.00	750	2001	12
11350	Pinot Noir	11	30.00	24.00	750	2001	12
11475	Pinot Noir	1	22.00	17.50	750	2001	48
12380	Pinot Noir	20	21.00	18.00	750	2000	24
12383	Chardonnay	20	18.00	12.00	750	2000	36
12384	Fume Blanc	20	17.49	11.00	750	2001	36

f. Enforce referential integrity between the tables.

g. Print the Relationships report.

h. Add a Picture field for OLE objects to the Wine Products table.

i. Add pictures to the Wine Products table for products 11475, 12384, 12895, 14539, and 15347. (*Note:* Pictures for these products are provided and are labeled with the SKU number.)

j. Establish a phone number input mask for the Phone field of the Buyer table, and then change all the phone numbers in the table to include an area code of 805.

k. Create a validation rule for the Price field of the Wine Products table, making the price field required and making sure the price is no less than $1 but no more than $100. Create your own feedback statement and enter it as the validation text. Save the changes you made.

l. When creating your validation rule, you might well have checked to see if the data already stored actually met that rule. If you did check, you found that the validation rule was in conflict with some of the existing data. Change the rule so that the price must be no less than $1 but now no more than $200. Create your own feedback statement and enter it as the validation text. Save the changes you made.

m. Establish a default value of 750 for the Size field of the Wine Products table.

n. Resize the column width of the Wine Products table so that it can fit on one page when printed in landscape orientation.

o. Print each table.

p. Print documentation on the properties of the Phone field of the Buyer table and the Price field of the Wine Products table.

q. Make sure you keep a copy of this file for use in the next chapter.

Queries

In this chapter you will learn:

- Use a query to display selected records
- Use character data in criteria in a query
- Use wildcards in criteria
- Edit a query
- Use comparison operators and sorting
- Use compound criteria and limit output
- Perform calculations
- Use computed fields
- Compute statistics
- Use an action query to update records
- Use a parameter query
- Use an action query to delete records
- Print a query

Case: **Coast Jewelers, Inc.**

Kyle decides to take Meagan and Nathan to the next level of database use by explaining the query process.

"What good is all this information if you can't use it?" Kyle asks. "Access provides you tables as a holder of information, but queries are used to ask questions of the data and to retrieve a subset of the total information available."

"Do we have to learn a special language in order to ask questions of the database?" asks Meagan.

"No, but you do need to know some characteristics of the data so that you can use Access's Query By Example (QBE) method of inquiry," he responds.

Kyle decides that he'll begin by explaining how to go about querying the database for specific information, such as what necklaces Coast has in inventory, and then continue with more complicated queries, such as which necklaces Coast has in inventory that are above one price but below another.

Querying Selected Records

Kyle explains that the querying you accomplished in your introduction to Access involved listing specific data from various tables. In these queries you didn't establish any criteria to select specific records; you just specified what specific information you wanted from all records. The next level of inquiry requires that you establish specific criteria for certain fields to narrow down your search for particular records. These are referred to as *select* queries.

"We'll begin with character data, wildcards, and numbers to specify what records we're looking for," Kyle explains.

Using Character Data in a Select Query

Queries can be generated either by using the Query Wizard (as was done in our introduction to Access) or by using the Design view, which is more sophisticated and flexible. Kyle suggests you use the Design view to create a simple query of your inventory file, which has been updated to include a total of 20 records. If a customer were looking for a specific item that she saw elsewhere, then she might ask if you have a particular watch in stock. You could look that item up in your database by generating a query asking for a specific match to a specific name.

"Why don't we ask the database if it has a specific Seiko watch with a product number of SMA113?" asks Meagan.

"Good idea," Nathan responds. "Let's create such a query that displays the product number, name, and supplier."

To create a query using character data:

1   Start Access.

2   Click the **Microsoft Office** button and then click **Open.**

3   Navigate the Open window to the location of this text's student files. (The location would be the CD provided with the text or from your computer lab's server.)

4   Double-click **ch10-01**, which should be located in a Ch 10 folder. (This is a modified version of the completed Coast Jewelers Inventory file from Chapter 9.)

5   Click the **Microsoft Office** button and then place the mouse over the words **Save As.**

6   Click **Access 2007 Database** under the section Save the database in another format.

7   Navigate the Save As window to the location where you want to save this file and type **Ch10-01_student_name** in the File Name: text box, replacing "student_name" with your name.

8   Click **Save.**

9   Click **Query Wizard** from the Other group on the Create tab of the Ribbon.

10   Click **Simple Query Wizard** and then click **OK.**

11   Click **Table: Product Table** from the drop-down list of Tables/Queries.

12 Double-click **Product Number** and **Product Name** from the list of available fields.

13 Click **Table: Supplier Table** from the drop-down list of Tables/ Queries.

14 Double-click **Supplier Name** from the list of available fields.

15 Click **Next** and then type **Product Query 1** as the title for the query and then click **Finish.**

16 Double-click the space between each field name to resize the columns so that all information is visible. Your screen should look like Figure 10.1

Figure 10.1

Product Query 1

Product Number	Product Name	Supplier Name
LGR29	Engagement Ring	Johnson Wholesale Jewelry Supply
P44R	Diamond Heart Slide	Johnson Wholesale Jewelry Supply
CJ-2275-7	Diamond Wedding Ring	Johnson Wholesale Jewelry Supply
PRLN652	Pearl Necklace	Johnson Wholesale Jewelry Supply
CR313	Tanzanite Ring	Johnson Wholesale Jewelry Supply
BTZ129	Blue Topaz Ring	Johnson Wholesale Jewelry Supply
ER-764	Diamond Earrings	Jewelry Inc.
1235	Diamond Pendant	Jewelry Inc.
ER-800	Diamond Studs	Jewelry Inc.
SR23RB	Diamond Solitare Earrings	Jewelry Inc.
LZP014-AM	Amethyst Pendant	Jewelry Inc.
SMA113	Seiko Kinetic Auto Relay Titanium	Seiko USA
SKA040	Le Grand Sport	Seiko USA
SMA075	Seiko Kinetic Auto Relay	Seiko USA
SKA041	Seiko Dive Watch	Seiko USA
136305	Flower Drop Earrings	Robert Rose
LZN003-BT	Topaz Necklace	Robert Rose
DW004B-4V	G-Shock	Casio USA
24277	Swiss Army Watch	Casio USA
RSUB	Rolex Oyster Submariner	Rolex

17 Click the **Home** tab of the Ribbon; click **View** and then click **Design View.**

18 Type **SMA113** in the criteria section of the query in the ProductNumber column of the design grid, as shown in Figure 10.2.

19 Click **Run** from the Results group of the Design tab of the Ribbon.

20 Resize the column widths if necessary to view all of the information provided. The resulting Datasheet view of the query should look like the query solution in Figure 10.3.

21 Close the Query window and click **Yes** to save changes.

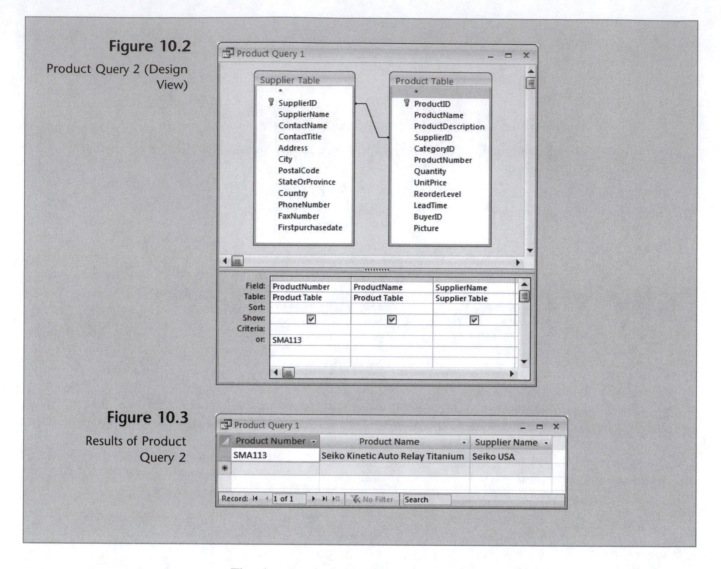

Figure 10.2

Product Query 2 (Design View)

Figure 10.3

Results of Product Query 2

The character-based queries work well when you have a specific name or set of characters (like the product number) you are looking for. However, Access users are often in search of records that match some—but perhaps not all—of a specific criteria. Wildcards provide this capability.

Using Wildcards in a Select Query

Queries using wildcards allow the user to find such things as field values, records, or filenames. The asterisk (*), which matches any number of characters, can be used as a wildcard in the first, last, or first *and* last position of the character string. For example, if Nathan wanted to list all the products he had in inventory that contained the text "diamond" in the product name, he would type *diamond* as the criteria under the ProductName column.

Kyle points out that there is a way to create a new query other than by using the Query Wizard. This method, which Kyle actually prefers, is called *query by design* and uses a different tool called the Query Design tool. He suggests you try this method out next to practice your use of wildcards.

To search for a product using wildcards using the Query Design tool:

1 Click **Query Design** from the Other group on the Create tab of the Ribbon.

2 Double-click **Product Table** from the list of tables in the Tables tab of the Show Table window to add the Product table to the query, and then click the **Close** button.

3 Resize the Product Table window so that all fields are visible by clicking and holding the lower right-hand corner of the window and dragging down and to the right.

4 Double-click the **Product Name** and **Unit Price** fields from the Product table shown in the query.

5 Type *diamond* in the criteria section of the query in the ProductName column of the design grid, as shown in Figure 10.4.

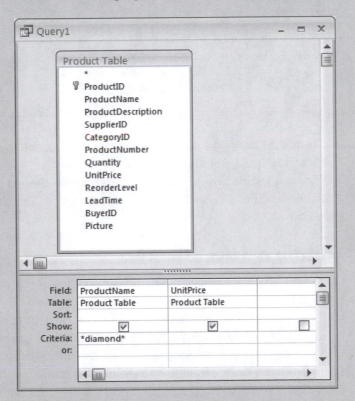

Figure 10.4

Using Wildcards in a Query

6 Click **Run** from the Results group in the Design tab of the Ribbon. The resulting Datasheet view of the query should look like the query solution in Figure 10.5.

7 Click **View** and then **Design View.** Note that the Criteria has changed to Like "*diamond*", which is the proper syntax to be used when searching in a query.

8 Click the **Microsoft Office** button and then click **Save As.**

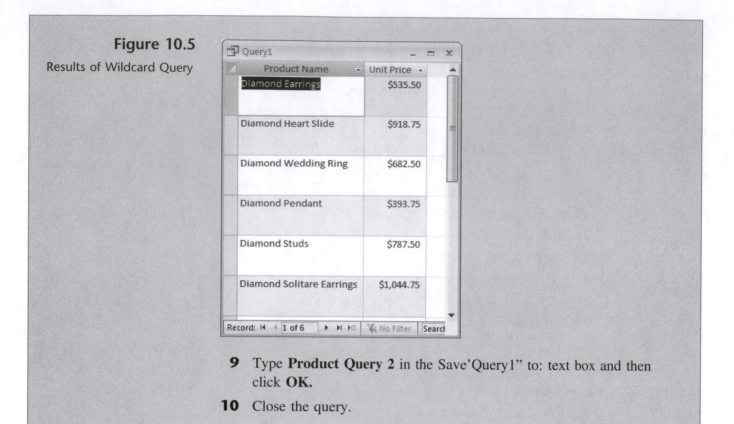

Figure 10.5

Results of Wildcard Query

9 Type **Product Query 2** in the Save'Query1" to: text box and then click **OK.**

10 Close the query.

"That's all well and good," Meagan says. "But what if I wanted to add more fields to my query solution?"

"Good question," Kyle responds. "It's easy to change your existing query, but you'll notice that Access has saved your query in a slightly different form from how you created it.

Editing a Select Query

Once you've saved a query, it can be re-run any number of times. For instance, Product Query 2—which looked up a particular product number from the database—could be run again for the same or a different product number. Product Query 3 could be run again using the same criteria but asking for different fields of information.

Kyle suggests you demonstrate the query editing features of Access by modifying Product Query 2 to look up a different product number (LGR29) and adding the buyer's name to the result. He also suggests you modify Product Query 3 to look up all product names containing the word "earrings" and adding the category name to the result.

To edit existing queries:

1 Right-click **Product Query 1** from the Query listing and then select **Design View** from the shortcut menu.

Trouble? You may have to resize the query window, tables, and so forth in order to view all the information. To do this, place the cursor over the edges you wish to resize.

2 Click **Show Table** from the Query Setup group on the Design tab of the Ribbon.

3 Double-click **Buyers Table** and then close the Show Table window.

4 Move the table windows around so that all fields and tables are viewable.

5 Double-click the **Buyer Name** field from the Buyers table shown in the query to add that field to your query.

6 Type **LGR29** in the criteria section of the query in the Product Number column as shown in Figure 10.6.

Trouble? Before typing the new criteria specified for this query, note that the previous product number has automatically been placed in quotes. You don't need to type the quotes in before making this query, but Access knows that quotes are needed for future instances of the query.

Figure 10.6

Editing Product Query 1

7 Click **Run** from the Results group in the Design tab of the Ribbon. The resulting Datasheet view of the query should look like the query solution in Figure 10.7.

Figure 10.7

Results of the Newly
Modified Product Query 1

Product Number ▾	Product Name ▾	Supplier Name ▾	Buyer Name ▾
LGR29	Engagement Ring	Johnson Wholesale Jewelry Supply	Farley

Record: I◄ ◄ 1 of 1 ► ►I ►⧉   🛇 No Filter   Search

8 Click **Save As** from the Microsoft Office button.

9 Type **Product Query 3** as the new name and then click **OK.**

10 Close the Query window.

11 Right-click **Product Query 2** from the Query listing and then select **Design View** from the shortcut menu.

12 Click **Show Table** from the Query Setup group on the Design tab of the Ribbon.

13 Double-click **Category Table** and then close the Show Table window.

14 Move the table windows around so that all fields and tables are viewable.

15 Double-click the **CategoryName** field from the Category table shown in the query.

16 Type ***earrings*** in the criteria section of the query in the ProductName column as shown in Figure 10.8.

Figure 10.8

Editing Product Query 2

17 Click **Run** from the Results group in the Design tab of the Ribbon. The resulting Datasheet view of the query should look like the query solution in Figure 10.9.

Figure 10.9

Results of the Newly Edited Product Query 2

18   Click **Save As** from the Microsoft Office button.

19   Type **Product Query 4** as the new name and then click **OK.**

20   Close the Query window.

"Don't we have four earrings as products in the Product Table?" Meagan asks.

"Yes, but only three of them have the word earrings in the product name. The fourth one, whose product name is Diamond Studs, is classified as in the category of earrings but the text "earrings" is not in its product name." Kyle responds.

"How do we delete fields from a query?" Meagan asks.

"Let me show you by removing the unit price field from the Product Query 4 we just created," Kyle answers.

To delete a field from a query:

1   Double-click **Product Query 4** to reopen the query you just worked on.

2   Click **View** and then click **Design View.**

3   Click the top of the UnitPrice field until it is selected (turns black).

4   Press the [**Delete**] key. Note that the Unit Price field is removed.

5   Close Product Query 4 but do not save changes.

"I'm impressed!" exclaims Meagan. "This query stuff isn't so difficult; in fact, it's rather intuitive."

Kyle continues with his explanation of queries by showing additional examples of the query process. So far he has used characters in his queries. Now it is time to demonstrate the use of numbers in queries and show how comparison operators can be used in a select query.

Using Comparison Operators and Sorting in a Select Query

Kyle asks if you would like to track items you're running short of or items that you need to place on sale.

If so, he suggests you create a select query to find all inventory items for which quantity balances are running low (less than or equal to two items, for instance). To do so, Kyle explains that you simply modify your criteria to include comparison operators like the < symbol, which signifies "less than". He cautions you, however, that the less-than symbol, just like the greater-than symbol (>), is not inclusive of the number specified. Thus, in order to generate a query that selects those records for which inventory quantities are less than or equal to a certain number, you must include both the < and the = symbols.

To select records for which inventory quantities are less than or equal to two:

1 Click **Query Design** from the Other group on the Create tab of the Ribbon.

2 Double-click **Product Table** from the list of tables in the Tables tab of the Show Table window to add the Product table to the query; then click the **Close** button.

3 Resize the Product Table window so that all fields are visible.

4 Double-click **Product Name** and **Quantity** fields for this query.

5 Type **<=2** in the criteria row of the Quantity field of the design grid.

6 Click **Run.** Your results should look like Figure 10.10.

Figure 10.10

Query Results for Products with a Quantity of 2 or Less

Product Name	Quantity
Diamond Earrings	2
Seiko Kinetic Auto Relay	1
Seiko Dive Watch	0
Rolex Oyster Submariner	2
*	0

Record: ◄ ◄ 5 of 5 ► ►I ► No Filter   Search

7 Click **Save As** from the Microsoft Office button.

8 Type **Product Query 5** as the new name and then click **OK.**

9 Close the Query window.

"Wouldn't you get the same results if you set the criteria as <2?" Nathan asks. "No, you wouldn't," responds Kyle. "Let me demonstrate."

To select records with criteria of <2:

1 Right-click **Product Query 5** and then click **Design View.**

2 Type **<2** in the criteria row of the Quantity field of the design grid, replacing the <=2.

3 Click **Run.** Your results should look like Figure 10.11.

Figure 10.11

Query Results for Products with a Quantity of Less Than 2

Product Query 5		
Product Name ▾	Quantity ▾
Seiko Kinetic Auto Relay	1
Seiko Dive Watch	0
*	0
Record: ◄ ◄ 1 of 2 ► ►I ►❉ ☒ No Filter S	

4 Close the query but do not save changes.

Kyle compares the two query results to demonstrate to Nathan the differences. He explains that the equal sign was important so that all records with a quantity of two or fewer were selected.

"What other comparison operators are available in Access?" asks Meagan.

Kyle responds that, in addition to the < and = symbols, Access allows you to select records using any combination of <, =, or >. For instance, you could ask for records in which the price was between $500 and $1,000 by using the < and > symbols together. Or you could not use the symbols and simply ask for the records in which the unit price was between 500 and 1000.

"Could we also sort the results from lowest to highest price?" asks Meagan.

"Yes," Kyle answers. "Access queries allow for sorting the results in either ascending or descending order.

To select records with a price between $500 and $1,000 and sort the results:

1 Click **Query Design** from the Other group on the Create tab of the Ribbon.

2 Double-click **Product Table** from the list of tables in the Tables tab of the Show Table window to add the Product table to the query, and then click the **Close** button.

3 Resize the Product Table window so that all fields are visible.

4 Double-click **Product Name** and **UnitPrice** fields for this query.

5 Type **>500 And <1000** in the criteria row of the UnitPrice field of the design grid.

6 Click **Ascending** from the drop-down menu in the Sort cell of the UnitPrice field, as shown in Figure 10.12.

Figure 10.12

Design View for Comparison Query

7 Click **Run.** Your results should look like Figure 10.13.

Figure 10.13

Results of Unit Price Query

8 Type **Between 500 And 1000** in the criteria row of the UnitPrice field.

9 Click **Run.** Your results should still look like Figure 10.13.

10 Click **Save As** from the Microsoft Office button.

11 Type **Product Query 6** as the new name and then click **OK.**

12 Close the Query window.

Kyle explains that so far you've specified criteria for only one field. Access allows you to specify criteria for more than one field using specific or comparison operators.

Using Compound Criteria and Limiting Output in a Select Query

Compound criteria allow you to select records from a database using more than one field. These criteria can be applied to require that all criteria be met or they can be applied such that only one criterion need to be met before record is selected. The field upon which the criteria are applied must be included in the query but need not be included in the output.

"Let's create a query that includes product name and unit price for all products with a unit price greater than $500 and a buyer ID of 1 or 3 sorted by product name," suggests Kyle.

"Do we have to include the Buyers table in this query?" Meagan asks.

"No, since the buyer ID is a part of the Product table, it won't be necessary to include the Buyers table," answers Kyle.

To create a query that includes product name and unit price for all products with a unit price greater than $500 and a buyer ID of 1 or 3:

1 Click **Query Design** from the Other group on the Create tab of the Ribbon.

2 Double-click **Product Table** from the list of tables in the Tables tab of the Show Table window to add the Product table to the query, and then click the **Close** button.

3 Resize the Product Table window so that all fields are visible.

4 Double-click **Product Name**, **Unit Price** and **Buyer ID** fields for this query.

5 Type **>500** in the criteria row of the Unit Price field of the design grid. Make sure the Show check box in the Unit Price field of the design grid is selected.

6 Type **1 Or 3** in the criteria row of the Buyer ID field of the design grid.

7 Unselect the **Show** check box under the Buyer ID field.

8 Click **Ascending** from the drop-down menu in the Sort cell of the Product Name field. Your screen should look like Figure 10.14.

9 Run the query. Your results should look like Figure 10.15.

10 Click **Save As** from the Microsoft Office button.

11 Type **Product Query 7** as the new name and then click **OK**.

Figure 10.14

Query Design of Products with Unit Price Greater than $500 *and* Purchased by Buyer 1 or 3

Figure 10.15

Query Results for Products with Unit Price Greater than $500 *and* Purchased by Buyer 1 or 3

As an alternative Kyle explains that the criteria specified on multiple fields can require that all records satisfy all criteria or that the criteria specified on multiple fields satisfy one or more criteria. For example, the previous query asked for all records in which the unit price was greater than $500 *and* for which the buyer was 1 or 3. Another query might ask for all records in which the unit price was greater than $500 *or* for which the buyer was 1 or 3. These variations, as you will see, yield different results.

To create a query that includes product name, unit price, and buyer ID for all products with a unit price greater than $500 or a buyer ID of 1 or 3:

1 Using Product Query 7 that you just created, click **View** and then click **Design View.**

2 Click **1 Or 3** from the Criteria: row of the Buyer ID field and then press the [**Delete**] key.

3 Type **1 Or 3** in the or: row of the Buyer ID field, as shown in Figure 10.16.

Figure 10.16

Query Design of Products with Unit Price Greater than $500 *or* Purchased by Buyer 1 or 3

4 Select the **Show** check box under the Buyer ID field.

5 Click **Run.** Your results should look like Figure 10.17.

Figure 10.17

Query Results for Products with Unit Price Greater than $500 *or* Purchased by Buyer 1 or 3

6 Click **Save As** from the Microsoft Office button.

> **7** Type **Product Query 8** as the new name and then click **OK.**
>
> **8** Close this query.

   Kyle points out that, in this modified query, the G-Shock record is present (even though its unit price is less than $500) because its buyer ID is 1 or 3. Likewise, the Diamond Wedding Ring record is present (even though its buyer ID is 4) because its unit price is greater than $500.

Performing Calculations

Kyle remarks that there are many types of calculations you can perform in a query. For example, you can calculate the sum or average of the values in one field, multiply the values in two fields, or calculate the date three months from the current date. When you display the results of a calculation in a field, the results aren't actually stored in the underlying table. Instead, Microsoft Access reruns the calculation each time you run the query so that the results are always based on the most current information in the database.

Displaying the Results of Calculations in a Field

To demonstrate the use of computations and the creation of a computed field, Kyle suggests that you and Nathan create a query that calculates the cost of each item in inventory. He explains that to begin you'll need to create a query that includes the field's product name, quantity, and unit price. Then you'll need to create a computed field to calculate the product of the quantity and the unit price fields. In order to create a computed field, you'll need to type the name of the newly created field in a blank field row followed by the two fields used to compute total cost. Each field used must be surrounded by brackets, as with [Quantity]. After you've created the computed field, you'll often need to format the field to a number or currency depending on how you want it displayed.

To create an inventory cost query:

1 Click **Query Design** from the Other group on the Create tab of the Ribbon.

2 Double-click **Product Table** from the list of tables in the Tables tab of the Show Table window to add the Product table to the query, and then click the **Close** button.

3 Resize the Product Table window so that all fields are visible.

4 Double-click **Product Name, Unit Price** and **Buyer ID** fields for this query.

5 In the fourth column on the Field row of the design grid, type **Cost: [Quantity]*[UnitPrice].** (In this case Cost is the name of the new field and [Quantity] and [UnitPrice] are the two fields being used to calculate the value for the newly created Cost field.

6 Right-click the newly created **Cost** field and then click **Zoom** to enlarge the formula.

7 Click **Font** and then click **16** in the Size column; then click **OK** to make the Zoom window text increase in size. Your Zoom window should look like Figure 10.18.

Figure 10.18
Creating a Calculated Field

8 Click **OK** to close the Zoom window after you verify its contents.

9 Right-click the **Cost** field again and then click **Properties**, which takes you to the Property Sheet window.

10 Click in the text box next to Format and then select **Currency** from the drop-down list of formats; then close the Property Sheet window.

11 Click **Run** to run the query to yield the results shown in Figure 10.19.

Figure 10.19
Query with a Calculated Field

Product Name	Unit Price	Buyer ID	Cost
Flower Drop Earrings	$6.30	3	$63.00
Seiko Kinetic Auto Relay Titanium	$446.25	3	$1,785.00
Le Grand Sport	$288.75	4	$1,443.75
G-Shock	$51.45	1	$514.50
Engagement Ring	$420.00	4	$5,040.00
Diamond Earrings	$535.50	3	$1,071.00
Diamond Heart Slide	$918.75	1	$3,675.00
Diamond Wedding Ring	$682.50	4	$3,412.50
Swiss Army Watch	$183.75	4	$551.25
Diamond Pendant	$393.75	3	$2,756.25
Diamond Studs	$787.50	1	$2,362.50
Pearl Necklace	$99.75	1	$1,496.25
Diamond Solitare Earrings	$1,044.75	3	$3,134.25
Tanzanite Ring	$467.25	1	$4,205.25
Blue Topaz Ring	$261.45	4	$1,830.15
Topaz Necklace	$393.75	3	$1,968.75
Amethyst Pendant	$204.75	5	$1,638.00
Seiko Kinetic Auto Relay	$414.75	5	$414.75
Seiko Dive Watch	$367.50	5	$0.00
Rolex Oyster Submariner	$3,148.95	5	$6,297.90
*		0	

Record: 1 of 20   No Filter   Search

12 Click the **Microsoft Office** button and then click **Save As.**

13 Type **Product Query 9** as the name of the new query and then click **OK.**

14 Close the query.

Once again, the resulting value established in the Cost field is there only temporarily and cannot be used in a later report or form unless this query is run as well. In addition to creating a computed field, Access will allow you to perform statistics and summations from within a query.

Computing Statistics

Access will allow you to calculate various statistical measures of your database, including (for example) sum, average, maximum, and minimum.

"What if I needed to know my total inventory cost?" asks Nathan.

"No problem," Kyle responds. "Access has a sum function that will work on the cost variable we just created. All we need to do is turn on the sum function and then create a sum query using the cost field we defined. To do so, we must select the query we just created instead of an existing table."

To create a sum query:

1 Click **Query Design** from the Other group on the Create tab of the Ribbon.

2 Double-click **Product Query 9** from the list of queries in the Queries tab of the Show Table window then click the **Close** button.

3 Resize the Product Query 9 window so that all fields are visible.

4 Double-click **Cost.**

5 Click **Totals** from the Show/Hide group of the Design tab on the Ribbon.

6 Click **Sum** from the drop-down list in the Total row, as shown in Figure 10.20.

7 Click Run to generate a summation of all inventory cost, as shown in Figure 10.21.

8 Click the **Microsoft Office** button and then click **Save As.**

9 Type **Product Query 10** as the name of the new query and then click **OK.**

10 Close the query.

Figure 10.20

Creating a Sum Query

Figure 10.21

Sum Of Inventory Cost Query

"Is there any way to find the total cost of inventory by category?" asks Nathan.

"Yes," Kyle answers. "Access uses the concept of grouping to provide statistical information on a database."

Kyle goes on to explain that, since the field he summed previously was a calculated field, it is imperative that the category field be a part of that query before a sum query is run. He suggests that you edit the inventory cost query to include the category field before modifying the inventory cost summary query you just created.

To create a sum query by category:

1   Right-click **Product Query 9** and then click **Design view** from the shortcut menu.

2   Click **Show Table** from the Query Setup group on the Design tab of the Ribbon.

3   Double-click **Category Table** and then close the Show Table window.

4   Double-click the **Category Name** field to add it to the query.

5 Close and save the revised query.

6 Right-click **Product Query 10** and then click **Design view** from the shortcut menu.

7 Click and drag the **Category Name** field to the left of the Cost field, as shown in Figure 10.22.

Figure 10.22

Modifying a Query to Group Totals by Category

8 Click **Run** to generate a summation of all inventory cost by category, as shown in Figure 10.23.

Figure 10.23

Results of a Query to Group Totals by Category

CategoryName	SumOfCost
Earrings	$6,630.75
Necklaces	$11,534.25
Rings	$14,487.90
Watches	$11,007.15

Record: 1 of 4   No Filter

9 Click the **Microsoft Office** button and then click **Save As.**

10 Type **Product Query 11** as the name of the new query and then click **OK.**

11 Close the query.

"That's great information," says Nathan. "Is there a way to find out how many watches, necklaces, et cetera we have on hand or how many different products we have in each category?"

"Sure," responds Kyle. "We can use the sum feature again to sum up the quantity of each category and the count feature to count the number of products we have by category."

Kyle explains that the sum feature in this case can be used on the product and category tables because the information we want to display and sum is found in the tables and not in any particular query. Likewise, the count feature is used on the same two tables. He recommends that you and Meagan give it a try.

To create a sum query of quantities by category:

1 Click **Query Design** from the Other group on the Create tab of the Ribbon.

2 Double-click **Category Table** and **Product Table** from the list of tables in the Tables tab of the Show Table window then click the **Close** button.

3 Resize the window so that all fields are visible.

4 Double-click the **Category Name** and the **Quantity** fields to add them to the query.

5 Click **Totals** from the Show/Hide group of the Design tab on the Ribbon.

6 Click **Sum** from the drop-down list in the Total row of the Quantify field; then click **Group By** from the drop-down list in the Total row of the CategoryName field, as shown in Figure 10.24.

Figure 10.24

Design View of Query to Sum Quantities by Category

7 Click **Run** to generate a summation of all quantities by category, as shown in Figure 10.25.

Figure 10.25

Results of a Query to Group Quantities by Category

Query1	□ ✕
CategoryName ▾	SumOfQuantity ▾
Earrings	18
Necklaces	39
Rings	33
Watches	25

Record: ◄ ◄ 1 of 4 ► ►► ☒ No Filter

8 Click the **Microsoft Office** button and then click **Save As.**

9 Type **Product Query 12** as the name of the new query and then click **OK.**

10 Close the query.

"That was fairly easy," Meagan says. "Let's let Nathan see if he can create the count query."

To create a query to count the number of products by category:

1 Click **Query Design** from the Other group on the Create tab of the Ribbon.

2 Double-click **Category Table** and **Product Table** from the list of tables in the Tables tab of the Show Table window; then click the **Close** button.

3 Resize the window so that all fields are visible.

4 Double-click the **Category Name** and the **Quantity** fields to add them to the query.

5 Click **Totals** from the Show/Hide group of the Design tab on the Ribbon.

6 Click **Count** from the drop-down list in the Total row of the Quantify field and then click **Group By** from the drop-down list in the Total row of the CategoryName field, as shown in Figure 10.26.

7 Click **Run** to generate a count of all products by category, as shown in Figure 10.27.

8 Click the **Microsoft Office** button and then click **Save As.**

9 Type **Product Query 13** as the name of the new query and then click **OK.**

10 Close the query.

Figure 10.26

Design View of Query to Count Products by Category

Figure 10.27

Results of a Query to Count Products by Category

Next Kyle will explain the process of using action queries to affect many records at one time.

Action Queries (Update, Parameter, and Delete)

An action query is a query that makes changes to many records in just one operation. There are three types of action queries that Kyle would like to explain: update, parameter, and delete. An *update query* makes global changes to a group of records in one or more tables. For example, you can raise costs or sales prices by 10 percent for all products, or you can raise salaries by 5 percent for the people within a certain job category. With an update query, you can change data in existing tables. A *parameter query* is a query that, when run, displays its own dialog box prompting you for information—such as criteria for retrieving records or a value you want to insert in a field. A *delete query* removes a group of records from one or more tables. With delete queries, you always delete entire records, not just selected fields within records.

Update Queries

Nathan would like to use an update query to increase the cost of all products by 5 percent. To do so he'll need to use an update query that includes the Product table and the field UnitPrice. You should always back up your database before you run an update query, because you cannot undo the results of an update query. Making a backup ensures that you can always reverse your changes.

To back up a database and then create an update query to increase the cost of all products by 5 percent:

1   Click the **Microsoft Office** button.

2   Place the mouse over the text **Manage** and then click **Back Up Database**

3   Accept the file name provided, which should be Ch 10-01_student_name_ today's date, with your name replacing student_name and with the current date (e.g., 2008-10-18).

4   Navigate the window to the location where you want to save your backup file, and then click **Save.**

5   Click **Query Design** from the Other group on the Create tab of the Ribbon.

6   Double-click **Product Table** from the list of tables in the Tables tab of the Show Table window; then click the **Close** button.

7   Resize the window so that all fields are visible.

8   Double-click the **Unit Price** to add it to the query.

9   Click **Update** from the Query Type group of the Design tab of the Ribbon.

10 Type **[UnitPrice]*1.05** in the Update To: row of the design grid, as shown in Figure 10.28.

11 Click **Run** and then click **Yes** to update 20 records.

12 Click the **Microsoft Office** button and then click **Save As.**

13 Type **Product Query 14** as the name of the new query and then click **OK.**

14 Close the query.

15 Double-click **Product Query 2** to see unit prices for all products with the word "diamond" in the Product Name, as shown in Figure 10.29.

16 Note that the unit prices have all been increased by 5 percent as compared with the previous time you ran this query. (See Figure 10.13 for comparison.)

17 Close the query.

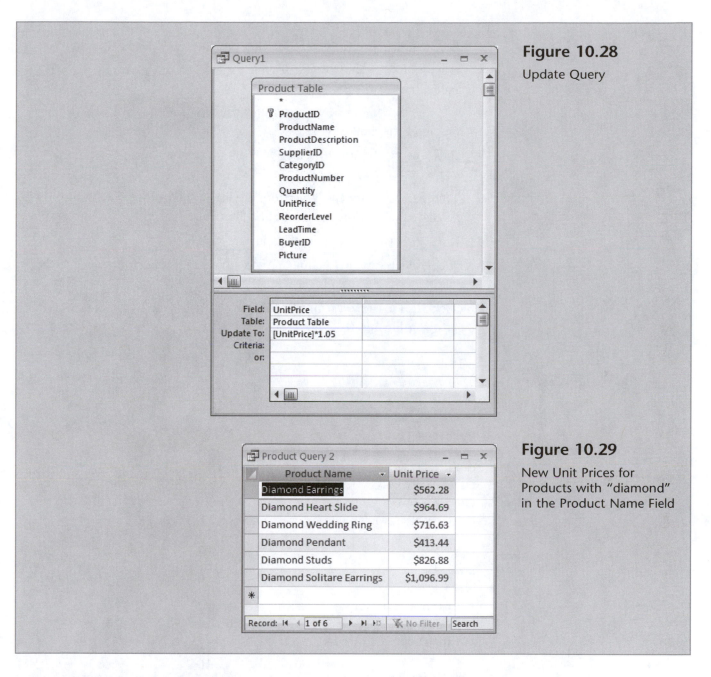

Figure 10.28
Update Query

Figure 10.29
New Unit Prices for Products with "diamond" in the Product Name Field

"Very slick and efficient!" says Meagan. "This software will be very helpful for us in maintaining our inventory. But do we always have to update all records, or can we limit an update to just a few records?"

"You can limit your update by setting criteria for the update, just as with a select query," Kyle answers. "Let's have you update all records that have a reorder level of 2 to reflect a new reorder level of 4."

To create an update query to update reorder levels:

1 Click the **Microsoft Office** button.

2 Place the mouse over the text **Manage** and then click **Back Up Database**

3 Accept the file name provided, which should be of the form Ch 10-01_ student_name_today's date.

4 Navigate the window to the location where you want to save your backup file, and then click **Save.**

5 Click **Query Design** from the Other group on the Create tab of the Ribbon.

6 Double-click **Product Table** from the list of tables in the Tables tab of the Show Table window; then click the **Close** button.

7 Resize the window so that all fields are visible.

8 Double-click **Product Name** and **Reorder Level** to add the fields to the query.

9 Click **Run** to view a listing of all products and their reorder level, as shown in Figure 10.30.

Figure 10.30

Products and Reorder Level

Query1		
Product Name	Reorder Level	
Flower Drop Earrings	5	
Seiko Kinetic Auto Relay Titanium	2	
Le Grand Sport	2	
G-Shock	2	
Engagement Ring	2	
Diamond Earrings	2	
Diamond Heart Slide	2	
Diamond Wedding Ring	2	
Swiss Army Watch	3	
Diamond Pendant	2	
Diamond Studs	2	
Pearl Necklace	3	
Diamond Solitare Earrings	2	
Tanzanite Ring	2	
Blue Topaz Ring	2	
Topaz Necklace	2	
Amethyst Pendant	2	
Seiko Kinetic Auto Relay	2	
Seiko Dive Watch	2	
Rolex Oyster Submariner	2	

Record: 1 of 20   No Filter   Search

10 Click the **Microsoft Office** button and then click **Save As.**

11 Type **Product Query 15** as the name of the new query and then click **OK.**

12 Close the query.

13 Click **Query Design** from the Other group on the Create tab of the Ribbon.

14 Double-click **Product Table** from the list of tables in the Tables tab of the Show Table window, and then click the **Close** button.

15 Resize the window so that all fields are visible.

16 Double-click the **ReorderLevel** to add it to the query.

17 Click **Update** from the Query Type group of the Design tab of the Ribbon.

18 Type **4** in the Update To: row and then type **=2** in the Criteria row of the design grid as shown in Figure 10.31.

Figure 10.31

Update Query to Change ReorderLevel

19 Click **Run** and then click **Yes** to update 17 records.

20 Click the **Microsoft Office** button and then click **Save As.**

21 Type **Product Query 16** as the name of the new query and then click **OK.**

22 Close the query.

23 Double-click **Product Query 15** to see the new reorder level for all affected products, as shown in Figure 10.32.

24 Compare Figure 10.32 with Figure 10.30 and note that all products that previously had a recorder level of 2 now have a reorder level of 4.

25 Close the query.

Figure 10.32

New Reorder Levels for All Products

Product Name	Reorder Level
Flower Drop Earrings	5
Seiko Kinetic Auto Relay Titanium	4
Le Grand Sport	4
G-Shock	4
Engagement Ring	4
Diamond Earrings	4
Diamond Heart Slide	4
Diamond Wedding Ring	4
Swiss Army Watch	3
Diamond Pendant	4
Diamond Studs	4
Pearl Necklace	3
Diamond Solitare Earrings	4
Tanzanite Ring	4
Blue Topaz Ring	4
Topaz Necklace	4
Amethyst Pendant	4
Seiko Kinetic Auto Relay	4
Seiko Dive Watch	4
Rolex Oyster Submariner	4

Product Query 15

Record: 1 of 20   No Filter   Search

Parameter Queries

Another type of action query is the parameter query, in which the query prompts the user with a dialog box asking for some criteria information to select records.

"When would I want to use this type of query?" Meagan asks.

"These queries," Kyle explains, "are used when you're not sure what criteria the user wants to specify for record selection. They provide flexibility in the query process and will be handy in the future when forms and reports are generated for users who aren't that familiar with Access."

"Let's create a parameter query to provide information on who is responsible for buying each product," suggests Nathan. "Can this query just give us information on one buyer?"

"Yes," responds Kyle. "I suggest you and Meagan create this query now."

To create a parameter query for buyers:

1 Click **Query Design** from the Other group on the Create tab of the Ribbon.

2 Double-click **Product Table** and **Buyers Table** from the list of tables in the Tables tab of the Show Table window, and then click the **Close** button.

3 Resize the window so that all fields are visible.

4 Double-click the **BuyerName**, **ProductName**, and **Quantity** fields to add them to the query.

5 Type **[Enter Buyer's Name]** in the Criteria: row of the Buyer Name field of the design grid, as shown in Figure 10.33.

Figure 10.33

Creating a Parameter Query

6 Click **Run**.

7 Type **Lopez** in the Enter Parameter Value dialog box presented, as shown in Figure 10.34.

Figure 10.34

Enter Parameter Value Dialog Box

8 Click **OK** to produce the results, as shown in Figure 10.35.

9 Click the **Microsoft Office** button and then click **Save As.**

10 Type **Product Query 17** as the name of the new query and then click **OK.**

Figure 10.35

Products and Quantity for Lopez

11 Close the query.

The last action query Kyle wants to demonstrate deletes specific records from your database.

Delete Queries

"Occasionally," Kyle explains, "you might want to delete some records from your database based on specific criteria. For example, you may want to delete all records in a table that have a quantity balance of zero."

"I'll bet you set the criteria to = 0, right?" asks Meagan.

"Well, almost," Kyle answers. "First you must create a specific delete query, include all the fields from the table, and specify the criteria that must be met for deletion of a record. But just as with the update queries you created previously, it always makes sense to back up your database before making massive changes."

"Let's give it a try," says Nathan.

To back up a database and then create a delete query to delete specific records:

1 Click the **Microsoft Office** button.

2 Place the mouse over the text **Manage** and then click **Back Up Database**

3 Accept the file name provided (of the form Ch 10-01_student_name_ today's date).

4 Navigate the window to the location where you want to save your backup file, and then click **Save.**

5 Double-click on **Product Table.**

6 Scroll down the table and note that ProductID 19 (Seiko Dive Watch) has a quantity of 0.

7 Close the Product Table.

8 Click **Query Design** from the Other group on the Create tab of the Ribbon.

9 Double-click **Product Table** from the list of tables in the Tables tab of the Show Table window; then click the **Close** button.

10 Resize the window so that all fields are visible.

11 Double-click * (asterisk) to add all fields in the product table to the query.

12 Double-click **Quantity.**

13 Click **Delete** from the Query Type group of the Design tab of the Ribbon. Note that "From" appears on the Delete: line of the design grid under the field Product Table.* and that "Where" appears on the Delete: line under Quantity.

14 Type **0** in the Criteria: row of the design grid under the column Quantity, as shown in Figure 10.36.

Figure 10.36

Creating a Delete Query

15 Click **Run** and then click **Yes** (in the dialog box presented) to delete one record from the Product table.

16 Click the **Microsoft Office** button and then click **Save As.**

17 Type **Product Query 18** as the name of the new query and then click **OK.**

18 Close the query.

19 Double-click **Product Table** and note that there are no more products with a quantity of 0. (Product ID 19 has been removed.)

20 Close the Product table.

Print a Query

All that is left is to print a query. Kyle explains that printing a query is similar to printing a table (as you did in the previous chapter), but he'll review the process anyway.

To print a query:

1 Double-click **Product Query 17** (as an example).

2 Type **Farley** as the Buyer's Name then click **OK.**

3 Click the **Microsoft Office** button and then click **Print.**

4 Click **OK** to print. The printed query should look like Figure 10.37.

Figure 10.37

Printed Product Query 17

Product Query 17

Buyer Name	Product Name	Quantity
Farley	Le Grand Sport	5
Farley	Engagement Ring	12
Farley	Diamond Wedding Ring	5
Farley	Swiss Army Watch	3
Farley	Blue Topaz Ring	7

End Note

In this chapter you have learned how to use select queries with characters, numbers, wildcards, comparison operators, and compound criteria. You've also performed calculations, computed statistics, created computed fields, and created parameter queries and action queries to update and delete records. In the next chapter you will learn how to create forms.

Chapter 10 Questions

1 Describe the difference between the Query Wizard and Design view methods of creating a query.

2 Describe the process for using criteria in a query using the Design view method.

3 How and why are wildcards used in a query?

4 Describe the process for adding to an existing query a field that exists in a table not currently included in the query.

5 What are the three key comparison operators used in a query?

6 What will compound criteria allow you to accomplish in Access?

7 Are the results of a calculation stored as a field in a table?

8 What is an action query? Give examples.

9 What is a parameter query?

10 When might you use a delete query?

Chapter 10 Assignments

1 Create additional select queries for Coast Jewelers using specific criteria (use the Ch10-02 file)

   a. Create and print a select query for Coast Jewelers that lists the buyer name, buyer phone number, and product name of product number ER-800. Save this query as Ch 10 Assignment 1a before you print it.

   b. Create and print a select query for Coast Jewelers that lists the category name, product name, product number, and lead times for all products with a lead time in excess of 20 days. Save this query as Ch 10 Assignment 1b before you print it.

2 Create additional select queries for Coast Jewelers using wildcards

   a. Create and print a select query for Coast Jewelers that lists the product name, quantity, supplier contact name, and supplier phone number for any product name that includes the text "ring". Save this query as Ch 10 Assignment 2a before you print it.

   b. Create and print a select query for Coast Jewelers that lists the supplier name, city, and phone number for any supplier located in the city of New York. Save this query as Ch 10 Assignment 2b before you print it.

3   Edit select queries for Coast Jewelers

   a.   Edit Query1 by adding the field PostalCode and deleting the field StateorProvince. Save this query as Ch 10 Assignment 3a before you print it.

   b.   Edit Query2 to include the field Category Name and to include only the category Rings, sorted by product name in ascending order. Save this query as Ch 10 Assignment 3b before you print it.

4   Create additional select queries for Coast Jewelers using comparison operators

   a.   Create and print a select query for Coast Jewelers that lists the product name, unit price, supplier name, and supplier contact name for any unit price between $300 and $600, sorted in descending order by unit price. Save this query as Ch 10 Assignment 4a before you print it.

   b.   Create and print a select query for Coast Jewelers that lists the product name, unit price, and category name for any unit price less than or equal to $200, sorted in ascending order by unit price. Save this query as Ch 10 Assignment 4b before you print it.

5   Create additional select queries for Coast Jewelers using computed fields

   a.   Create and print a select query for Coast Jewelers that lists the product name and sales price for all watches, sorted in ascending order by sales price. (*Hint:* You'll need to create a computed field titled Sales Price whose formula is the product's unit price times 1 plus the sales markup; format the computed field to Currency and include the Category table and the Product table in the query.) Save this query as Ch 10 Assignment 5a before you print it.

   b.   Open the query just created; then modify and print a select query for Coast Jewelers that lists the product name, sales price, quantity, and sales value for all rings. (*Hint:* You'll need to create another computed field, Sales Value, whose formula is the previously computed sales price times quantity; change the criteria from watches to rings and format the computed field to Currency.) Sort the query by sales price in descending order. Save this query as Ch 10 Assignment 5b before you print it.

6   Create additional select queries for Coast Jewelers using statistics

   a.   Create and print a select query for Coast Jewelers that calculates the total sales value of all watches in inventory. (*Hint:* You'll need to use your completed query from assignment 5b as the source for this query; format this computed field to Currency with two decimal places.) Save this query as Ch 10 Assignment 6a before you print it.

   b.   Create and print a query for Coast Jewelers that includes all products and lists category name, product name, sales price, and sales value. To do this, create two computed fields: Sales Price (unit price times 1 plus the sales markup) and SalesValue (sales price times quantity). Save this query as Ch 10 Assignment 6b before you print it.

c. Next create and print a query that sums the sales value of each category, using the query just created in assignment 6b as the source. Format this totaled value as Currency with two decimal places. Save this query as Ch 10 Assignment 6c before you print it.

7 Create action queries for Coast Jewelers (after backing up your file)

a. Create and run an action query for Coast Jewelers that increases the sales markup 5 percent for all categories. (*Hint:* You'll need to use an update query that adds .05 to the existing sales markup.) Save this query as Ch 10 Assignment 7a. Print the resulting category table.

b. Create a parameter query for Coast Jewelers that lists products purchased from a particular supplier. The query should ask "Enter supplier's name:" and list the supplier name, product name, quantity, and unit price. Save this query as Ch 10 Assignment 7b. Run and print the query entering Casio USA as the supplier.

c. Create and run a delete query for Coast Jewelers that deletes all products where Supplier ID = 1. Save this query as Ch 10 Assignment 7c. Create and print a query listing the supplier ID and product name for all products still in the database, in ascending order by supplier ID. Save this query as Ch 10 Assignment 7c 1.

Chapter 10 Case Problem 1:
KELLY'S BOUTIQUE

Note: You must have completed this case in the previous chapter in order to complete this case.

In the last chapter you added and modified some tables for Kelly's Boutique. She would now like you to create, run, and print some select, parameter, and action queries. Make the following changes for Kelly using the ch9-03_student_name file you created in Chapter 9. (*Note:* open your ch9-03_student_name file and then save it as ch10-03_student_name before making the indicated changes.)

Add a field Quantity (Data Type = Number) to the Book Table and then enter values as follows:

Book Title	Quantity
Angela's Ashes	18
Betsy - Tacy	4
Blueberries for Sal	5
Caddie Woodlawn	4
Deep End of the Ocean	2
Divine Secrets of the YaYa Sisterhood	3

Book Title	Quantity
Green Eggs and Ham	15
Harry Potter and the Chamber of Secrets	10
Harry Potter and the Prisoner of Azkaban	8
Harry Potter and the Sorcerer's Stone	6
Hop on Pop	8
The Cat in the Hat	4
The Notebook	3

Add a field Markup (Data Type = Number, Field Size = Decimal, Format = Percent, Scale = 2, Decimal Places = 0) to the Dept Table and then enter values as follows:

Dept	Markup
Adult	100%
Children	50%

a. Create and print a select query that lists the author and book title for all books written by Seuss. Save this query as Ch 10 Kelly Case a before you print it.

b. Create and print a select query that lists the book title and author for all books purchased and supervised by Barbara Manchester, sorted in ascending order by book title. Save this query as Ch 10 Kelly Case b before you print it.

c. Create and print a select query that lists the book title and list price for all book titles that start with Harry. Save this query as Ch 10 Kelly Case c before you print it.

d. Edit the query you just created. Add fields for author and for publisher and delete the list price field. Change the criteria from "starting with Harry" to "containing the word Secrets". (*Hint:* Place a wildcard character in front of and behind the word.) Save this query as Ch 10 Kelly Case d before you print it.

e. Create and print a select query that lists the book title and the publisher contact person and phone number for all books with a list price greater than $17. Save this query as Ch 10 Kelly Case e before you print it.

f. Create and print a select query that lists the ISBN, book title, and list price for all books with a list price greater than $20 or less than $10, sorted in ascending order by list price. Save this query as Ch 10 Kelly Case f before you print it.

g. Create and print a select query that lists the book title, list price, quantity, and retail value (a computed field equal to list price multiplied by quantity), sorted in descending order by retail value. Be sure to format the field as Currency. Save this query as Ch 10 Kelly Case g before you print it.

h. Create and print a select query that lists book title, list price, markup, unit cost, quantity, and cost. Unit cost is a computed field (list price divided by 1 plus markup). Cost is another computed field (unit cost times quantity). Be sure to format both computed fields as Currency and to sort the query alphabetically by book title. Save this query as Ch 10 Kelly Case h before you print it.

i. Create and print a select query that sums the total cost of the book inventory. (*Hint:* Use the query just created in part 1h as your source for this new query and use the currency format.) Save this query as Ch 10 Kelly Case i before you print it.

j. Modify the query created in part 1h so that it includes the Department field. Save the query as Ch 10 Kelly Case h 1, and then use that modified query as the source for a query that sums the cost of inventory by department. Save this latter query as Ch 10 Kelly Case j before you print it.

k. Create and run an action query that increases all books' list price by 5 percent. Be sure to back up your file first! Save this query as Ch 10 Kelly Case k. Create another query that lists the book title and list price for all books, sorted alphabetically by book title. Save this query as Ch 10 Kelly Case k 1 and then print it.

l. Create a parameter query that lists books from a particular publisher. The query should ask "Enter publisher's name:" and then list the publisher, book title, and quantity for that publisher. Save this query as Ch 10 Kelly Case l. Run and print the query after entering "Harper Collins" as the publisher.

m. Create and run a delete query that deletes all products with a quantity of 0. Save this query as Ch 10 Kelly Case m.

n. Create a query listing the book title and quantity for all the remaining books in inventory, sorted by quantity in descending order. Save this query as Ch 10 Kelly Case n and then print it.

Make sure you keep a copy of this file for use in the next chapter.

Chapter 10 Case Problem 2:
WINE DEPOT

Note: You must have completed this case in the previous chapter in order to complete this case.

In the last chapter you modified some tables for the Wine Depot. Now Barbara would like you to help her create some queries to extract some information from the database. Make the following changes for Barbara using the ch9-04_student_ name file you created in Chapter 9. (*Note:* Open your ch9-04_student_name file and then save it as ch10-04_student_name before making the indicated changes.)

a. Create a select query that lists the type, winery, and price for all wines on hand from winery #4. Save this query as Ch 10 Wine Depot Case a and then print it.

b. Create a select query that lists the type, winery name, and price for all wines whose buyer name is Michael Jackson. Save this query as Ch 10 Wine Depot Case b and then print it.

c. Create a select query that lists the SKU and type for wines types that contain the word "Blanc". Save this query as Ch 10 Wine Depot Case c and then print it.

d. Edit the query you just created in part 2c. Add fields for cost and vintage and remove the SKU field. Change the criteria of the query from "types that include the word Blanc" to "types that begin with the letter S". Save this query as Ch 10 Wine Depot Case d and then print it.

e. Create a select query that lists type, price, winery name, buyer name, and phone number for all wines with a price greater than $35. Save this query as Ch 10 Wine Depot Case e and then print it.

f. Create a select query that lists type, price, winery name, buyer name, and phone number for all wines with a price greater than $35 but less than $50. Save this query as Ch 10 Wine Depot Case f and then print it.

g. Create a select query that lists SKU, type, winery name, price, quantity, and retail value (a computed field: quantity times price, formatted as currency) for all Chardonnay wines, sorted in descending order by retail value. Save this query as Ch 10 Wine Depot Case g and then print it.

h. Create an update query that changes the price of all wines to be 150% of cost. (Remember to back up your file first.) Save this query as Ch 10 Wine Depot Case h.

i. Create a parameter query that lists SKU, type, winery name, price, and retail value. The query should ask "What type of wine?". Sort the query in descending order by price. Save this query as Ch 10 Wine Depot Case i. Run the query for Pinot Noir wines and then print it.

j. Create a select query that sums the total retail value of the Chardonnay wine inventory, formatted as currency. Be sure to list the wine type in your query. (*Hint:* Use the Ch 10 Wine Depot Case g query you created previously as the source for this new query.) Save this query as Ch 10 Wine Depot Case j and then print it.

k. Create a select query that lists SKU, type, winery name, cost, quantity, and total cost (a computed field: quantity times cost, formatted as currency) for all wines, sorted in ascending order by SKU. Save this query as Ch 10 Wine Depot Case k and then print it.

l.   Create a select query that sums the cost of wine inventory by type (in currency format), sorted by type. (*Hint:* Use the Ch 10 Wine Depot Case k query as the source for your new query.) Save the new query as Ch 10 Wine Depot Case l and then print it.

Make sure you keep a copy of this file for use in the next chapter.

Forms

Case: Coast Jewelers, Inc.

Nathan and Meagan are now ready to expand the use of forms in their rapidly expanding database. They recall that forms have a variety of purposes. Previously they created a form to capture additional information about their products. Now Kyle suggests they create a form with more features.

Kyle tells them that they can add functionality to forms with such features as calculated controls, check boxes, option buttons, list boxes, combo boxes, and subforms.

"Once again this sounds like more than we need!" Nathan exclaims.

"Don't panic," says Meagan. "Kyle seems to know just how much of this stuff we can take. Give him a chance."

Kyle thanks Meagan for her confidence and convinces them that, in the long run, using forms in their database will allow them to use their product database more efficiently and to improve the integrity of the data input.

Labels and Text Box controls

In this section you will become familiar with the steps necessary to modify a form's labels and text box controls. Forms are often created using the Forms Wizard, but once created they often need to be customized. Customization includes moving controls and labels and resizing the form itself.

Kyle suggests that you modify a form that was previously created using the Forms Wizard. This would yield a form more like the one Nathan used to keep on each supplier.

"That would be helpful," Nathan comments. "I feel more comfortable using an electronic version of a form I've already worked with on paper."

Kyle explains that the purpose of this exercise is to become familiar with the process for moving controls and labels around a form.

To modify the Suppliers form:

1 Start Access.

2 Click the **Microsoft Office** button and then click **Open.**

3 Navigate the Open window to the location of this text's student files. (The location would be the CD provided with text or from your computer lab's server.)

4 Double-click **ch11-01**, which should be located in a Ch 11 folder. (This is a modified version of the completed Coast Jewelers Inventory file from previous chapters.)

5 Click the **Microsoft Office** button and then place the mouse over the words **Save As.**

6 Click **Access 2007 Database** under the section Save the database in another format.

7 Navigate the Save As window to the location you wish to save this file and type **Ch11-01_student_name** in the File Name: text box (replacing student_name with your name).

8 Click **Save.**

9 Double-click **Supplier** to view the form shown in Figure 11.1.

Figure 11.1

Existing Supplier Form

10 Click **View** and then click **Design View.**

11 Click and hold in the lower right corner of the Supplier form to reveal the dragging tool, then move the window down and to the right to reveal the Form Footer. The process will expand the size of the Form Design view window so that you can manipulate all the objects on the form.

12 Click on the edge of the **Postal Code** control until the four-arrow icon appears; then move the control approximately two inches to the right, as shown in Figure 11.2. This process will move the control around the form.

Figure 11.2

Moving Controls around the Form

13 Click on the upper left corner of the **Postal Code** label and then move it up and to the right, as shown in Figure 11.3. This process is will separate the label from the control.

14 Click on the upper left corner of the **Postal Code** label again and then press the [**Delete**] key; this will delete the label from the window.

15 Remove the City, State or Province, and Country labels in the same way.

16 Click on the far right edge of the City control, and then drag the control to the left in order to reduce its width.

17 Resize controls and remove labels until your form looks like Figure 11.4.

Figure 11.3

Separating a Label from a Control

Figure 11.4

Modified Supplier Form

18 Click **View** to view the form in Form View. The form should look like Figure 11.5.

19 Click the **Microsoft Office** button and then click **Save As.**

20 Type **Supplier A** as the new form name and then click **OK.**

21 Close the form.

Figure 11.5

Form View of Modified Form

"Modifying a form's labels and controls was fairly intuitive," Meagan comments, "although it was a bit difficult to line up labels and controls so they were properly aligned."

Kyle agrees and now suggests that you and Nathan explore the use of form controls—such as list and combo boxes—to help simplify the data entry process and improve the integrity of information captured in your database. He will also show you how to specify locations of controls more precisely.

List Box and Combo Box Controls

The form you just modified included a series of text box controls containing information such as a supplier's name, address, and so on. These text boxes are referred to as a type of *form control*. You use text boxes on a form or report to display data from a record source. This type of text box is called a *bound* text box because it's bound to data in a field. In this case, for example, the text box control Supplier Name was bound to the field Supplier Name in the Supplier table. Text boxes can also be unbound. For example, you can create an unbound text box to display the results of a calculation or to accept input from a user. Data in an unbound text box isn't stored anywhere, but we will discuss unbound text boxes later.

Kyle explains that it's often quicker and easier to select a value from a list than to remember a value when using a form to enter new information, such as a new supplier. A list of choices also helps to ensure that the value entered in a field is correct. If you have enough room on your form to display the list at all times, you might want to use a list box. If you want to create a control that displays a list but requires less room then you would use a combo box, which provides the combined functionality of a list box and a text box.

"Which should we use, and when?" asks Meagan.

"Well, let's try something simple first, like modifying an existing text box control in our supplier form to a list box," answers Kyle.

List Box Control

Kyle explains that modifying a control on a form simply requires changing the form control (from text to list) and creating the list of choices.

"Let's modify the Country text box control on our previously created supplier form to a list box control," suggests Kyle. "We will also add a new supplier from the United Kingdom."

To change the Country text box control to a list box control and add a new supplier:

1 Double-click **Supplier A.**

2 Click **View** and then click **Design View.**

3 Right-click the **Country** text box control; then click **Change To** and click **List Box,** as shown in Figure 11.6.

Figure 11.6

Shortcut Menu to Transform a Text Box Control to a List Box Control

4 Right-click the **Country** list box control; then click **Properties.**

5 In the Property Sheet for List Box: Country, click the **Data** tab, click **Value List** in the Row Source Type section, and then type **USA; CAN; UK** in the Row Source (see Figure 11.7).

6 Close the Property Sheet window. The form should now look like Figure 11.8.

Figure 11.7

Modifying the Row Source Properties of the Country Control

Property Sheet	▼ ×
Selection type: List Box	
Country	⌄

Format	**Data**	Event	Other	All

Control Source	Country
Row Source	USA;CAN;UK
Row Source Type	Value List
Bound Column	1
Allow Value List Edits	No
List Items Edit Form	
Inherit Value List	No
Show Only Row Source Value	No
Default Value	
Validation Rule	
Validation Text	
Enabled	Yes
Locked	No
Smart Tags	

Figure 11.8

Modified Form with List Box Control for Country

7 Click **View** and then click **Form View.**

8 Enter a new supplier by clicking on the **New (blank) record** button located at the bottom of the form and then typing the information provided in Figure 11.9. Observe that, in order to specify the country for this new supplier, all you had to do was click **UK.**

9 Click the **Microsoft Office** button and then click **Save As.**

10 Type **Supplier B** as the name of the new form and then click **OK.**

11 Close the form.

Figure 11.9

New Record

You have now modified an existing form to include a list box control. Now Kyle suggests you look at the combo box control as an alternative.

Combo box Control

Once again, a combo box control is a control that is used on a form and provides the combined functionality of a list box and a text box. In this situation, someone entering a new supplier using the Supplier form can either type new information into a combo box control (like a text box control) or select from an existing list of information (like a list box control) without taking up much space.

Kyle suggests you try out a combo box control by changing the State text box control to a combo box control that lists the four most common states in which your suppliers reside. He also suggests that you try this combo box control out by entering a new supplier.

To change the State text box control to a combo box control and then add a new supplier:

1 Double-click **Supplier B.**

2 Click **View** and then click **Design View.**

3 Right-click the **State Or Province** text box control; then click **Change To** and click **Combo Box.**

4 Increase the size of the StateOrProvince combo box control slightly.

5 Right-click the **State Or Province** combo box control and then click **Properties.**

6 Click the **Data** tab.

7 Click **Value List** from the Row Source Type drop-down list.

8 Type **CA;NY;MA;NJ** in the Row Source section. The Properties Sheet should look like Figure 11.10.

Figure 11.10

Property Sheet for the State Combo Box Control

Property Sheet	▼ ×
Selection type: Combo Box	
StateOrProvince	⌄

Format	Data	Event	Other	All

Control Source	StateOrProvince
Row Source	CA;NY;MA;NJ
Row Source Type	Value List
Bound Column	1
Limit To List	No
Allow Value List Edits	No
List Items Edit Form	
Inherit Value List	No
Show Only Row Source Value	No
Input Mask	
Default Value	
Validation Rule	
Validation Text	
Enabled	Yes
Locked	No
Auto Expand	Yes
Smart Tags	

9 Close the Properties window.

10 Click **View** and then click **Form View.**

11 Enter a new supplier by clicking on the **New (blank) record** button located at the bottom of the form and then typing the information provided in Figure 11.11. Note that, to specify the state for this new supplier, all you had to do was click **NJ** from the combo box control.

Figure 11.11

Entering a New Supplier with a new State Combo Box Control

Supplier	_ □ ×

Supplier ID	8	Phone Number	(908) 555-4244
Supplier Name	Made to Order		
Contact Name	Sarah Hoffman	Fax Number	908-555-4243
Contact Title	Sales Representative	First Purchase	
Address	44 Main Street		
	Clinton	NJ ⌄ 08809	USA / CAN / UK

Record: 8 of 8 ▶ ▶I ▶✱ No Filter   Search

"When I tab through the form's fields, why do they skip from the city to the zip code and then back to the state?" Nathan asks.

"That is because of the order in which the fields were entered," Kyle explains. Let me show you how to change the tab order."

To change the tab order:

1 Click **View** and then click **Design View**.

2 Right-click anywhere in the Supplier B form and then click **Tab Order**.

3 Click the far left-hand side of the **State Or Province** control and move it up above the PostalCode control, as shown in Figure 11.12.

Figure 11.12

Changing the Tab Order

4 Click **OK** to save the changed tab order.

5 Click **View** and then click **Form View**.

6 Now enter a new supplier (who doesn't reside in one of the states listed in the combo box) as follows: Seawear, Dan Patrick, Consultant, 5405 Skalak Drive, Williamsburg, VA, 23188, USA, 757-555-1000, 757-555-5186. Observe that, after you entered the city, pressing [**Tab**] to move to the next control took you to the StateOrProvince control. Then you could simply type **VA** to specify the state for this new supplier.

7 Click the **Microsoft Office** button and then click **Save As**.

8 Type **Supplier C** as the form name, and then close the form.

You have now created a combo box control on a form to ease the creation of new supplier records, and you have found that it acts like both a text box and list box control. Now it is time to experiment with other features, such as calculated controls.

Calculated Controls

A calculated control uses an expression as its source of data. An *expression* is any combination of mathematical or logical operators, constants, functions, names of fields, controls, and properties that evaluate to a single value. For example, an expression can use data from a field in an underlying table, from a query of a form or report, or from another control on the form or report.

Bound controls obtain their data from fields in a table, whereas unbound controls don't have any particular data source other than an expression. Kyle explains that, in order to calculate the total cost invested in any particular product, Nathan would have to multiply the units on hand times the unit cost. He demonstrates that both the units on hand and the unit cost are already on the product form as bound controls Quantity and UnitPrice. However, creating a control on the form that calculates the total cost will require that Nathan create an unbound control (referred to in this case as a calculated control) to calculate the product of Quantity times Unit Price.

"Bound, unbound, I'm bound up just thinking about these," Meagan complains. "Do we really have to understand this to create a useful form?"

"Well," responds Kyle, "I think you'll find them useful in many forms you might create and they are really not that difficult. Here, let me show you."

To add a control to calculate the total cost in inventory of each item:

1 Double-click **Products.**

2 Click **View** and then click **Design View.**

3 Click the **Text Box** control from the Controls group on the Design tab of the Ribbon, as shown in Figure 11.13.

Figure 11.13

Form Design Tools on the Ribbon

4 Click and drag the new **Text Box** control from the Ribbon to a location under the Unit Price control, as shown in Figure 11.14.

5 Right-click the **Unit Price** control; then click the **Unit Price** label control and click **Properties.**

6 Click the **All** tab to view format properties for the Unit Price label control. A portion of the Format Properties window is shown in Figure 11.15.

Figure 11.14

Adding a New Text Box Control to the Products Form

Figure 11.15

A Portion of the Properties Window for the Unit Price Label Control

7   Note the width, height, and left properties. (Width defines how wide the label should be, height defines how tall the label should be and the left defines how far from the margin the label should be.)

8   Click the newly created text box control and then click the newly created text box label control; note how the Property Sheet now reflects properties for the new text box label control.

9   Click the **All** tab.

10   Type **Total** as the name property of the new text box label.

11   Type **Total** as the caption property of the Total text box label.

12   Type **0.83333** as the width property.

13   Type **1.875** as the height property.

14   Type **2.5417** as the top property.

15   Type **0.0417** as the left property. Your Properties window should look like Figure 11.16.

Figure 11.16

A Portion of the Properties Window of the Total Text Box

16 Click the **Unit Price** control. A portion of the Format Properties window for the unit price control is shown in Figure 11.17.

Figure 11.17

A Portion of the Properties Window for the Unit Price Control

17 Note the width, height, and left properties.

18 Click the **Unbound** text box control and observe that the Property Sheet now reflects properties for this text box control.

19 Type **Total Amount** in the Name box.

20 Type **=[Quantity]*[UnitPrice]** in the Control Source box.

21 Select **Currency** as the format property.

22 Type **0.75** as the width property.

23 Type **1.875** as the height property.

24 Type **2.5417** as the top property.

25 Type **0.875** as the left property. Your Properties window should now look like Figure 11.18.

26 Close the Properties window.

Figure 11.18

A Portion of the Properties
Window for the Total
Amount Text Box

| Property Sheet ▾ × |
| Selection type: Text Box |

Total Amount

| Format | Data | Event | Other | **All** |

Name	Total Amount
Control Source	=[Quantity]*[UnitPrice]
Format	Currency
Decimal Places	Auto
Visible	Yes
Text Format	Plain Text
Datasheet Caption	
Show Date Picker	For dates
Width	0.75"
Height	0.1875"
Top	2.5417"
Left	0.875"

27 Click **View** and then click **Form View.** Your new form should look like Figure 11.19.

Figure 11.19

New Product Form with
a Total Control

| Products | — ☐ X |

ID	1	Lead Time	10
Name	Flower Drop Earrings	Buyer ID	3
Description	These elegant earrings have a classy, refined look. The crystal stone top is attention-getting marcasite look,	Picture	
Supplier	4		
Category	4		
Number	136305		
Quantity	10	Reorder	5
Unit Price	$6.62		
Total	$66.20		

Record: ◄ ◄ 1 of 19 ► ►► ►* ☒ No Filter Search

Trouble? If you did not type the expression exactly as specified, then you may end up with the message "#Name?" in the text box where you expected to see the $66.20 cost. Reexamine the Control Source section of the Properties window for the total text box to verify that you've typed the expression correctly.

28 Click the **Microsoft Office** button, and then click **Save As.**

29 Type **Products A** as the new form name and then click **OK.**

30 Close the form.

You've now seen the process for creating a calculated control. Both Nathan and Meagan seem more comfortable with the terms and processes and are anxious to know if there are any other useful controls available in Access.

Check Box Control

When implemented on a form, the check box control gives the user the choice of activating all, none, or some of the check boxes. In each case, a check box control returns a Yes value if checked and returns a No value if unchecked. This control, like other controls, can be bound or unbound. To create a bound check box control, you must be working in a form or report that is bound to a record source.

Kyle asks Meagan if there are any situations in which she thinks a control like this might be helpful on a form. She suggests that, in the Buyers table, it would be nice to know who specializes in what category of product. For instance, some buyers specialize in only one category, like rings, while others specialize in several categories.

"Would a check box control be appropriate here?" she asks.

"Yes," you respond. "But if you want to store this information for later use, doesn't it have to be a bound control? And if so, don't we have to create some new fields in the Buyers table?"

Kyle compliments you on your comprehension of this topic. He agrees that this is a situation where a bound control is appropriate, but he points out that the buyer table fields must first be created and set up in a data type called Yes/No.

To create additional fields in the Buyers table:

1 Right-click **Buyers Table** and then click **Design View**.

2 Add five new fields to the table and specify each as a Yes/No data type, as shown in Figure 11.20.

Field Name	Data Type
BuyerID	AutoNumber
BuyerName	Text
BuyerPhone	Text
Watches	Yes/No
Rings	Yes/No
Necklaces	Yes/No
Earrings	Yes/No
Bracelets	Yes/No

Figure 11.20

Modifying the Buyers Table

3 Close the Buyers Table. Click **Yes** to save changes.

Now that the Buyers table includes the field for data storage, you offer to modify the Buyers form to include check boxes for quick data entry.

"How do I create check boxes on the form?" you ask.

"All you'll need to do is add the fields you just created in the Buyers table to the Buyers form. Because they are of the data type Yes/No, they will automatically be added to the form as a check box control," Kyle responds.

To create a check box control bound to a field:

1 Right-click the **Buyers** form and then click **Design View**.

2 Click **Add Existing Fields** from the Tools group of the Design tab on the Ribbon.

3 Resize and move the Buyers form and Field list windows so that your screen looks like Figure 11.21.

Figure 11.21

Modifying the Buyers Form

4 Click and drag all five fields you just created, one at a time, to the Buyers form (see Figure 11.22).

5 Click **View** and then click **Form View**.

6 Update each record from the Buyers form to indicate in what category each buyer specializes. Buyer 1 specializes in watches, necklaces, and earrings. After updating Buyer ID 1, your Buyers form should look like Figure 11.23.

7 Continue your update. Buyer 3 specializes in necklaces and earrings. (*Note:* Buyer 2 was previously deleted.) Buyer 4 specializes in watches and rings. Buyer 5 specializes in watches only.

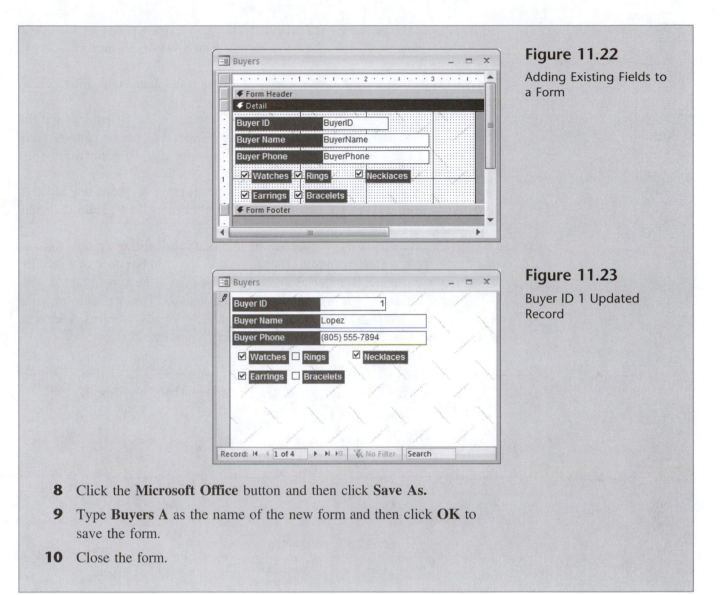

Figure 11.22

Adding Existing Fields to a Form

Figure 11.23

Buyer ID 1 Updated Record

8 Click the **Microsoft Office** button and then click **Save As.**

9 Type **Buyers A** as the name of the new form and then click **OK** to save the form.

10 Close the form.

"I like using these new controls," comments Meagan. "But I still have a question on the combo box controls we did before. Is there a way to give our database users a choice of options that change as our company grows?"

"There sure is," Kyle responds. "I'll introduce you to special combo box controls next."

Special Combo Box Control

An additional possible use of a combo box control would be to give the user a choice of options that change as a function of other changes that may occur in the database. For instance, let's say you want to give the user the option of selecting a specific supplier for each product but that you want the list to be dynamic, not static. In other words, you'd like the user's available choices to be limited to those suppliers currently in your Supplier table. Thus, when you add a supplier the list expands and, of course, when you delete a supplier the list contracts.

"That would be perfect for our product form," you suggest. "I can see using that form to add new products and then choosing from a list of existing suppliers to provide the product."

"How is that different from what we just did with the state and country combo boxes?" Meagan asks.

"In those situations," Kyle explains, "we provided a list of choices for the combo list. However, the user could type in a different state or country from those we listed. Plus, the list never changes unless we physically rewrite the list in the control.""So where do we create the list?" you ask.

"Actually, we just point the control to the Supplier table. As names are added to or removed from that table, the combo box control changes," says Kyle. "Nathan, let me show you how it is done."

Kyle explains that Nathan's goal will be to modify the existing Product form so that the Supplier text box control is transformed to a combo box control with a list containing the supplier ID numbers and names that exist in the Supplier table. This will require that the existing relationship between the Product table and the Supplier table be temporarily eliminated (since it currently enforces referential integrity) and that the data type of the SupplierID fields be changed.

To modify the Product table and change the Supplier ID field's data type:

1 Click **Relationships** from the Show/Hide group on the Database Tools tab of the Ribbon.

2 Resize the windows so that your screen looks like Figure 11.24.

Figure 11.24

Existing Relationships

3 Right-click the relationship between the Product table and the Supplier table; click **Delete** and then click **Yes** in the dialog box that appears in order to confirm your deletion.

4 Close the Relationships window and click **Yes** to save changes.

5 Right-click **Product Table** and then click **Design View.**

6 Click **Lookup Wizard** from the drop-down list of data types for the Supplier ID field, as shown in Figure 11.25.

Figure 11.25

Changing Data Type to Lookup Wizard

7 Click on the first option button (I want the lookup column to look up the values in a table or query) and then click **Next.**

8 Click **Table: Supplier Table** from the next Lookup Wizard dialog box; then click **Next.**

9 Double-click **Supplier ID** and **Supplier Name** in the list of Available Fields in order to move them to the list of Selected Fields, as shown in Figure 11.26.

10 Click **Next**; then click **Supplier Name** from the drop-down list in box 1 as the field to sort on.

11 Click **Ascending** as the sort order, and then click Next.

Figure 11.26

Identifying Fields to be
Included in the Lookup
Column

12 Uncheck the **Hide key column** check box and resize the column widths
to look like Figure 11.27.

Figure 11.27

Organizing Columns in
the Lookup Column

13 Click **Next.**

14 Click **Next** again to keep the Supplier ID as the field being stored.

15 Click **Finish** to keep Supplier ID as the label for your column.

16 Click **Yes** to save the table.

17 Close the modified Product table.

18 Once again, click **Relationships** from the Show/Hide group on the
Database Tools tab of the Ribbon.

19 Double-click the relationship between the Product table and the Supplier
table.

20 Click in the **Enforce Referential Integrity** check box and then click **OK.**

21 Close the Relationships window.

Kyle explains that now Nathan can modify the Products form to include the new and revised Supplier ID field as a combo box control. But first, he cautions, Nathan will have to remove the old Supplier ID text box control from the form.

To create a combo box control linked to the Supplier table:

1 Right-click **Products A** and then click **Design View.**

2 Click the existing **Supplier ID** text box control; then press the [**Delete**] key.

3 Click **Add Existing Fields** from the Tools group of the Design tab on the Ribbon.

4 Click and drag the **Supplier ID** field to the Products A form, as shown in Figure 11.28.

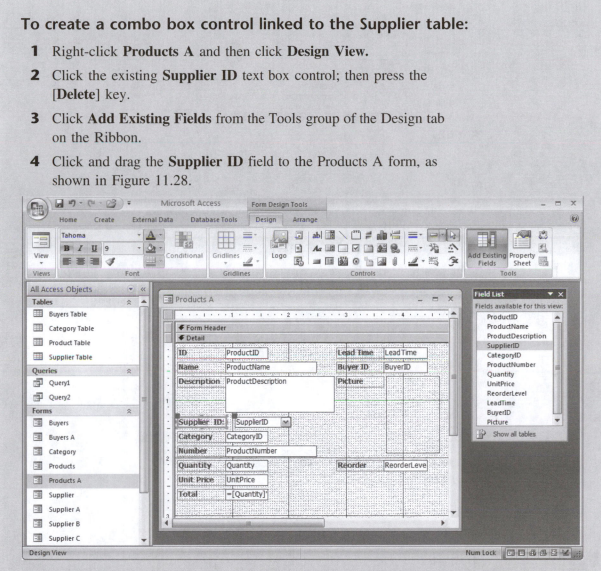

Figure 11.28

Adding the Newly Modified Supplier ID Field to the Products A Form

5 Close the Field List window.

6 Click **View** and then click **Form View.**

7 Note that the Supplier ID of record 1 in the Products A form is still specified at 4. Click on the drop-down list arrow of the Supplier ID combo box control to see the options available, as shown in Figure 11.29.

8 Click the **Microsoft Office** button and then click **Save As.**

Figure 11.29

Modified Product Form
with Lookup Capabilities
for Supplier ID

9 Type **Products B** as the name of the new form.

10 Go to record 7, the Diamond Heart Slide, and change the Supplier ID from 1 to 2 (Jewelry Inc.) as shown in Figure 11.30.

Figure 11.30

Modifying an Existing
Record

11 Now change the Supplier ID of the same record by typing 10 in the combo box control and then moving to the next record.

12 An alert dialog box should appear, indicating that this choice is not acceptable because a related record is required in the Supplier table. Since there is no supplier with an ID of 10, the system rejects your change. Click **OK.**

13 Change the Supplier ID of record 7 back to 2.

14 Close the form.

In addition to form controls, subforms are helpful in situations where a one-to-many relationship exists. Kyle suggests that understanding subforms may actually help resolve some of their previously expressed inventory tracking concerns.

Subforms

Subforms are simply forms within forms. Subforms require that information in one form have a one-to-many relationship with the information in another form. Kyle explains that users often like to see specific information on one form that has some common characteristic.

"For instance," says Kyle. "You have already established a relationship between the categories of your products and the products themselves, so we have a one-to-many relationship. One category, for example, includes many products."

"So we could create a form showing all the products we have that fall within any of our categories?" asks Meagan.

"That's it!" Kyle responds. "Let's have you create this form within a form using the Forms Wizard."

To create a form and subform of categories and products:

1 Click **More Forms** from the Forms group of the Create tab on the Ribbon.

2 Click **Forms Wizard**, as shown in Figure 11.31.

Figure 11.31

Starting the Forms Wizard

3 Select **Table: Category Table** from the list of Tables/Queries.

4 Click **Category Name** from the list of Available Fields; then click the > button to move Category Name from the list of Available Fields to the list of Selected Fields.

5 Select **Table: Product Table** from the list of Tables/Queries.

6 Click **Product Name** from the list of Available Fields and then click the > button.

7 Click **Quantity** from the list of Available Fields and then click the > button.

8 Double-click **Unit Price** from the list of Available Fields (note how this accomplishes the same task of moving the field from Available Fields to Selected Fields).

9 Click the **Next** button.

10 Click **by Category Table.**

11 Click the **Form with subform(s)** option button. Your window should look like Figure 11.32.

Figure 11.32

Creating Forms with Subforms

12 Click **Next.**

13 Click the **Data sheet** layout option button and then click **Next.**

14 Click the **Foundry** style option button and then click **Next.**

15 Type **Products by Category** as the form title and **Products Subform** as the subform title.

16 Click **Finish** to save the new forms. Your window should look like Figure 11.33.

17 Observe that not all products, quantities, or unit prices are visible. Click **View** and then **Design View.**

Figure 11.33

Newly Created Products by Category Form and Subform

18 Click the right-hand side of the form border, and drag to the right until the right side of the form is at the 7 mark (see Figure 11.34).

Figure 11.34

Increasing the Size of a Form

19 Click **View** and then **Layout View.**

20 Modify the width of each column by double-clicking between column titles until your window looks like Figure 11.35.

21 Click **View** and then **Form View.**

CategoryName	Watches		

Products

Product Name	Quantity	Unit Price
Seiko Kinetic Auto Relay Titanium	4	$468.56
Le Grand Sport	5	$303.19
G-Shock	10	$54.02
Swiss Army Watch	3	$192.94
Seiko Kinetic Auto Relay	1	$435.49
Rolex Oyster Submariner	2	$3,306.40
*	0	

Record: 14 ◄ 1 of 6 ► ►I ►⋈ No Filter Search

22 Navigate the newly created form by clicking on the category record navigator at the bottom of the form. The Watches category should look like Figure 11.36.

Products by Category ‑ ☐ ✕

Products by Category

CategoryName	Watches		

Products

Product Name	Quantity	Unit Price
Seiko Kinetic Auto Relay Titanium	4	$468.56
Le Grand Sport	5	$303.19
G-Shock	10	$54.02
Swiss Army Watch	3	$192.94
Seiko Kinetic Auto Relay	1	$435.49
Rolex Oyster Submariner	2	$3,306.40
*	0	

Record: 14 ◄ 1 of 6 ► ►I ►⋈ No Filter Search

Record: 14 ◄ 1 of 5 ► ►I ►⋈ No Filter Search

23 Click **Save** on the Quick Access toolbar.

24 Keep this form open for printing.

This newly created form and subform is ideal for viewing products by categories. Nathan is impressed.

Printing a Form

All that is left is to print a form. Kyle remarks that printing a form is much like printing a table or query, as you did in previous chapters. In this case he just needs you to print the first record (Watches).

To print a form:

1 With record 1 showing on the Products by Category form you just created; click the **Microsoft Office** button and then click **Print.**

2 Click the **Selected Record** option button and then click **OK.** The printed form should look like Figure 11.37.

Products by Category

CategoryName　　Watches

Products

Product Name	Quantity	Unit Price
Seiko Kinetic Auto Relay Titanium	4	$468.56
Le Grand Sport	5	$303.19
G-Shock	10	$54.02
Swiss Army Watch	3	$192.94
Seiko Kinetic Auto Relay	1	$435.49
Rolex Oyster Submariner	2	$3,306.40

Figure 11.37

Printed Products by Category Form for Watches

3 Close the Products by Category form.

Documenting a Form

Kyle suggests that you document all changes made to a form so that you can verify the underlying attributes that were changed in the course of creating or modifying the form. In particular, he suggests you examine and print the data properties that were changed when you converted a text box to a combo box for the StateOrProvince field in the supplier form.

To view and print the changes made in the State Or Province field in the supplier form:

1 Double-click **Supplier C.**

2 Click **Database Documenter** in the Analyze group of the Database Tools tab on the Ribbon.

3 Click the **Forms** tab in the Documenter window.

4 Click in the check box next to **Supplier C** (you may have to scroll down the window to find it).

5 Click **Options.**

6   Uncheck all check boxes listed under the **Include for Form** section title.

7   Click the **Names and Properties** option button under the Include for Sections and Controls section title. Your screen should look like Figure 11.38.

Figure 11.38

Selecting Print Form Definitions

8   Click the **Properties** button.

9   Deselect all Print Categories other than Data Properties, as shown in Figure 11.39.

Figure 11.39

Selecting Print Categories

10   Click **OK** in the Property Categories window.

11   Click **OK** in the Print Form Definition window.

12   Click **OK** in the Documenter window.

13   Click **Print** and then click **OK.** Page 2 of the printout should refer to the combo box control established for the StateOrProvince field, as shown in Figure 11.40.

14   Close the Print Preview window and then close the form.

Combo Box: StateOrProvince

AllowValueListEdits:	False	AutoExpand:	True
BoundColumn:	1	ControlSource:	StateOrProvince
Enabled:	True	InheritValueList:	False
LimitToList:	False	Locked:	False
RowSource:	CA;NY;MA;NJ	RowSourceType:	Value List
ShowOnlyRowSourceValues:	False		

Figure 11.40

Part of the Documenter for the Supplier C Form

End Note

In this chapter you have learned how to modify a form's labels and text box controls, how to use list box, combo box, calculated, and check box controls, how to create a form with a subform, and how to print document a form. Feeling fairly confident, you're ready to finish up with variations on report creation.

Chapter 11 Questions

1 What view of a form is used to edit an existing form?

2 What is the difference between bound and unbound controls?

3 Why are text box controls used on a form?

4 Why are list box controls used on a form?

5 Why are combo box controls used on a form?

6 Why are calculated controls used on a form?

7 Why are check box controls used on a form?

8 When is the Lookup Wizard used?

9 Why must an existing relationship be deleted before modifying a field's data type?

10 What type of relationship must exist if a subform is used on a form?

Chapter 11 Assignments

1 Using the Ch11-02 file, modify the Buyers form for Coast Jewelers so that it looks like Figure 11.41. Save this form as Ch 11 Assignment 1, and print record 1 using this form.

Figure 11.41

New Buyers Form

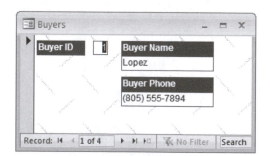

2 Modify the Category form by changing the sales markup text box control to a list box control that lists the choices as 100%, 125%, 150%, 175%, and 200%. Format the text box control to a percent format with decimal places = 0. Save the form as Ch 11 Assignment 2. Print the documenter page that documents the list box for SalesMarkup.

3 Modify the Category form by changing the sales markup text box control to a combo box control that lists choices of 100%, 125%, 150%, 175%, and 200%. Format the text box control to a percent format with decimal places = 0. Save the form as Ch 11 Assignment 3. Print the documenter page that documents the combo box for Sales Markup.

4 Modify the Products form by changing the BuyerID text box control to a combo box control, listing the choices of BuyerID and BuyerName from the Buyers table. (*Hint:* Be sure to first remove the relationship between the Product and Buyer tables and then, after you've created the combo box control, to reestablish the relationship and related referential integrity. Save the form as Ch 11 Assignment 4. Print the documenter page that documents the combo box for Buyer ID.

5 Salespeople earn a 7 percent commission on the price of each sale. Create a new unbound calculated control to compute the possible commission on each product. Modify the Products form by adding a calculated control called Commission. (The expression created should multiply the unit price by .07.) Format the control in a currency format. Save the form as Ch 11 Assignment 5. Print record 7 using this form.

6 Add a new field (Taxable) to the Products Table. Make the field a Yes/No data type. Add this new field to the Products form under the label Reorder. Make record 6 (Diamond Earrings) taxable. Save the form as Ch 11 Assignment 6. Print record 6 using this form.

7 For each buyer name, create a form (using the Forms Wizard) that contains the product name, quantity, and unit price of each product that the buyer is responsible for. Use the subform option with a datasheet layout and use Civic style. Save the form as Ch 11 Assignment 1f and the subform as Ch 11 Assignment 7 Subform. Format the subform so that columns fit in the form created. Print record 4 (Buyer = Szulczewski) using this form.

Chapter 11 Case Problem 1:
KELLY'S BOUTIQUE

Note: You must have completed this case in the previous chapter in order to complete this case.

In the last chapter you added and modified some queries for Kelly's Boutique. She would now like you to create some new forms. Make the following changes for Kelly using the ch10-03_student_name file you created in Chapter 10. (*Note:* Open your ch10-03_student_name file and then save it as ch11-03_student_name before making the indicated changes.)

a. Create a form to look like Figure 11.42. Save the form as Ch 11 Kelly Case a. Print record 3 (Hop on Pop).

b. Create a list box control using the form created in part a. This control should provide the user with a list of departments: Adult, Children. Move the picture control down to make room for the list box control. Save the modified form as Ch 11 Kelly Case b. Print record 7 (Green Eggs and Ham).

Figure 11.42

New Books Form

c. Create a combo box control using the form created in part a. This control should provide the user with a list of departments (as in part b) but with a combo box instead of a list box. Dept choices should be Adult, Children, and Teen. Save the modified form as Ch 11 Kelly Case c. Print the documenter page that documents the combo box for Dept.

d. Create a special combo box control using the Book Form. This control should provide the user with a dynamic list of publishers based on the publishers listed in the Publisher table. The combo box should list publisher number and name, and referential integrity must be enforced. Label the combo box column Publisher. Save the modified form as Ch 11 Kelly Case d. Print the documenter page that documents the combo box for Publisher.

e. Using the Book Form, create a calculated control to compute the total retail value of each book in stock. First add the quantity field to the form and then add the calculated control. Format the control in currency, and label the control Total Retail Value. Save the modified form as Ch 11 Kelly Case e. Print the record containing the book title "Harry Potter and the Prisoner of Azkaban."

f. Using the Book Form, create a check box control to indicate whether or not the text is a bestseller. Label the field and control Best Seller. Mark the book Green Eggs and Ham as a bestseller using your new form. Print the record that contains the book title "Green Eggs and Ham" and then save the modified form as Ch 11 Kelly Case f.

g. Create a form and subform that shows all books by publisher, listing ISBN and Book Title in datasheet layout and in Civic style. Then save the modified form and subform as Ch 11 Kelly Case g and Ch 10 Kelly

Case g Subform. Print the record with Arthur A. Levine Books as the publisher.

Make sure to keep a copy of this file for use in the next chapter.

Chapter 11 Case Problem 2:
WINE DEPOT

Note: You must have completed this case in the previous chapter in order to complete this case.

In the last chapter you modified some queries for the Wine Depot. Now Barbara would like you to help her create some new forms. Make the following changes for Barbara using the ch10-04_student_name file you created in Chapter 10. (*Note:* Open your ch10-04_student_name file and then save it as ch11-04_student_name before making the indicated changes.)

a. Change the Type field in the Wine Products table to a text type with a field size of 30. Use the Forms Wizard to create a new form from the Wine Products table and Winery Table that includes the following fields: SKU, Cost, Price, Quantity, Size, Vintage, Type, Picture, and Winery Name. Use a justified layout with Metro style and entitle the form Wine Products; then modify the form to look like Figure 11.43. Save this form as Ch 11 Wine Depot Case a. Navigate to SKU 14539 and print that selected record only. (*Hint:* Be sure to set the picture properties field to size mode "zoom" by right-clicking the picture object in the design view, selecting properties, and choosing zoom as the size mode.)

Figure 11.43

New Wine Products Form

b. Modify the form you created and saved in part a by changing the Type text box to a list box control that provides a list of all wine types: Cabernet Sauvignon, Chardonnay, Fume Blanc, Merlot, Pinot Noir, Sauvignon Blanc, Syrah, Red Chianti, and Zinfandel. Save the modified form as Ch 11 Wine Depot Case b. Print the record containing SKU 12895 only.

c. Modify the form you created in part b by replacing the Winery Name field with a Winery field (from the Winery Table). Then change the Winery text box to a combo box control that provides a drop-down list of all 21 wineries. Your new combo box should contain a value list that you create listing each winery by number. For example: 1,2,3 etc. Save the modified form as Ch 11 Wine Depot Case c. Print the documenter page that documents the combo box for Winery.

d. Modify the form you created in part c by deleting the Winery combo box control and replacing it with a Winery combo box control based on the winery and name fields in the Winery Table. The field should use the winery and name fields of the Winery Table and then list the winery name when requested. (Don't forget to modify the relationships window first and then to reestablish referential integrity!) Save the modified form as Ch 11 Wine Depot Case d. Print the documenter page that documents the new combo box for Winery.

e. Modify the form you created in part d by adding a check box control in the lower right-hand corner of the form to indicate if this product has been recommended by the *Wine Spectator* (a noted magazine of wine-tasting professionals). Label the field and control "Wine Spectator Recommended". (*Hint:* Don't forget to create a field in the Wine Products Table first.) Only three wines currently have that designation: SKU 11475, 13883, and 15347. Save the modified form as Ch 11 Wine Depot Case e, and print the record containing SKU 15347 only.

f. Modify the form you created in part e by adding a calculated control below the Winery Name to compute the total cost in inventory of each product (cost times quantity). Format the control in currency and label the control Total Cost. Save the modified form as Ch 11 Wine Depot Case f. Print the record containing SKU 11475 only.

g. Create a new form with a subform using the Winery Table and Wine Products Table. Use the Winery Name field from the Winery Table and the SKU and Type fields from the Wine Products table. View the data by winery in a datasheet layout and Metro style. Use the default names provided for the form and subform. Save the modified form as Ch 11 Wine Depot Case g. Print the record containing the Melville winery only.

Make sure you keep a copy of this file for use in the next chapter.

Reports

12

In this chapter you will learn:

- Use a query to create a report
- Use grouping and summarizing in a report
- Modify an existing report design
- Export a report to MS Word and/or Excel

Case: **Coast Jewelers, Inc.**

You, Nathan, and Meagan are feeling rather confident in using Access. So far you've created and modified tables, queries, and forms in your database, but you are anxious to see some results of your work in a more formal presentation.

"How are reports different from queries and forms?" Meagan asks.

"Remember that forms are used to view and update information in the database," Kyle answers. "Queries are your means of asking questions about the data, and reports are your means of expressing that information in a usable fashion."

He reminds you that, when exploring queries, you were able to use select, update, and delete queries to locate certain information and were also able to compute totals and statistics. However, those queries when printed were not formatted very well. Although they could be sorted, they didn't have the header, footer, grouping, or summarizing features of reports.

Kyle suggests that you start with using a query as your basis for a report and as a means to learn more about the available reporting features of Access.

Use a Query to Create a Report

To demonstrate the use of queries in a report, Kyle creates a simple select query that lists the category name, product name, quantity, unit price, and total retail value of all products in inventory with a unit price greater than $100. We can now create a report using this query. The first question he asks is what information from this query needs to be displayed in a report.

"Well, if you ask me," says Nathan, "I'd like to see a report of our products that cost more than $100 sorted alphabetically by product name. And I'd like to see each product's quantity, unit price, and total cost."

"Could we also add information to the report like the category name for each item?" Meagan asks.

"Sure," Kyle responds.

He then explains the process for creating such a report and offers to demonstrate it to you now.

To create a report using a query:

1   Start Access.

2   Click the **Microsoft Office** button and then click **Open.**

3   Navigate the Open window to the location of this text's student files. (The location would be the CD provided with the text or from your computer lab's server.)

4   Double-click **ch12-01**, which should be located in a Ch 12 folder. (This is a modified version of the completed Coast Jewelers Inventory file from previous chapters.)

5   Click the **Microsoft Office** button and then place the mouse over the words **Save As.**

6   Click **Access 2007 Database** under the section Save the database in another format.

7   Navigate the Save As window to the location where you wish to save this file and type **Ch12-01_student_name** in the File Name: text box (replacing student_name with your name).

8   Click **Save.**

9   Click **Report Wizard** in the Reports group of the Create tab on the Ribbon.

10   Select **Query: Product Query** from the Tables/Queries drop-down list.

11   Click **>>** to select all fields for inclusion into this report, as shown in Figure 12.1.

Figure 12.1

Existing Supplier Form

12   Click **Next.**

13   Click **<** to remove the automatic grouping (more on this later), as shown in Figure 12.2.

14   Click **Next** , then select **Product Name** from the drop-down list 1 when asked about sorting; this will sort your report by product name.

Figure 12.2

Using the Report Wizard

15 Click **Next**; then check the Adjust the field width check box so that all fields fit on a page.

16 Click **Tabular** under the Layout section and **Portrait** under the Orientation section; then click **Next.**

17 Click **Flow** as the report style and then click **Next.**

18 Type **Report 1** as the title of your report, click the **Modify the report's design** option button, and then click **Finish.** Your window should look like Figure 12.3.

Figure 12.3

Design View of Report 1

19 Resize the Total Value, Unit Price, and Product Name fields and titles as shown in Figure 12.4.

20 Click **View** and then click **Report View.** The top of your finished report, created from a query, should look like Figure 12.5.

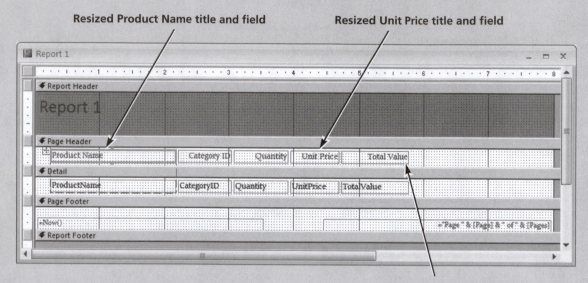

Resized Product Name title and field

Resized Unit Price title and field

Resized Total Value title and field

Figure 12.4

Modified Design View of Report 1

Product Name	Category ID	Quantity	Unit Price	Total Value
Amethyst Pendant	3	8	$214.99	$1,719.92
Blue Topaz Ring	2	7	$274.52	$1,921.64
Diamond Earrings	4	2	$562.28	$1,124.56
Diamond Heart Slide	3	4	$964.69	$3,858.76
Diamond Pendant	3	7	$413.44	$2,894.08
Diamond Solitare Earrings	4	3	$1,096.99	$3,290.97
Diamond Studs	4	3	$826.88	$2,480.64
Diamond Wedding Ring	2	5	$716.63	$3,583.15
Engagement Ring	2	12	$441.00	$5,292.00
Le Grand Sport	1	5	$303.19	$1,515.95
Pearl Necklace	3	15	$104.74	$1,571.10
Rolex Oyster Submariner	1	2	$3,306.40	$6,612.80
Ruby Pendant	3	10	$250.00	$2,500.00

Figure 12.5

Top Portion of Report 1

> **21** Close the report and click **Yes** to save changes.

Kyle further explains that it is best to create a report from a query that has all the information you need. Kyle suggests that you learn more about reports by working on grouping and summarizing information.

Use Grouping and Summarizing in a Report

Kyle explains that *grouping* arranges the records in your report. When you group records, each group that shares a common characteristic is displayed together. You can group based on one or several characteristics. Furthermore, Kyle explains that —once a report has groups assigned—those groups can be summarized in many ways, including subtotals, grand totals, average, and so on.

"Can I get a report that lists my inventory by category and also subtotals each group?" Nathan asks.

"Sure," says Kyle. "But I suggest we learn how to group first and then worry about summarizing later."

Grouping

"Let's create a report similar to the one we just created but grouped by category name," suggests Kyle.

To create a report using grouping:

1 Click **Report Wizard** in the Reports group of the Create tab on the Ribbon.

2 Select **Query: Product Query** from the Tables/Queries drop-down list.

3 Click **>>** to select all fields for inclusion in this report.

4 Click **Category ID** in the Selected Fields section, then click **<** to remove the Category ID field from the list.

5 Select **Table: Category Table** from the Tables/Queries drop-down list.

6 Double-click **Category Name** to add that field to the Selected Fields list.

7 Click **Next** and then double-click **by Category Table** to add a grouping level.

8 Click **Next** two times.

9 Select **Product Name** from the drop-down list 1 when asked about sorting; this will sort your report by product name.

10   Click **Next**; then check the Adjust the field width check box so that "All fields fit on a page."

11   Click **Stepped** under the Layout section and **Portrait** under the Orientation section; then click **Next**.

12   Click **Flow** as the report style and then click **Next**.

13   Type **Report 2** as the title of your report and then click **Finish**. Your window should look like Figure 12.6.

CategoryName	Product Name	Quantity	Unit Price	Total Value
Watches				
	Le Grand Sport	5	$303.19	$1,515.95
	Rolex Oyster Submariner	2	$3,306.40	$6,612.80
	Seiko Kinetic Auto Relay	1	$435.49	$435.49
	Seiko Kinetic Auto Relay Titaniu	4	$468.56	$1,874.24
	Swiss Army Watch	3	$192.94	$578.82
Rings				
	Blue Topaz Ring	7	$274.52	$1,921.64
	Diamond Wedding Ring	5	$716.63	$3,583.15
	Engagement Ring	12	$441.00	$5,292.00
	Tanzanite Ring	9	$490.62	$4,415.58
Necklaces				
	Amethyst Pendant	8	$214.99	$1,719.92
	Diamond Heart Slide	4	$964.69	$3,858.76
	Diamond Pendant	7	$413.44	$2,894.08
	Pearl Necklace	15	$104.74	$1,571.10
	Ruby Pendant	10	$250.00	$2,500.00
	Topaz Necklace	5	$413.44	$2,067.20
Earrings				

Figure 12.6

Partial View of Report 2

14   Close the report.

"Is it possible to group more than once?" Meagan asks.

"Yes," explains Kyle. "Access will let you group on any number of fields."

He suggests you create a report listing the product name and quantity by category and by supplier. In this way you can see what products are in each category as well as which suppliers provide them.

To create a report using multiple field grouping:

1 Click **Report Wizard** in the Reports group of the Create tab on the Ribbon.

2 Select **Table: Product Table** from the Tables/Queries drop-down list.

3 Double-click **Product Name** and **Quantity** from the list of available fields.

4 Select **Table: Category Table** from the Tables/Queries drop-down list.

5 Double-click **Category Name** from the list of available fields.

6 Select **Table: Supplier Table** from the Tables/Queries drop-down list.

7 Double-click **Supplier Name** from the list of available fields; then click **Next.**

8 Click **by Category Table** as your data view and then click **Next.**

9 Double-click **Supplier Name** to add a grouping level. Your window should look like Figure 12.7.

Figure 12.7

Multiple Grouping Levels

10 Click **Next** and the select **Product Name** from the drop-down list 1 when asked about sorting; this will sort your report by product name.

11   Click **Next**; then check the Adjust the field width check box so that "All fields fit on a page."

12   Click **Stepped** under the Layout section and **Portrait** under the Orientation section; then click **Next.**

13   Click **Flow** as the report style and then click **Next.**

14   Type **Report 3** as the title of your report and then click **Finish.** Your window should look like Figure 12.8.

Report 3

CategoryName	SupplierName	Product Name	Quantity
Watches			
	Casio USA		
		G-Shock	10
		Swiss Army Watch	3
	Rolex		
		Rolex Oyster Submariner	2
	Seiko USA		
		Le Grand Sport	5
		Seiko Kinetic Auto Relay	1
		Seiko Kinetic Auto Relay Titanium	4
Rings			
	Johnson Wholesale Jewelry Supply		
		Blue Topaz Ring	7
		Diamond Wedding Ring	5

|◄ ◄ 1   ► ►| ►| ❦ No Filter   ◄   ▐▐▐▐▐   ►

Figure 12.8

Partial View of Report 3

15   Close the report.

"I can imagine all sorts of reports I would like to generate in our business," says Meagan. "But you said we could summarize as well, right?"

"Correct," Kyle responds. "Let me introduce you to the summarizing process."

Summarizing

Kyle explains that Access will automatically provide summaries on numeric fields in your report if you use the Report Wizard and establish groups. He tells you that a group is a collection of records, along with any introductory and summary information displayed with the records, such as a header. A group consists of a group header, nested groups (if any), detail records, and a group footer. Grouping allows you to separate groups of records visually and to display introductory and summary data for each group. The available functions include summation, average, minimum, and maximum. Access will also calculate the percent of total for sums if you like.

"It's important to remember that Access won't let you sum text or other non-numeric fields, for obvious reasons," says Kyle. "So if you accidentally set up a field in a table that contains numeric values but identify the field as a data type other than number, you won't be able to use the summary features."

He suggests creating a product value by category report that sums the total value of products in each category.

To create a report using grouping and summary options using the Report Wizard:

1 Click **Report Wizard** in the Reports group of the Create tab on the Ribbon.

2 Select **Query: Product Query** from the Tables/Queries drop-down list.

3 Double-click **Product Name**, **Quantity**, **Unit Price**, and **Total Value** from the list of available fields.

4 Select **Table: Category Table** from the Tables/Queries drop-down list.

5 Double-click **Category Name** from the list of available fields; then click **Next.**

6 Double-click **by Category Table** as your data view, and then click **Next** two times.

7 Click **Product Name** from the drop-down list 1 when asked about sorting; this will sort your report by product name.

8 Click the **Summary Options** button in the Report Wizard box.

9 Click **Sum** on the TotalValue row to direct Access to add the total value of each product by group.

10 Click **OK** in the Summary Options window,

11 Click **Next**; then check the Adjust the field width check box so that "All fields fit on a page."

12 Click **Stepped** under the Layout section and **Portrait** under the Orientation section; then click **Next.**

13 Click **Flow** as the report style and then click **Next.**

14 Type **Report 4** as the title of your report and then click **Finish.** Your window should look like Figure 12.9.

Figure 12.9

Partial View of Report 4

15 Close Print Preview but leave the Report window open.

Kyle further explains the nature of the report just generated. In addition to the total provided for each category, the report created a grand total value of all products (see Figure 12.8). However, the description of the summary amount is a bit odd, and the value amounts are shown as ###.

"To help you understand how this summary was created, I think it's best to show you the Report Design view of this report," Kyle suggests. "Let's open up the report, take a look, fix these problems, and print the report."

To examine the sum functions created in the previous report and then print the report:

1 Click **View** and then **Design View** to view the design view of Report 4, as shown in Figure 12.10.

Sum label control in the CategoryID footer   Sum control in the CategoryID footer

Figure 12.10

Design View of Report 4

2 Note the Sum label control and the =Sum([TotalValue]) formula in a text box control, both located in the Category ID footer.

3 Also note the Grand Total label control and the =Sum ([TotalValue]) formula in a text box control, both located in the Report footer.

4 Click the left side of both Sum controls and drag to the left to increase their size, as shown in Figure 12.11.

5 Right-click the **=Sum([TotalValue])** control in the Category ID footer; then click **Properties** to reveal the Property Sheet window.

6 Click the **All** tab to view the Property Sheet window, as shown in Figure 12.12.

7 Observe that the formula in the Control Source section of the Properties window contains the formula to sum the TotalValue field of the report.

8 Close the Properties window.

9 Click **View** and then click **Report View.**

Click and drag the Sum control in the
CategoryID footer to make it larger

Figure 12.11

Increasing the Size of a Report Control

Figure 12.12

Partial View of the Properties Window of the Sum ([TotalValue]) Control

Control Source Formula

Property Sheet

Selection type: Text Box

Sum Of TotalValue

| Format | Data | Event | Other | **All** |

Name	Sum Of TotalValue
Control Source	=Sum([TotalValue])
Format	
Decimal Places	Auto
Visible	Yes
Text Format	Plain Text
Datasheet Caption	
Width	1.4583"
Height	0.1875"
Top	0.1875"
Left	6.5"

10 Click the **Microsoft Office** button, click **Print**, and then click **OK** to print the report. It should look like Figure 12.13.

11 Close the Report window. Click **Yes** to save the changes.

Report 4

CategoryName	Product Name	Quantity	Unit Price	Total Value
Watches				
	Le Grand Sport	5	$303.19	$1,515.95
	Rolex Oyster Submariner	2	$3,306.40	$6,612.80
	Seiko Kinetic Auto Relay	1	$435.49	$435.49
	Seiko Kinetic Auto Relay Titanium	4	$468.56	$1,874.24
	Swiss Army Watch	3	$192.94	$578.82
Summary for 'CategoryID' = 1 (5 detail records)				
Sum				11017.3
Rings				
	Blue Topaz Ring	7	$274.52	$1,921.64
	Diamond Wedding Ring	5	$716.63	$3,583.15
	Engagement Ring	12	$441.00	$5,292.00
	Tanzanite Ring	9	$490.62	$4,415.58
Summary for 'CategoryID' = 2 (4 detail records)				
Sum				15212.37
Necklaces				
	Amethyst Pendant	8	$214.99	$1,719.92
	Diamond Heart Slide	4	$964.69	$3,858.76
	Diamond Pendant	7	$413.44	$2,894.08
	Pearl Necklace	15	$104.74	$1,571.10
	Ruby Pendant	10	$250.00	$2,500.00
	Topaz Necklace	5	$413.44	$2,067.20
Summary for 'CategoryID' = 3 (6 detail records)				
Sum				14611.06
Earrings				
	Diamond Earrings	2	$562.28	$1,124.56
	Diamond Solitare Earrings	3	$1,096.99	$3,290.97
	Diamond Studs	3	$826.88	$2,480.64
Summary for 'CategoryID' = 4 (3 detail records)				
Sum				6896.17
Grand Total				47736.9

Figure 12.13

Printed Report 4

"Placement of these controls determines what gets summed," Kyle explains. "The first control, placed in the CategoryID footer, sums the total value for each category, while the second control, placed in the report footer, sums the total value for the whole report."

"Why is Total Value in brackets?" asks Meagan, "and why are the sum amounts and totals without commas, dollar signs or full decimals?"

"The brackets indicate that a field name is being used in a formula," explains Kyle. "The Sum function will sum all the fields named Total Value located within the CategoryID detail section. The formatting of the controls is something we can take care of next."

Kyle now advises you to learn more about reports by modifying an existing report.

Modify an Existing Report

Not all reports you create with the Report Wizard will look the way you want or present the information you need. It is therefore important that you be able to modify an existing report. Kyle has explained how placement of controls in the various sections of a report dictate the information displayed. He suggests that you learn about each report section by creating controls to count and sum and then modifying those control's properties.

Counting and Summing in Report Sections

Kyle explains that all reports have a detail section, but a report can also include a report header, a page header, a group header, group footer, page footer, and a report footer section. Each section has a specific purpose and prints in a predictable order in the report.

In Design view, sections are represented as bands, and each section that the report contains is represented once. In a printed report, some sections might be repeated many times. You determine where information appears in every section by placing controls such as labels and text boxes.

The *Report header* appears once at the beginning of a report. You can use it for items such as a logo, report title, or print date. The Report header is printed before the Page header on the first page of the report. The *Page header* appears at the top of every page in the report; you use it to display items such as column headings. The *Detail section* contains the main body of a report's data. This section is repeated for each record in the report's underlying record source. The *Page footer* appears at the bottom of every page in the report; you use it to display items such as page numbers. The *Report footer* appears once at the end of the report. You use it to display items such as report totals. The Report footer is the last section in the report design but appears before the Page footer on the last page of the printed report.

Kyle explains that the CategoryID footer generated by the Report Wizard created a text box control for this report that specified not only which CategoryID was being totaled but also how many detail records were in each category section. This was accomplished by using the field name in the control and using the Count function to add up the number of detail records in each category section. The CategoryID Header describes the field information being grouped below it. In this case you chose to group information by CategoryID. Alternatively, you could have chosen to group the product information by buyer name or supplier name for example.

The formula used in the text box control was ="Summary for " & " 'Category ID' = " & " " & [CategoryID] & " (" & Count(*) & " " & IIf(Count(*)=1,"detail record","detail records") & ")" In the report, this text box control printed the following result for the first category: "Summary for 'CategoryID' = 1 (5 detail records)". The most important part of the formula is the function Count. To count records in a section, the formula Count (*) is used. The & symbol is used to separate text from fields, and the IIf function changes the final text to read either record or records, depending on whether one or more records were counted.

The CategoryID footer also included a text box control to sum the total value for each category (note that the Report footer included the identical text box control). The placement of the control in the CategoryID footer caused the control to calculate the total value for each category, while the control placed in the Report footer caused that control to calculate the total value for the entire report.

"Why don't you use the report you just created to experiment on modifying report sections by adding a control to sum the quantity of each category and adding a control to count all detail records in the entire report?" Kyle suggests.

To modify report sections to sum and count:

1 Right-click **Report 4** and then click **Design View**.

2 Right-click the **Sum** control in the CategoryID footer, click **Properties**, and change the format to currency (see Figure 12.14).

Figure 12.14

Formatting the Sum Control

Property Sheet	▼ ✕
Selection type: Text Box	
Sum Of TotalValue	⌄

Format	Data	Event	Other	**All**

Name	Sum Of TotalValue
Control Source	=Sum([TotalValue])
Format	Currency
Decimal Places	Auto
Visible	Yes
Text Format	Plain Text
Datasheet Caption	
Width	1.4583"
Height	0.1875"
Top	0.1875"
Left	6.5"

Select currency from this drop-down list

3 With the Property Sheet still open, click the Sum control in the Report footer and change the format of this control to currency as well.

4 Close the Property Sheet window.

5 Select the **Textbox** button in the Controls group of the Design tab of the Ribbon.

6 Click and drag your mouse in the Category ID footer to create a new text box control, as shown in Figure 12.15.

7 Click inside the new text box control (labeled Unbound) and type **=Sum([Quantity]).**

8 Delete the new text box control label by clicking in the upper left corner of the label, and then press the [**Delete**] key.

9 Move and resize the newly created text box to line up with Quantity in the detail section.

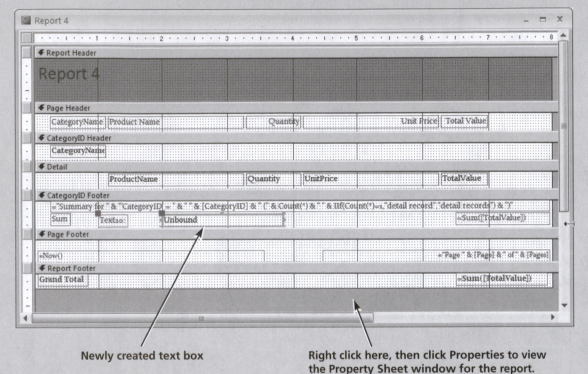

Newly created text box

Right click here, then click Properties to view the Property Sheet window for the report.

Figure 12.15

Creating a New Control in a Report

10 Click the top of the **Grand Total** label control in the Report footer to see a move cursor; then, holding the mouse button down, move the label to the right and place it next to the Grand Total amount.

11 Type **Report 5** in the Report header, replacing the old title Report 4.

12 Click the **Microsoft Office** button, click **Save As**, type **Report 5** as the new report title, and then click **OK** .

13 Right-click in the light blue section of the Design view under the Report footer and click **Properties** to display the Property Sheet.

14 Type **Report 5** as the caption, replacing the text Report 4.

15 Select the **Textbox** button in the Controls group of the Design tab of the Ribbon.

16 Click and drag your mouse in the Report footer to create a new text box control.

17 Click inside the new text box control (labeled Unbound) and type **=Count(*)**.

18 Type **Total detail records** in the new text box control label.

19 Move and resize the newly created text box to line up with records count in the detail section.

20 Click **View** and then click **Layout View.** (This allow you to see the report in a view with the data provided and often makes it easier to align fields and labels.)

21 Click **View** and then **Report View.** Your screen should look like Figure 12.16.

Figure 12.16

Bottom Half of Report 5 in Report View

22 Close the report, saving your changes.

Having added controls to Count records and Sum different values, it is now time to modify various properties of those controls like borders, lines, fonts, and so forth.

Lines, Borders, and Formatting in Report Sections

Access allows you to modify reports by adding lines and modifying properties of existing controls like the font name, size, and weight. Kyle suggests that you and Nathan look over the report you just modified and determine what changes you think would add to its look and usefulness.

"I think it would be nice to better separate each category section with a line," Nathan comments, "and get rid of that border around the grand total."

"I agree," you respond. "We should also have a line above each total for the sum of watches, earrings, et cetera. Plus I would like to change the font style of the controls in the Report footer to Times New Roman, size 10, bold, and italicized."

"How about making the total cost of each category look like currency?" Meagan suggests.

"Go for it!" Kyle exclaims.

To add lines, modify borders, and change formatting:

1 Right-click **Report 5** and then click Design View.

2 Type **Report 6** in the Report header, replacing the old title Report 5.

3 Click the **Microsoft Office** button, click **Save As**, type **Report 6** as the new report title, and then click **OK** .

4 Right-click in the grayed-out section of the Design view under the Report footer and click **Properties** to display the Property Sheet.

5 Type **Report 6** as the caption, replacing the text Report 5; then close the Property Sheet.

6 Click the **Line** tool located in the Controls group of the Design tab of the Ribbon.

7 Click the **Line Type** tool (also located in the Controls group of the Design tab) and then select **Solid.**

Line added here

Report 6				
CategoryName	Product Name	Quantity	Unit Price	Total Value
Watches				
	Le Grand Sport	5	$303.19	$1,515.95
	Rolex Oyster Submariner	2	$3,306.40	$6,612.80
	Seiko Kinetic Auto Relay	1	$435.49	$435.49
	Seiko Kinetic Auto Relay Titanium	4	$468.56	$1,874.24
	Swiss Army Watch	3	$192.94	$578.82
Summary for 'CategoryID' = 1 (5 detail records)				
Sum		15		$11,017.30
Rings				
	Blue Topaz Ring	7	$274.52	$1,921.64
	Diamond Wedding Ring	5	$716.63	$3,583.15
	Engagement Ring	12	$441.00	$5,292.00
	Tanzanite Ring	9	$490.62	$4,415.58
Summary for 'CategoryID' = 2 (4 detail records)				
Sum		33		$15,212.37
Necklaces				
	Amethyst Pendant	8	$214.99	$1,719.92
	Diamond Heart Slide	4	$964.69	$3,858.76

Line added here

Figure 12.17

Adding Lines to Report 6

8 Click the **Line Thickness** tool (also located in the Controls group) and then select **1 pt.**

9 Click the **Line Color** tool (also located in the Controls group) and then select a black square.

10 Click and drag the mouse cursor from just under the label Sum in the Category ID footer to just under the lower right corner of the =Sum ([Total]) text box. A line should appear.

11 Click the **Line** tool again.

12 Add a short line just above the =Sum([Quantity]) control in the Category ID footer. A line should appear.

13 Click **View** and then **Layout View.** Your screen should look like Figure 12.17.

14 Type **Products by Category** (in place of Report 6) in the Report header.

Products by Category

CategoryName	Product Name	Quantity	Unit Price	Total Value
Watches				
	Le Grand Sport	5	$303.19	$1,515.95
	Rolex Oyster Submariner	2	$3,306.40	$6,612.80
	Seiko Kinetic Auto Relay	1	$435.49	$435.49
	Seiko Kinetic Auto Relay Titanium	4	$468.56	$1,874.24
	Swiss Army Watch	3	$192.94	$578.82
Summary for 'CategoryID' = 1 (5 detail records)				
Sum		15		$11,017.30
Rings				
	Blue Topaz Ring	7	$274.52	$1,921.64
	Diamond Wedding Ring	5	$716.63	$3,583.15
	Engagement Ring	12	$441.00	$5,292.00
	Tanzanite Ring	9	$490.62	$4,415.58
Summary for 'CategoryID' = 2 (4 detail records)				
Sum		33		$15,212.37
Necklaces				
	Amethyst Pendant	8	$214.99	$1,719.92
	Diamond Heart Slide	4	$964.69	$3,858.76
	Diamond Pendant	7	$413.44	$2,894.08
	Pearl Necklace	15	$104.74	$1,571.10
	Ruby Pendant	10	$250.00	$2,500.00
	Topaz Necklace	5	$413.44	$2,067.20
Summary for 'CategoryID' = 3 (6 detail records)				
Sum		49		$14,611.06
Earrings				
	Diamond Earrings	2	$562.28	$1,124.56
	Diamond Solitare Earrings	3	$1,096.99	$3,290.97
	Diamond Studs	3	$826.88	$2,480.64
Summary for 'CategoryID' = 4 (3 detail records)				
Sum		8		$6,896.17
Total detail records:	18		Grand Total	$47,736.90

Figure 12.18

Printed Products by Category Report

15 Click **Save** in the Quick Access toolbar to save changes to Report 6.

16 Click the **Microsoft Office** button and the click **Print.**

17 Click **OK** in the Print window to print your report. The printed report should look like Figure 12.18.

18 Close the report window.

"Wow, that was a lot of work," Meagan complains. "Why can't the Report Wizard do all this for us in the first place?"

"Good question," Kyle answers. "Reports have so many variations that the Report Wizard can only begin to create reports. The rest is up to us!"

End Note

In this chapter you have learned how to use a query to create a report, how to use grouping and summarizing to enhance a report's usefulness, and how to modify a previously generated report so that it will be more useful. Now you are ready to take on the world and create your own solutions to database organization and reporting problems.

Chapter 12 Questions

1 Why create a report from a query? Why not just print your query results?

2 Can you always add a field from any table to a report based on a query?

3 When creating a report, what does grouping accomplish?

4 When creating a report, what does the process of summarizing accomplish?

5 Is it possible to group more than one item?

6 What do the [ ] (brackets) signify in an Access formula?

7 How do you determine where information appears in a report?

8 What type of control is used in a report to add values?

9 What function is used (and how is it written) to count records in a report?

10 Describe the process of adding lines to a report.

Chapter 12 Assignments

1 Using the Ch12-02 file, create a report using all the fields present in the Buyer Query. View the data by Buyers Table with no grouping or summarization in a stepped layout with portrait orientation and adjusting the field width so all fields fit on a page, Median style. Title and save the new report as Ch 12 Assignment 1. Print the new report.

2 Create a report using the BuyerName, ProductName, Quantity, UnitPrice, and Total Value fields present in the Buyer query. View the data by Buyers Table and group by BuyerName. Use the summary option feature of Access to the sum Total Value, showing detail and summary in a stepped layout with portrait orientation and adjusting the field width so all fields fit on a page, Median style. Title and save the new report as Ch 12 Assignment 2. Make sure all values are visible, and then print the new report.

3 Open the report created in Assignment 2. Change the title of the report to Products by Buyer. Add lines to separate each buyer. Add a line above the grand total amount. Save the new report as Ch 12 Assignment 3. Make sure all values are visible and then print the new report. Your printed report should look like Figure 12.19.

Figure 12.19

Completed Product by
Buyer Report

Product by Buyer					
Buyer Name	Product Name	Quantity		Unit Price	Total Value
Lopez					
	Diamond Studs	3		$826.88	$2,480.64
	G-Shock	10		$54.02	$540.20
	Diamond Heart Slide	4		$964.69	$3,858.76
	Tanzanite Ring	9		$490.62	$4,415.58
	Pearl Necklace	15		$104.74	$1,571.10
Summary for 'BuyerID' = 1 (5 detail records)					
Sum					$12,866.28
Fortier					
	Seiko Kinetic Auto Relay Tit	4		$468.56	$1,874.24
	Diamond Earrings	2		$562.28	$1,124.56
	Flower Drop Earrings	10		$6.62	$66.20
	Diamond Pendant	7		$413.44	$2,894.08
	Diamond Solitare Earrings	3		$1,096.99	$3,290.97
	Topaz Necklace	5		$413.44	$2,067.20
Summary for 'BuyerID' = 3 (6 detail records)					
Sum					$11,317.25
Farley					
	Blue Topaz Ring	7		$274.52	$1,921.64
	Diamond Wedding Ring	5		$716.63	$3,583.15
	Engagement Ring	12		$441.00	$5,292.00
	Le Grand Sport	5		$303.19	$1,515.95
	Ruby Pendant	10		$250.00	$2,500.00
	Swiss Army Watch	3		$192.94	$578.82
Summary for 'BuyerID' = 4 (6 detail records)					
Sum					$15,391.56
Szulczewski					
	Rolex Oyster Submariner	2		$3,306.40	$6,612.80
	Amethyst Pendant	8		$214.99	$1,719.92
	Seiko Kinetic Auto Relay	1		$435.49	$435.49
Summary for 'BuyerID' = 5 (3 detail records)					
Sum					$8,768.21
Grand Total					$48,343.30

Chapter 12 Case Problem 1:
KELLY'S BOUTIQUE

Note: You must have completed this case in the previous chapter in order to complete this case.

In the last chapter you added and modified some forms for Kelly's Boutique. She would now like you to create some new reports. Make the following changes for Kelly using the ch11-03_student_name file you created in Chapter 11. (*Note:* Open your ch11-03_student_name file and then save it as ch12-03_student_name before making the indicated changes.)

a. Kelly would like you to modify an existing query (Ch 10 Kelly Case h) to include the publisher name and then to save the new query as Ch 10 Kelly Case o. Use this new query to generate a report listing all of the field names provided in the query and grouped by publisher, sorted by book title, with no summarizing, in a stepped layout with portrait orientation and in Equity style. Save the newly created report as Ch 12 Kelly Case a and then print the report, making sure that all fields of information are clearly readable before printing.

b. Next, Kelly would like you to add some grouping to the report created in Case 1a. Rather than modify the existing report, create a new report using the Ch 10 Kelly Case o query to generate a report listing only the publisher, book title, quantity, and cost, grouped by publisher and sorted by book title, summing cost in a stepped layout with portrait orientation in Flow style. Save the newly created report as Ch 12 Kelly Case b and then print the report, making sure that all fields of information are clearly readable before printing.

c. Next, Kelly would like you to use the parameter query created previously (Ch 10 Kelly Case l) to create a report containing the fields book title and quantify for a specified publisher and viewed by Book Table, sorted by book title, in a tabular layout with portrait orientation and in Office style. Save the newly created report as Ch 12 Kelly Case c. Add a field to count the number of titles for the publisher specified and then sum the quantity of books for that publisher. Add line controls, change the report title, and move controls around so that your report looks like Figure 12.20.

Books Published by Random House

Book Title	Quantity
Green Eggs and Ham	15
Hop on Pop	8
The Cat in the Hat	4

Number of Titles: 3   Quantity of books: 27

Figure 12.20

Report Example for Kelly Case C

Run the report for Random House and then print the report, making sure that all fields of information are clearly readable before printing.

Chapter 12 Case Problem 2:
WINE DEPOT

Note: You must have completed this case in the previous chapter in order to complete this case.

In the previous chapter you modified some forms for the Wine Depot. Now Barbara would like you to help her create some new reports. Make the following changes for Barbara using the ch11-04_student_name file you created in Chapter 11. (*Note:* Open your ch11-04_student_name file and then save it as ch12-04_student_name before making the indicated changes.)

a. Use the Report Wizard to create and print a new report based on the query created in Chapter 10 (Ch 10 Wine Depot Case b),which listed all wine products purchased by Michael Jackson. Include all the fields available from the query, view the data by wine products with no grouping, sorted by type in ascending order, in a tabular layout with portrait orientation and in Apex style. Title the report Ch 12 Wine Depot Case a and then print the report, making sure that all fields of information are clearly readable before printing.

b. Create a new report that lists the following fields: buyer name, type, winery name, vintage, and quantity. View your data by buyer and then by winery name, in ascending order by type, in stepped layout with portrait orientation and ing Apex style. Title the report Ch 12 Wine Depot Case b and then print only page 1 of the report, making sure that all field of information are clearly readable before printing.

c. Create a new report of product total cost by winery. Using your previous query (Ch 10 Wine Depot Case k) as the basis for this report, include all the fields in that query and view them by winery. Sort the detail by type in ascending order, and add a summary option for total cost (in a Currency format) that shows detail and summary in a stepped layout with portrait orientation and in Apex style. Title the report Ch 12 Wine Depot Case c and then print only the last page of the report, making sure that all fields of information are clearly readable before printing.

d. Modify your previous query (Ch 10 Wine Depot Case k) to be a parameter query by asking the user to specify a type of wine. Save the new query as Ch 10 Wine Depot Case m. Use that query to create a report of costs by type of wine. The report should include all the fields from the query except type. View the data by winery name, in ascending order by SKU, and in a stepped layout with portrait orientation in Apex style. The report should calculate the sum of total cost for the wine selected. Run the report for Pinot Noir wines. Modify the report to look like Figure 12.21 by adding a line and a Grand Total in the report footer. Then title the report as Ch 12 Wine Depot Case d and print it, making sure that all fields of information are clearly readable before printing.

Ch 12 Wine Depot Case d

Name	SKU	Cost	Quantity	Total Cost
Babcock				
	11475	$17.50	48	$840.00
Melville				
	11350	$24.00	12	$288.00
Robert Mondovi				
	12380	$18.00	24	$432.00
			Grand Total	$1,560.00

Figure 12.21

Total Cost of Wines by Name

Index

Excel Chapters (1–6)

SUM function, 28–29
Sum-of-the-year's digits method, 84, 85–86

T

Tabs, 6
Trial balance, 17
and enter data into worksheet, 23–25

U

User interface, 4

V

Values, 23
Vertical analysis
on balance sheet, 55–57
on income statement, 53–55, 59
View Toolbar, 7

W

What-if analysis
with depreciation function, 78–79
and goal seek
with bond amortization
schedule, 105–107
with cash budget, 136
Workbook, 8
Worksheet, 9
appearance of data, 27–28
column width and row height,
change, 25–26
data
edit, 26–27
enter, 23–25
formula
edit, 30–31
enter, 30–31, 28–29

manipulate data and structure,
31–40
Autofill, 31–32
headers and footers, 39–40
insert and delete columns and
rows, 34–35
relative and absolute references, 32–34
work with multiple work-
sheets, 35–39
using function, 28–29
Wine Depot, case problem, 49–51, 73,
94, 115–116, 141–142